THE MYSTERY OF HISTORY

When God Became Man

by:

Pastor John David Shanks
David Shanks

1 Timothy 3: 16 And without controversy great is the mystery of godliness: God was manifest in the flesh, justified in the Spirit, seen of angels, preached unto the Gentiles, believed on in the world, received up into glory.

Dedications

To **the Lord Jesus Christ:** the mystery of history, the mystery of godliness, God made manifest in the flesh, our perfect sin sacrifice, who loved us, died for us, and rose again that we might have everlasting life.

To **Beulah Baptist Church:** in remembrance of our "goodly heritage" of over 100 years of Christian service and looking forward to God's blessings yielding a great harvest of souls as we continue to share the gospel around the world.

Pastor John David Shanks

To my uncle**, Curtis Blaine Bitner:** Uncle Curtis went to be with the Lord in August of 2020 and left us with a victorious Christian testimony and a godly example to follow.

David Shanks

Special Acknowledgements

We want to express our deep appreciation to **Charlene Jessee** for her tremendous assistance in the editing of this book.

Pastor John David and David Shanks

Thank you to **Dr. Ralph Sexton Jr.** for your teaching about Migdal Eder and for answering my questions concerning it.

Pastor John David Shanks

Thank you to **Pastor Roy Yelton** and the people of **Oakland Avenue Baptist Church** who provided the funding for my journey to the Holy Land in 2018.

Pastor John David Shanks

Thank you to **Rachel Renee Shanks** for your technical assistance, grammar knowledge, and formatting information.

David Shanks

Thank you to **Pam Shanks** for proofreading and suggestions.

David Shanks

Contents

Introduction/Preface
The Mystery of History—When God Became Man

📖 **1 Timothy 3: 16 And without controversy great is the mystery of godliness: God was manifest in the flesh, justified in the Spirit, seen of angels, preached unto the Gentiles, believed on in the world, received up into glory.**

The incarnation of Christ, His virgin birth, the union of the divine and human natures, form a mystery revealed to us through the word of God. Christians believe this mystery. We do not know the science of how. However, God has given us a wealth of information in Holy Writ surrounding the process of this mysterious work of God becoming man. That is what Christmas is all about.

History abounds with mysterious idolatrous religions and their various myths of man working to become God. Every generation is included. Christianity stands alone, apart from and above the religions of the world when God becomes man.

Surely, there are enough Christmas books to fill a small library. Do we need another one? Yes! All of them are different and so is ours. Our book will offer a combination of the following special dynamics that make this book unique revealing many mysteries surrounding Christmas:

☑ **Presents the pure gospel on multiple occasions with evangelism being a major emphasis**

☑ **Provides critical, historical information about the times of Christ and some of the biblical characters**

☑ **Provides additional historical and cultural supplemental information not published in most Christmas books**

☑ **Gives a chronological review of the timeframe of the birth of Jesus**

☑ **Covers a detailed review of the Virgin Birth and many of its various connections to the titles, names, and person of Christ**

☑ **Investigates and explains the technical legal rights of Jesus to rule on the throne of David**

☑ **Documents the genealogical records that divinely positions Christ as the kinsman redeemer for all mankind**

☑ **Refutes some common serious doctrinal errors connected to the Christmas story**

☑ **Demonstrates some excellent Bible study methods**

☑ **Confirms that the writers believe in the inspiration and the preservation of scriptures. Our approach will be God honoring and Bible believing as we place our faith in the accuracy of the Scriptures.**

Christmas needs to be a time of **evangelization.** There is no better time to present the gospel. Soul winning Christians understand that portions of the Christmas story open the door for a gospel witness to almost everyone.

Christmas needs to be a time of **celebration.** Jesus Himself said that He came that we might have life and have it more abundantly. Christmas is a great time for families and churches to joyfully assemble and worship and celebrate who we are in Christ.

Christmas needs to be a time of **glorification.** We need to give God the glory for all He has done for us. We can praise God for salvation, daily provisions, the blessings of life, finances, freedom, homes, family, churches, pastors, kinfolk... Ah! There is no end!

Merry Christmas to you and good tidings of great joy to all people!

Chapter 1
The Mystery of Christmas Celebration

Should we celebrate Christmas? The mystery here is the tremendous disagreement on the subject among Christians. There is certainly a wide array of professing Christians from various denominations and groups that do not think we should celebrate Christmas. Those who believe you should not celebrate Christmas are quick to point out that there is no direct Bible teaching instructing Christians to celebrate Christmas. They note that God has specifically given instructions for things like the Old Testament feasts, baptism, and the Lord's supper. So, should we celebrate Christmas? We will take a few minutes and look at an overview of the Bible and see if we can come up with some conclusions.

Christians understand the Bible is divinely inspired, without error and the sole authority for Christian faith and practice. The Bible is first and foremost a history of God's dealings with His created subjects. The Bible is the most complete book ever written covering subjects of importance to all men, cultures, and societies. The Bible is brief and to the point, yet thorough, when dealing with the subjects of morality, law, government, love and marriage, business and finance, the future of mankind and nations, personal and public relations, eternal things, and hundreds of other major and minor topics that this writer does not have the time or place to discuss in this format. Due to the divine nature of the Bible and the evil present in this world and in man, the Bible is the most criticized, the most hated, and the most attacked piece of literature in the history of mankind.

On the other side, the Bible is the most praised, discussed and written about book in history exerting influence extending from the homes of average citizens to the mansions of nobility. The Bible is replete providing many infallible proofs that it is the very word of God standing alone and above all other books. The Bible is first and foremost a history of God's dealings with man. The Bible contains the complete divine revelation from a Holy God to man.

At this junction, let us look at the Bible from a summative and wide-angle perspective. The Bible begins at the beginning with God creating the heaven and the earth. The Bible says plainly that God did his creative work in six days and rested on the seventh day. God crowned his creation with the first man and woman–Adam and Eve.

Adam and Eve was placed in the perfect paradise of the garden of Eden. Adam was put in charge of God's creation and he and Eve were given complete freedom in the garden. There was only one prohibition. Adam and Eve were not to eat of the Tree of Knowledge of Good and Evil and we are told that if they did eat, they would surely die. They disobeyed and acquired the knowledge of good and evil. Per the Bible, Eve was deceived, but Adam willingly followed Eve in this sinful transgression. Adam was primarily responsible for this sin because of his appointed position as head of God's creation. Adam's sin brought death into the world. The Bible teaches that Adam's sin nature or tendency to sin has been passed to all men. The world is reaping the consequences of that sin and this is evidenced through the death of all men and women.

God came seeking the erring pair in the garden. After acknowledging their sin, God provided Adam and Eve with coats of skins showing His continued love for them and revealing His willingness to cover and forgive their sin. A "seed" or future heir was promised that would bring deliverance from sin and defeat to Satan. This seed was to provide the ultimate redemption for all mankind. From this time forward, man in the Bible will look forward to the coming of this redemptive seed.

It is interesting that the first prophecy of Christ is found in **Genesis 3:13-15:**

📖 **Genesis 3:13-15, And the LORD God said unto the woman, What is this that thou hast done? And the woman said, The serpent beguiled me, and I did eat. 14And the LORD God said unto the serpent, Because thou hast done this, thou art cursed above all cattle, and above every beast of the field; upon thy belly shalt thou go, and dust shalt thou eat all the days of thy life: 15And I will put enmity between thee and the woman, and between thy seed and her seed; it shall bruise thy head, and thou shalt bruise his heel.**

Adam and Eve now knew about good and evil and had to learn about the consequences of sin. They were cast out of the garden of Eden and were told they would have to make their living by the sweat of their face. Adam and Eve were directed to go forth and multiply and subdue the earth.

As stated previously, the children of Adam bore his sin nature. After a few generations, the earth was filled with people and the Bible records that the earth was filled with violence and the imagination of man's heart was evil continually. Mankind was so wicked and thoroughly corrupted that God was provoked to bring judgment upon his creation. God brought a worldwide flood upon the earth and the earth was destroyed. However, Noah had found grace in God's sight, and he and his family of eight souls were spared through God's instruction and providence of the ark.

When the waters of the flood were abated, God gave his rainbow in the sky as a unilateral covenant to mankind, that He would never destroy the earth by flood again. Mankind starts over. God instructs Noah to institute human government. Capital punishment is authorized as a deterrent for sin.

Noah's family begins to multiply and in a few short generations becomes exceedingly wicked, arrogant, and hostile to God. Under the leadership of Nimrod, the men of that age built the tower of Babel. Their idea was to usurp the authority of God and become one people with one religion and one world government. Despite their arrogance, God still had to come down and deal in judgment with his created beings. As a deterrent for sin, God confounded their language so that they could not understand one another's speech and scattered the people across the face of all the earth.

Soon after, God chose Abraham and made a covenant with him to deliver the promised seed through his family. God told Abraham that through this seed, **"All the families of the earth would be blessed (Genesis 22:18)."** God told Abraham, **"Get thee out of thy country, and from thy kindred, and come into the land which I shall shew thee (Genesis 12:1)."** Abraham moved out of the land of the Chaldeans and dwelt in Charran: and from thence to the promised land called Canaan at that time and known as Israel today. Thus, we have the children of Israel to be established as "God's chosen people" in the land of Israel, also called the "promised land." Make no mistake, the promise of the promised seed of the promised chosen people in the promised land was to be the Messiah or the Christ.

During this time, God has His prophets to preach and teach to His people, to record his word, and to prophesy what God is going to do.

God continues to confirm his promise to Abraham's son Isaac, and Isaac's son Jacob. There is a famine in the promised land and the children of Israel moved to the land of Egypt. The sojourning of the people of God in Egypt was 430 years and they grew to a great nation of several hundred thousand in Egypt. In God's time, God chooses Moses to bring the children of Israel out of Egypt, and to establish them in the promised land.

When the children of Israel come out of Egypt, they camp at Mount Sinai and are given the law. The law was given in three sections: God's moral law or the Ten Commandments, God's civil law governing the affairs of day-to-day life, and God's ceremonial law or religious law of worship. The tabernacle is built, and Old Testament worship is centered around God's ceremonial law and the ordinances of the tabernacle.

Upon the institution of the ceremonial law, God established 7 feast days to be observed in three gatherings (one in spring, one in summer and one in fall) each year. These three times mirrored the agricultural harvest seasons. The families of the children of Israel would gather as a group from various parts of the country and travel to Jerusalem to worship. These feast times were joyous occasions set aside for worship and fellowship with God and one another. Remember, that the temple, sacrifices, and the feasts are all symbolic and metaphoric pictures of Christ.

Leviticus chapter 23 is God's summary of His seven Feasts. It is interesting to note that each of these feasts are both memorial and prophetic in nature. Leviticus chapter 23 provides a prescriptive summary of these feasts. These feasts, taken as a unit, prophetically portray God's plan and program for all mankind. A feast is, by definition, an appointment at a fixed time or season, specifically a yearly festival. A feast is a God called assembly for His congregation at His place of meeting. A Convocation is a *called* out, public *meeting* for reading and *rehearsal.*

Each of these feasts have a threefold application. 1) They are a memorial looking back at what God has done. 2) They provide instruction and blessing to God's people attending these feasts and to those who read and understand God's feasts. 3) All the feasts are prophetic in nature. Note:

☑ God Declares the end from the beginning... Isaiah 46:9-11
☑ All these things happened unto them for our ensamples... 1 Corinthians 10:11
☑ These Scriptures are filled with instruction and doctrine... 2 Timothy 3:16

In short and in brief, each of these feasts is God telling us about His Son. These feasts are filled with typology, symbolism and patterns with prescriptive detail, specifics, and precision. Each aspect of the feasts and modes of offerings speak of the coming of Christ.

You will recall that at the feast of Pentecost in the book of Acts, there were devout men from every nation under heaven there to worship. History records tens of thousands traveling to the feast days during New Testament times.

Let us move on with our summary. The children of Israel rebelled against God in the wilderness and God chastises the children of Israel by allowing them to wonder in the wilderness for forty years. Under Joshua, the promised land is occupied.

The children of Israel were governed by judges for several generations and desired a king. Their first king was Saul who miserably failed. Then, God appointed David as king who was a man after God's own heart. God made a covenant with David and the promises of God for the promised seed were renewed and confirmed. The promises were in turn extended to David's son Solomon.

The children of Israel again sin. The nation is divided, and Israel is captured by the Babylonians and carried out of the promised land to Babylon. Afterward, the children of Israel suffered under the chastening hand of God for seventy years in Babylon. From Babylon, God scattered the children of Israel throughout the world and synagogues were used as places of worship and study of the holy Scriptures. God uses Cyrus by special decree to allow a remnant of the children of Israel to reoccupy the promised land. This reoccupation was done under the leadership of Ezra and Nehemiah. God continues to reconfirm his promises after this reoccupation. Then, as though the lights went out, God sent no special revelation for 400 years.

Ah! But God shows up again and the promises began to be a reality. The New Testament era begins at God's appointed time. The New Testament says, **"But when the fulness of the time was come, God sent forth his Son, made of a woman, made under the law," (Galatians 4:4).**

God had prepared the world to receive His Son. Throughout the world, there were little colonies of Jews and their synagogues. Each synagogue possessed a copy of the Holy Scriptures—our Old Testament. The scriptures foretold of the great expectation of the coming Saviour. God had planned for this very period in history in which He would send His Son to be born, to walk among sinful men, to live a sinless life, to go to an old rugged cross, to die for you and me, to raise from the dead and then to depart back into heaven.

The world had one world government and one common language—Greek. Greek was the common language of choice in the business and government circles of that day. God would use this language to write the New Testament and to spread His good news of the coming of His Son. Let us look at the many infallible proofs that God has graciously left us.

The reference to "her seed" pointing to Christ has been hailed throughout New Testament times to refer to the virgin birth. Thus, the teaching of the virgin birth starts in the book of Genesis and the virgin birth finds its fruition and fulfillment in the Christmas story.

Every Bible Christian who has a remedial understanding of the Bible knows that the Old Testament is all about Jesus. In chapter 5 of the gospel of John in the New Testament, Jesus said of Himself that Moses **"wrote of me."** On the Emmaus Road the gospel of Luke says of Jesus, **"And beginning at Moses and all the prophets, he expounded unto them in all the scriptures the things concerning himself" (Luke 24:27).** So, the Old Testament is all about Jesus.

Now let us move to the New Testament and examine some of the claims of Christ. Note that the Bible teaches us that in the Old Testament we see a shadow of good things to come. In the New Testament we have the very substance. John teaches us that Jesus is the Eternal God and the Word of God who was made flesh **(John 1:1-3 & 14).** Jesus, in a heated conversation with the Jews said that Moses **"wrote of me."** The New Testament clearly states that Jesus was the creator of all things **(John 1:1-3, Ephesians 3:9, Colossians 1:16).**

Here is Luke's account of Christ on the Emmaus Road after Christ's resurrection, **"And beginning at Moses and all the prophets, he expounded unto them in all the scriptures** (that is the old testament scriptures) **the things concerning himself" (Luke 24:27).** And the Lord said to the eleven disciples later that day, **"These are the words which I spake unto you, while I was yet with you, that all things must be fulfilled, which were written in the law of Moses, and in the prophets, and in the psalms, concerning me" (Luke 24:44).** Scholars report that our Lord fulfilled 351 Old Testament prophesies in the New Testament.

No man has seen God the Father at any time, but God the Son has kept a full schedule of His appearances to man. You see, it is the Lord Jesus Christ who steps out of heaven to reveal His Father to man **(John 14:9, John 1:18, Colossians 1:15 et al.).** It is easy for us to see Jesus revealing His Father in the New Testament, but the pre-incarnate Christ is the revelation and word of God in the Old Testament. He marches in and out of history as if He owned it. Yes, He does own history. We are His Creation. History is His Story. Christophanies bring blessings and judgments in their appearance. Christophanies always teach us about the character of God and about the way man should respond to God. The Christophanies start in the garden... **"And they heard the voice of the LORD God walking in the garden in the cool of the day: and Adam and his wife** hid themselves from the presence of the LORD God amongst the trees of the garden" (Genesis 3:8). The terms "angel of God" (thirteen mentions) and "the angel of the LORD" (sixty-eight mentions) are used in many cases to designate a Christophany. Dr. John Walvoord in his book, Jesus Christ Our Lord says, "It is safe to assume that every visible manifestation of God in bodily form in the Old Testament is to be identified with the Lord Jesus Christ." Are these appearances really the LORD God?

Isaiah the prophet, prophesied in some rough and tough times. Isaiah proceeds to proclaim a prophecy of deliverance which is recorded in **Isaiah 7:14, "Therefore the Lord himself shall give you a sign; Behold, a virgin shall conceive, and bear a son, and shall call his name Immanuel."** Isaiah never saw that deliverance.

However, God has let us see the Son of deliverance and we know that sign to be the virgin born Son of God who will deliver us. Isaiah delivered this prophecy over 700 years before the birth of Christ.

Chronologically, Luke opens the New Testament when Gabriel appeared unto Zacharias at the altar of incense. Zacharias means "God remembers" and Elisabeth means "His oath." You remember that Elisabeth is passed the time of childbearing. Gabriel appears to notify Zacharias that God has remembered His promises and is ready to bring a fulfillment of the prophesied Messiah. Through a miracle, Elisabeth will conceive and bare John the Baptist who will become the forerunner of Christ.

Zacharias does not believe God and thus God strikes Zacharias dumb until the fulfillment of the promises made by Gabriel. You know the story. John the Baptist is born, and Zachariah delivers his Psalm and prophecy of praise. Christians have entitled the song of Zacharias as the "Benedictus." It is found in **Luke 1:67-79.** When Zacharias finally speaks, he is not about to be denied his song of praise. Zacharias praises God as powerful and faithful to His promises. God accepted the praise of Zacharias and recorded it in His book.

Gabriel appears again to deliver God's message to Mary. There is no hesitation as Mary responds, **"Behold the handmaid of the Lord; be it unto me according to thy word."** Mary is elated and filled with joy and immediately sets out to visit her cousin Elisabeth. Mary, Elisabeth, and John the Baptist are all moved of the Holy Ghost. The praises of Mary and Elisabeth are certainly worth noting and God recorded the praises of each for us.

Time passes, Joseph and Mary travel to Bethlehem, Mary brings forth the Christ child, and God has an announcement to make. 📖 **Luke 2:8-20, And there were in the same country shepherds abiding in the field, keeping watch over their flock by night. ⁹And, lo, the angel of the Lord came upon them, and the glory of the Lord shone round about them: and they were sore afraid. ¹⁰And the angel said unto them, Fear not: for, behold, I bring you good tidings of great joy, which shall be to all people. ¹¹For unto you is born this day in the city of David a Saviour, which is Christ the Lord. ¹²And this shall be a sign unto you; Ye shall find the babe wrapped in swaddling clothes, lying in a manger. ¹³And suddenly there was with the angel a multitude of the heavenly host praising God, and saying, ¹⁴Glory to God in the highest, and on earth peace, good will toward men. ¹⁵And it came to pass, as the angels were gone away from them into heaven, the shepherds said one to another, Let us now go even unto Bethlehem, and see this thing which is come to pass, which the Lord hath made known unto us. ¹⁶And they came with haste, and found Mary, and Joseph, and the babe lying in a manger. ¹⁷And when they had seen it, they made known abroad the saying which was told them concerning this child. ¹⁸And all they that heard it wondered at those things which were told them by the shepherds. ¹⁹But Mary kept all these things, and pondered them in her heart. ²⁰And the shepherds returned, glorifying and praising God for all the things that they had heard and seen, as it was told unto them.**

On the birthdate of Jesus, God sends out the heavenly host. God lights up the sky and announces the birth of His Son. The Angels praise God. This writer believes they were singing. One spiritual commentator pointed out that the Bible does not say the angels were singing. Part of the Angels praise was "Glory to God in the highest." The Greek word for glory is "doxa." We get our English word "doxology from this Greek word. The author has heard several doxologies. All have been sung.

The shepherds arrive, see the Lord Jesus, and return glorifying and praising God. These shepherds, in turn, share this news with everyone they encountered.

Joseph and Mary, on the fortieth day after the birth of Jesus, travel up to the temple in Jerusalem to fulfill the required religious ceremonies. While they are there, Simeon blesses the holy family and prophesies. Immediately as Simeon ceases, Anna the prophetess walks in, worships the Lord Jesus, and gives thanks.

Joseph and Mary return to Bethlehem. Around this time, the Wise Men come from afar seeking the baby King. "We are from a far distance and bring precious gifts of gold, frankincense, and myrrh."

In summation, the first prophecy was related to Christmas. The Old Testament feast days of worship all look forward to the coming of the Lord Jesus Christ. Each ceremony, each sacrifice, each act of worship and fellowship ultimately speak of the Lord Jesus Christ. It is as though God was using the Old Testament worship ordinances to brag about His Son. That is exactly what He is doing.

When we get to the New Testament, God dispatches Gabriel to make various announcements concerning the birth of His Son to Zacharias, Mary, and Joseph. Then we have the songs of praise by Zacharias, Elisabeth, and Mary. Jesus is born and the world receives God's angelic announcement. The shepherds come to the manger and glorify and praise God. Simeon and Anna shower their blessings and praise on the Lord Jesus. Then came the Wise Men carrying precious gifts and worshiping the Lord.

Now, nowhere in the Bible does it state that we are to celebrate Christmas. However, it seems as though God is quick to look forward to the Christmas story and the virgin birth when He proclaims "her seed" to the fallen pair in the garden. God chooses Abraham and his family to bring the Christ child into the world. God initiates the famous Jewish festivals that in the simplest sense seem to celebrate the coming and incarnation of our Saviour. It seems to me, that God the father appreciates the celebratory efforts of the Angels, the shepherds, the Wise Men, and Simeon and Anna in their Christmas worship of the Christ child.

No, we do not find any specific instructions for the celebration of Christmas in the Bible. No, we do not know the definite birthday of Jesus. No, we do not find instances of Christmas celebrations in the New Testament epistles. However, God made a big deal of the birth of His Son.

Many of the favorite memories of my lifetime have been received through the celebration of Christmas. Christmas has always been a church centered time with sermons, cantatas, plays, dinners, and gatherings. Christmas has always been a family time with Bible reading, meals, reunions and yes—plenty of gifts. Christmas has always been a time of national observance with schools, businesses, and governments doing their part. Sure, the Scrooges have abounded, but the Christians have prevailed at Christmas time.

To the somber Christian professors, who do not believe that we should celebrate Christmas, be careful and stay out of the plague of the Christmas spirit. Keep your mule face. Cheer yourself and rejoice that you have a better way. You can take great satisfaction that you will have not have any indigestion from the gluttony of Christmas.

Around our house, if God gives us peace and grace and life, we are going to get together and read our Bible, pray, eat, give gifts, and go to church and start all over again. The year after that we will do the same again, and again the year after that, and again the year after that, and.... It should be no mystery to you that our family is going to celebrate Christmas.

Chapter 2
The Times of the First Christmas

Galatians 4:4-5, But when the fulness of the time was come, God sent forth his Son, made of a woman, made under the law, To redeem them that were under the law, that we might receive the adoption of sons.

Pam and I were married forty-three years ago. Without any construction experience, we built our house. We contracted pouring the basement concrete and the brickwork. Our family helped us, and the rest we completed ourselves. When we moved in, there was no carpet, a $40 refrigerator, and two electric skillets. When we found out that Pam was expecting our first child, John David, there was just an unfinished empty room. We went to Dalton, Georgia, to buy a carpet remnant, secured the loan of a baby bed, and prepared the nursery.

At first glance when we examine the advent of our Lord Jesus Christ, it looks as though God handled things in a haphazard manner. Not so. God sent His Son in the fullness of time—that is the exact, precise, and premeditated time. The world was the nursery for God's Son. God prepared the world with a double fold purpose in mind. God readied this world to receive His Son, and subsequently, the message of His Son, the gospel, the death, burial, and resurrection of the Lord Jesus Christ.

Over 600 years before Christ, God gave the old prophet Daniel a panoramic view of the four world kingdoms that would rule the world. Daniel lived in the first kingdom, and Christ would live in the last. Daniel chapters 2 and 7 provide us with a prophetic look at four Gentile world kingdoms.

Daniel chapter two reveals these kingdoms from a human perspective. In **Daniel 2:29-35**, Nebuchadnezzar dreamed and saw a colossal statue of a man composed of various metals: the head was of gold, the upper body and arms of silver, the hips and thighs of bronze, the legs of iron, and finally the feet were mixed with iron and clay. In verses 36-45, Daniel interprets the dream to Nebuchadnezzar. World history would be dominated by four Gentile kingdoms that would rule the world. When man looks at these kingdoms, he takes glory in what he has done and in the truest sense, worships himself.

Daniel chapter seven reveals God's viewpoint. God exposes these kingdoms as vicious beasts that devour men's souls. Looking back on history, we can see God's prophecy of these kingdoms perfectly fulfilled. Note the historic setting of each of these kingdoms (referenced chapters and verses are from the book of Daniel):

1. **BABYLON** (612–539 BC)—symbolized by the head of gold (2:32) and a lion having the wings of an eagle (7:4)
2. **MEDO-PERSIA** (539–331 BC)—signified by the upper body of silver (2:32) and a bear (7:5)
3. **GREECE** (331–63 BC)—symbolized by the belly and thighs of bronze (2:32) and a leopard with four wings and four heads (7:6)
4. **ROME** (63 BC–AD 476; and vestiges of this kingdom still exist today in the Roman Catholic Church)—symbolized by legs of iron and continuing down through the feet and toes (2:33) and diverse composite beast with iron teeth and bronze claws (7:7).

As the controversial revolutionist Thomas Paine said, "these are times that try men's souls." Without the God of the Bible, these were times that would devour men's souls. It is the same today.

In 722 BC, the northern kingdom of Israel was destroyed by the Assyrians. Their people are taken captive and deported among the cities of the Medes. These Jews are known today as the Lost Ten Tribes of Israel. Judah was destroyed by the Babylonians in 598-582 BCE, and the Jews were carried away to Babylon.

After 70 years under the rule of the Medo-Persian empire, Cyrus the great allowed a remnant to return to Jerusalem. The exiles returned under the direction of Ezra and Nehemiah exactly fulfilling multiple prophecies. Over the next few years, Judah was repopulated. Babylon was the mecca of pagan idolatry. Despite all that God did for the children of Israel, their great sin was idolatry. God rubbed her nose in her idolatry, and that sin is not found in the Jew today.

Alexander the Great, the greatest military leader in history, conquered the Persian Empire in about 10 years and set up his world kingdom. The Greeks made a lasting impression and influenced the day-to-day lives of those who lived in the time of Christ. The Greeks brought to the world democracy, culture, mythical gods, architecture, and a worldwide language.

The first human author of our bible was Moses. He wrote in his native language, Hebrew. The Hebrew alphabet consisted of twenty-two letters. The Hebrew letters were all consonants, and there were no vowels. While there are a few chapters in Ezra and Daniel written in Aramaic, the majority of the Old Testament was written in Hebrew.

The New Testament, however, was written in Greek. The Greek letters consisted of both vowels and consonants. During the time of the composition of the New Testament, Greek was the language of government and business. This allowed for immediate transmission of the New Testament throughout the known world. The Greek of the New Testament was the common Greek dialect spoken and written by the ordinary people. God did not choose the classical Greek dialect that was used by scholars and academia.

The internal strife of the Grecian Empire finally destroyed the Empire from within and this allowed the Romans to establish their rule. Rome promoted itself as a peacemaker and expanded itself throughout the civilized world. Of course, many times they had to fight to establish peace. The Roman Empire was ruled by a legislative body and an executive or supreme leader. Legislative power was dispensed by the Chamber of Deputies and the Senate. The Chamber was made up of 200-300 members elected for a four-year term by direct, secret, and universal ballot. The Senate was composed of 120 members elected for a nine-year term with one-third of its members elected every three years. The Roman emperors got their job through their military achievements and inheritance.

The Roman empire had been established for about sixty years when Christ was born. Julius was the first Caesar. He became Caesar because of his military ability and success. Julius had a long, public, and military career but was Caesar for just a short period of time. The Senate saw their power diminishing when Caesar's was increasing. A rebellious group banded together and stabbed Caesar outside the Senate.

This left a power void. A series of civil wars broke out, and the constitutional government of the Republic was never fully restored. Caesar's adopted heir Octavian and the notorious and legendary Mark Antony competed for Emperor. Octavian, later known as Augustus, rose to sole power after defeating his opponents in the civil war.

As a note of interest, you may remember that Julius Caesar had a steamy love affair with Cleopatra. Historically, Cleopatra is regarded as the most desirable woman who ever lived. When Augustus was taken off the scene, Mark Antony was Cleopatra's next paramour. Mark Antony and Octavian shared the rulership of the Roman Empire for a period. Herod the Great and Mark Antony became friends. Herod secured Mark Antony's support to become ruler over Judea. Of course, Cleopatra was always using her charms, affections, and assets for political advantage. When Mark Antony ruled the western portion of the Roman empire, he gave Cleopatra a few small provinces near Judea, and one was Jericho. Cleopatra visited the region, and King Herod and his royal entourage provided Cleopatra with escort services. Remember that Cleopatra was Queen of Egypt. She had ambitions to rule Judea. Cleopatra tried to seduce Herod in hopes to gain some political advantage that would help her secure Judea as a part of her royal territory. Herod trusted no one and was not about to become entangled in Cleopatra's web.

It did not take long for Mark Antony and Octavian to figure out that the Roman empire was not big enough for them both. A naval battle would settle the matter. Octavian was at a tremendous disadvantage. Mark Antony had his navy ready, and Cleopatra also had her Egyptian Navy there to battle for Mark Antony. When the battle started, Cleopatra lost heart and her ships fled back to Egypt. Octavian was still at a disadvantage but held his own. When Mark Antony discovered that Cleopatra had sailed away, he lost his courage and will to fight and he fled to Egypt after Cleopatra. Thus, Octavian became ruler over the Roman empire and took the name Augustus Caesar.

When Jesus was born, Augustus Caesar was the Emperor of the Roman empire, and Herod the Great was king over Judea. The time in which Christ lived has been historically known as Pax Romana (Roman Peace). This was an age of comparative peace and stability across the Roman Empire. The era of Roman peace commenced in the time of Augustus and was maintained for over 200 years. There were always minor skirmishes and seditions that were generally brought on by the death of the governors, public kings, and rulers of the countries and provinces under Roman authority. This time of peace was a great asset to the spread of the gospel.

The Romans followed many of the astute governing practices of the Medo-Persian Empire which allowed each country to maintain a great deal of self-rule. Individual provinces could observe their religion and live according to their own ethnic culture and traditions. Rome was concerned with maintaining a constant flow of tax money—nothing new.

In New Testament times, travel from region to region and country to country was very commonplace especially among politicians, soldiers, and businessmen. Extensive road construction started during the time of the Medo-Persian Empire whose first king was Cyrus the great. This is the same Cyrus mentioned in the Bible who initiated the return of the Jews to Judea. The Romans would continue to improve the roads until there were over 50,000 miles of paved thoroughfares and 250,000 miles of crossroads and connectors. The major highways were engineered to go from point to point in a straight line. The highways were furnished with mile markers and signage. Travel from country to country was open to the public and commonplace. Roman currency was comprised of gold, silver, bronze, orichalcum, and copper coinage. Currency was standardized through the Roman Empire. The Romans were the first to use advanced skill to mine for minerals including iron, copper, tin, lead, and gold. The Romans had banking and finance systems that allowed for an open economy and free enterprise.

Among the coastal countries, shipbuilding was an advanced technological industry. Ships were designed for both cargo and war. Prior to the Roman Empire, large naval battles ensued involving dozens of ships on both sides.

A combination of a peaceful era, a common language, paved roads, mining, and banking created a system that allowed the economy to flourish during the time of Christ and New Testament years. Of course, agriculture and food related endeavors made up the major portion of occupations. The Roman empire was blessed with a large population, and the people had to eat.

Judea was heavily populated during the time of Christ. The total Palestinian population was thought to be around 500,000. When Jerusalem and the Temple were destroyed it 70 A.D., the Romans laid siege on Jerusalem during the Passover feast and the number of occupants was greatly increased by Jewish worshipers from other countries. Josephus estimated that 1.1 million people were slaughtered in the Jewish War, that 115,880 dead were carried out one of the gates during the month of Nisan in AD 70, and that 97,000 were taken as slaves. Reference: (Josephus, The Wars Of The Jews Book VI Ch 9 Sec 3).

Jewish people groups or sects that existed during the ministry of our Lord were made up of a combination of political, religious, social, racial, and vocational groups. The various amalgamations formed an interesting, complex, and volatile society.

The Samaritans were a mixed breed from the northern tribes of Israel who were left after the Assyrian captivity. They intermarried with the Assyrians to repopulate the area. They used the Pentateuch as the basis for the religion and worship on Mount Gerizim. The Jews and the Samaritans hated one another **(See Luke 9:52–56.)**

The Zealots were Jewish nationalists who despised Roman rule. The Zealots loathed the Roman gods and believed the Jews should not pay taxes to Rome nor allow Rome to rule over them. One of the 12 apostles, Simon, was a Zealot **(see Luke 6:15).** The Jews were a prideful and rebellious lot. Insurrectionist activities by various groups were a common occurrence and finally resulted in the complete destruction of Jerusalem and the Temple in 70 A.D.

The detested and ostracized publicans were native Jews who were employed in public positions as tax collectors of the Roman government. The apostle Matthew was a publican. Matthew penned the first gospel. **(See Matt. 9:9–10; Matt. 21:31–32; Mark 2:15.)**

The scribes provided secretarial services. Scribes had knowledge of the law and could draft legal documents (contracts for marriage, divorce, loans, inheritance, mortgages, the sale of land, and the like). They also copied sacred manuscripts and royal documents. Jewish scribes were well versed in the laws of Moses, making them the spiritual and temporal legal counselors of the period. Most, but not all, scribes were Pharisees and thus were frequently mentioned side-by-side in the Bible. Some scribes were affiliated with the Sadducees and other religious groups.

The Pharisees were the religious fundamentalists of their day. They believed in the resurrection, the written scriptures, and the oral traditions. They were the largest religious sect. The Apostle Paul was a Pharisee and educated by Gamaliel, one of the most prominent Pharisees of Jerusalem. **(See Matt. 23; Mark 7; Luke 11.)**

The Sadducees were an aristocratic, priestly class of Jews, influential in the temple and in the Sanhedrin. While they believed in the Pentateuch (Torah), they did not accept the oral law. The Sadducees denied the doctrine of the physical resurrection. **(See Mark 12:18–27; Acts 4.)**

The Essenes, while not mentioned in the Bible, have been given extensive notoriety today because of the discovery of the Dead Sea Scrolls, which formed the Essenes' library. They congregated in a communal, monastic lifestyle beside the Dead Sea. They dedicated themselves to living an ascetic life that included voluntary poverty and abstaining from worldly pleasures. Theologically, their beliefs had common elements of both the Pharisees and Sadducees. There are probably as many Essenes as Sadducees, but isolation limited their influence on the Jewish society during the ministry of Christ.

We also find among the Jewish population existing during Jesus's advent in ministry, a remnant of true worshipers. This devout residue was distributed throughout the various people groups mentioned above. They would be found in every location and each socioeconomic ladder in society. They were people who believed the law and observed the ordinances of the law. The law had given them the sense of their own sinfulness and demonstrated their need of a sin sacrifice. These were people who knew and understood the need for a Saviour. This faithful contingent looked forward to the coming of the Messiah. These were folks such as Joseph, Mary, Zacharias, Elisabeth, the shepherds, and the Wise Men.

Up to this point, we have talked about the different political, social, and religious labels attached to various groups of the Jews. There were also a few Gentiles in the land. Of course, Judah was not a big place, and Gentile countries surrounded Judah. Judah was just a speck compared to the rest of the world.

While the Jews certainly had business dealings with the Gentiles, the Gentiles were not highly thought of, and that is putting it mildly. The Jews abhorred and despised the Gentiles. After their exile in Babylon, the Jews, who were former idolaters, regarded the Gentiles as heathen and pagan idolaters. The Gentiles were considered unclean beasts that were not fit for babysitting duties. They were compared to oxen, dogs, jackasses, and other brute beasts that would fit the bill in their conversations.

In case you are wondering, the Herodians did not exist until after the birth of Christ and the death of King Herod. The Herodians wished to restore Herod's family to the rulership of Judea because of the immense economic prosperity and public building projects King Herod completed.

Now, we need to return to Herod the Great and review his tenure as King. Herod ruled from 37 B.C. to 4 B.C. No man in history ever ruled such a small kingdom and left such an indelible mark on history.

Herod was born in southern Palestine. His father, Antipater, was an Edomite or Idumaean from the line of Esau. Herod was raised in the Jewish religion. Of course, the Edomite heritage of Herod was obnoxious to the true Jew. In short, Herod was a Jew "wannabe."

The strong political ties of Herod's father allowed Herod to marry into the priestly line of the Jews. History records that Herod had 9 wives, and three were from the Jewish priestly line. There were several priests who served as both priest and king prior to the Roman empire.

Herod was politically astute and smart enough to use his political connections to advance himself and Judea. He took no prisoners and permanently destroyed his detractors. Herod oversaw an unparalleled amount of public building projects. He was an architectural genius and master builder. Judea quickly ascended to political and economic heights through his ambition and leadership. The prideful Herod was successful and spared no expense in displaying this success.

His greatest achievement was the restoration and for all practical purposes the rebuilding of the Temple in Jerusalem. Herod's Temple, as it was called, was an unexcelled architectural achievement. This magnificent structure tremendously boosted the respect for the Jewish religion. His desire was to endear himself to the people he ruled. Thus, the temple heightened the notoriety of Herod to the Roman world and increased his respect among the Jews. The temple was a symbolic masterpiece which mirrored the way Herod himself wanted to be perceived.

While the temple was Herod's greatest achievement, it is only one of many architectural masterpieces accomplished in his lifetime.

Regrettably, his blind ambition corrupted his core values, and Herod left a trail of innocent blood and carnage. In the end, Herod the Great was nothing more than a demented mental basket case and madman. Doris was the first wife of Herod the Great. After a nine- or ten-year marriage, Herod dismissed her along with their son so he could marry the Hasmonean heiress, Mariamne. He regarded this as a chance to climb the social ladder. Mariamne was his second wife and the love of his life. Despite his affection for Mariamne, jealousy poisoned his mind, and he had her killed. Herod also murdered her two sons, her brother, her grandfather, and her mother. Besides Doris and Mariamne, Herod had seven other wives and had children by six of them. He had a total of fourteen children.

When writing this section, the writer came across a video by a lady college professor who lectured on Herod. She plainly presented the truth about Herod's slaughter of his own family. She quoted the almost correct historical maxim, "it was better to be Herod's dog than a member of his family." Her statement was misquoted. The actual proverb was, "it was better to be Herod's hog than a member of his family."

Most secularists doubt that Herod really gave the order for the slaughter of the innocents. Secularists and skeptics do not want to believe that a man of Herod's political intellect and architectural genius could be guilty of such moral debauchery and killing. When Christ was born, Herod was a step away from his deathbed. He was sick in body with a variety of gross conditions, and he was an emotional wreck and mentally unstable. These were all a direct result of Herod's life of moral depravity.

Under his rule, Judea was not under a Roman army of occupation. Herod had the title of King and was strong enough in his own right to manage Judea without Roman help. After Herod's death, his kingdom was divided into three parts. You remember that when Jesus died, Pontius pilot served as the Roman prefect or governor of Judea. Pontius Pilate was a week puppet administrator and had to have an army of occupation. The size of the Army occupation continued to grow until 70 A.D. when Jerusalem and the Temple were destroyed.

What a terrible way to end this section. Ah! Our Lord Jesus came to the Roman empire and Bethlehem, a little town in Judea. Jesus came to give us hope over death, hell, the grave, and tyrants like Herod. Herod made a little mark on history. Jesus changed history. Herod moved men through fear. Jesus moves men through love. Herod had influence for a season. Jesus has influence today. Herod touched the lives of a few, some for better and some for worse. Jesus came to touch the world for the better. All that Herod had to offer was temporary. All that Jesus has to offer is eternal.

Chapter 3
The Mystery of the Memory of the Lord

Luke 1:57-66 Now Elisabeth's full time came that she should be delivered; and she brought forth a son. ⁵⁸And her neighbours and her cousins heard how the Lord had shewed great mercy upon her; and they rejoiced with her. ⁵⁹And it came to pass, that on the eighth day they came to circumcise the child; and they called him Zacharias, after the name of his father. ⁶⁰And his mother answered and said, Not *so;* but he shall be called John. ⁶¹And they said unto her, There is none of thy kindred that is called by this name. ⁶²And they made signs to his father, how he would have him called. ⁶³And he asked for a writing table, and wrote, saying, His name is John. And they marvelled all. ⁶⁴And his mouth was opened immediately, and his tongue *loosed,* and he spake, and praised God. ⁶⁵And fear came on all that dwelt round about them: and all these sayings were noised abroad throughout all the hill country of Judaea. ⁶⁶And all they that heard *them* laid *them* up in their hearts, saying, What manner of child shall this be! And the hand of the Lord was with him.

Chronologically, the New Testament opens with the above revelation. There is no record in the Bible of God having anything to say to His chosen people in the 400 years prior. The light of heaven had been switched off and the voice of God was mute. Four hundred long and tedious years had passed. But God, mysteriously in the tumultuous days of wicked King Herod, sends Gabriel with a special revelation to an unknown and unheralded priest named Zacharias. His story begins in **Luke 1:5**. Zacharias means **"whom the Lord remembers."** God had moved on the scene and the promise of Messiah is rekindled.

The Priests in Bible times ministered in the Temple on a rotating basis. Zacharias belonged to the course of Abijah. David had divided all the priests into twenty-four courses. In addition to the three feast seasons, each priest came from Sabbath to Sabbath twice a year to minister in the temple. This priest, Zacharias, lived in the hill country of Judea and came in his due course to minister before the Lord in the temple. He was married also to a high priestly daughter from the tribe of Levi. Her name was Elisabeth. They were holy and righteous people. They followed all the commandments of the Lord. But in their hearts, they had an unspoken and silent sadness; they had no child. The Bible tells us that both were old, that **"they both were now well stricken in years (Luke 1:7)."** That was a disastrous fate for any Jewish couple. For them to have no child was considered a sign of the displeasure of God. Zacharias the priest, and Elisabeth his wife bore this sorrow.

The priests of the course of Abijah would gather in the court of the priests to cast lots to decide who would go into the sanctuary, the Holy Place, to burn incense. Adam Clarke (1762-1832) in his commentary states: "We are informed in the Talmud, that it was the custom of the priests to divide the different functions of the sacerdotal office among themselves by lot: and, in this case, the decision of the lot was, that Zacharias should at that time burn the incense before the Lord, in the holy place." Once in a lifetime would such a privilege be given to a priest, and this day the lot fell upon Zacharias. When the time came to offer the sacrifice, Zacharias and two assistant-priests walked up the long ramp to the great altar of burnt offering. One of the assistant priests would use tongs to remove the burning coals from the altar and place them in a censer. They then walked back down the ramp. Zacharias took a golden bowl full of sweet incense, and they walked up the twelve steps to the door of the sanctuary. The three priests, (Zacharias with the assistant priests on each side) entered the Holy Place; the sanctuary was forbidden to all except the sons of Levi, the holy priests.

On one side would be the golden candlestick called the menorah. On the other side would be the table of showbread. In front of them would be the veil that separated the Holy of Holies from the Holy Place. In front of the veil was the golden altar of incense. As the three priests approach the sacred veil, one of them took away the coals that had been burned at a former offering and cleaned the golden altar. Then the other assistant carefully and evenly placed the burning live coals from off the altar of burnt offering. Then the two assistant priests bowed and went out, and Zacharias was before the Lord alone.

As he placed the incense evenly on the golden altar, the perfume began to rise. The Bible teaches this was a type of the prayers of the saints ascending unto God. Then a wonderful thing happened: on the right side of the golden altar, in the haze of smoke there appeared an angel of God **(Luke 1:11).** The angel said to Zacharias that he and his aged wife Elisabeth should have a son, and they were to name him John **(Luke 1:13)**; and he is to go before the Lord Jesus Christ announcing the kingdom of heaven **(Luke 1:17)**.

Zacharias should have rejoiced at such an announcement. Instead, he answered the angel in unbelief: **Luke 1:18 says, "And Zacharias said unto the angel, Whereby shall I know this? For I am an old man, and my wife well stricken in years."** Zacharias said, "We cannot have a son;" as though anything were too hard for God. The angel replied, "My name is Gabriel." Gabriel means "God is my strength." He said, **"I stand in the presence of God, and I am sent to speak unto thee these glad tidings that you do not believe and refuse to accept."** The angel Gabriel proceeds to declare, **"And, behold, thou shalt be dumb, and not able to speak, until the day that these things shall be performed, because thou believest not my words, which shall be fulfilled in their season"** (Luke 1:19-20).

The people who were worshiping outside could not understand why the priest was delayed in coming. When he finally appeared, Zacharias did not understand that the sign he had asked for had already come to pass. He could not speak. He did not realize that. Zacharias came to the edge of the steps that lead from the court of priests down to the court of Israel and raised his hands for the benedictory prayer. The benedictory prayer is found in **Numbers 6:24-26, "The Lord bless thee, and keep thee: The Lord make His face shine upon thee, and be gracious unto thee: The Lord lift up His countenance upon thee, and give thee peace."**

Zacharias came before the people and lifted his hands to speak the benediction and could not speak. The scripture says in **Luke 1:22, "And when he came out, he could not speak unto them: and they perceived that he had seen a vision in the temple: for he beckoned unto them and remained speechless."** The Greek word for beckoned indicates that he kept trying to talk, he kept trying to speak and he could not. He made signs, and he kept on making signs until the people realized he had seen a vision in the sanctuary.

In this chapter we are going to contrast this incident with that same Zacharias when his son was born. The Bible says they came on the eighth day to circumcise the child. At the circumcision ritual, Elisabeth's neighbors and cousins came to her and said, "We are going to name him Zacharias after his father." This was the tradition in Jewish families at that time. The child was usually given a family name. Elisabeth immediately rejected this saying, "His name is John." They reminded her, that there is none of her family or kindred by that name. Then they made signs to his father, "What shall his name be called?" In **Luke 1:63** it says, **"And he asked for a writing table, and wrote, saying, His name is John. And they marvelled all."**

Zacharias stated in faith and in adoration and in praise for what the angel had said, "His name is John." Zacharias is now full of faith, and **"immediately his tongue was loosed and he spake and praised God" (Luke 1:64).**

The point is that unbelief always silences praise and prophecy and the glory of God. Oh! But belief is always filled with the presence of the ability and power of God. Unbelief destroys testimony, and praise, and adoration, and understanding, and everything that pertains to the glory and the ableness and might of God. Unbelief shuts God out.

There are things you want to know. You can ask an unbeliever, a learned scientist, an intellectual, a teacher, or a professor and they cannot tell you about creation. You can ask the unbeliever and the infidel, "Where did this world come from and all that I see above me and around me?" He says, "I do not know. I have no answer. I am dumb. I am speechless." Finally, if you press him, he will say, "Possibly it came about with a big bang." Well, where did all the substance come from in the big bang? How could this universe come out of a catastrophic explosion? He does not know. He cannot answer. His voice is dumb.

You ask the infidel and the unbeliever, "What is the meaning of life? Does it have any purpose? "No, no," says the unbeliever and the infidel, "Life has no purpose, it has no meaning. You die and that is it. There's no meaning to life."

Then you ask about the world to come: "Is there a heaven? Is there some place where we'll see each other, where we will be together, where God is?" And he answers, "No, there is no life after death, there is no heaven, there is no gathering of God's saints. Death is the final blackened curtain that ends all existence." Unbelief silences testimony. Unbelief has nothing to say. Unbelief is dumb. Unbelief is speechless. Unbelief is silent.

When Zacharias expressed his belief, immediately his tongue was loosed, and he praised God. Unbelief is silenced, it is dumb; but belief, and acceptance, and adoration, and worship loose the tongue, and open the heart.

Where did this world come from? Look at all the glory that you see above you and around you. Gaze upon the stars of the firmament, and the beauty of the earth. Where did it all come from? Belief answers: **"In the beginning God created the heaven and** the earth" (Genesis 1:1). Belief answers: **"The heavens declare the glory of God; and the firmament showeth His handiwork" (Psalm 19:1).** Belief says that **"He is the image of the invisible God: and by Him were all things created, and in Him all things consist" (Colossians 1:15-17),** that means Jesus holds all things together. The Greeks called it the cosmos. Cosmos is the Greek word for order and beauty. The word "cosmetics" comes from it. The Greeks saw beauty and order in the created world around us and they called it the cosmos, the hand of God. If you have a heart of belief, you will see the hand of God everywhere. Every little flower, every rainbow, every star that shines, the rising of the sun, the beauty of the day, the falling rain is there for the one who has eyes opened to believe, God is everywhere.

Does life have purpose? Does it have meaning? Do you remember **Jeremiah 1:5?** The Lord said to Jeremiah: **"Before I formed thee in the belly I knew thee; and before thou camest forth out of the womb I sanctified thee, and I ordained thee a prophet unto the nations."** God has a plan and a purpose for your life. He knew you when you were in your mother's womb. He called you by your name, and you were born for a specific mission. God has a plan for every life. It is a wonderful thing to know that God has purposed for us a wonderful ministry. Even grief, sorrows, and disappointments have a purpose and help us grow. To the unbeliever they are meaningless; but to the believer every sorrow and hurt prepares him for God's service. When the Lord called Saul of Tarsus, He says in the ninth chapter of Acts, **"I will show him how great things he must suffer for My name's sake" (Acts 9:16).** There's purpose in every tear and every defeat. God can change your disappointments and setbacks into blessings for you.

What about death? Does God stand by us in death? Does death have a meaning? Is there a life beyond death? Is there a heaven? Shall we see one another again? Does Jesus await us on the other side? The unbeliever says: "No. Death is nothing but an open grave. Death is nothing but eternal darkness and night. Death is nothing but a final farewell and a forever goodbye." But belief says, "Death is the open door into heaven. It's our introduction to the glories that God hath prepared for those who love Him; and it's our entrance into our eternal and final home." Death is our entrance into heaven.

Some time ago when Dr. W. A. Criswell was pastor of the First Baptist Church of Dallas Texas, he told how on an airplane flight he was sitting beside and visiting with a well-known theologian. The man told how he had lost a son who, one day, had come home from school with a fever that he and his wife thought was just a childhood sickness. Sadly, it turned out to be meningitis. The doctor gave no hope for the boy's survival.

Near the end when the professor was sitting at his son's bedside, the child said, "Daddy, it's getting dark isn't it?" The professor answered, "Yes, son, it is getting dark, very dark." "Daddy, I guess it's time for me to go to sleep isn't it?" the boy continued. "Yes, son, it's time for you to go to sleep." As the child fixed the pillow on his bed the best he could in his weakened condition and, putting his head on his hands, said, "Good night, Daddy. I will see you in the morning." Those were the last words the professor's son said as he closed his eyes in death and passed from this life to enter God's heaven.

For a long time, Dr. Criswell said, the professor just sat looking out the window of the airplane. Later he turned again and, looking at Dr. Criswell, with tears in his eyes, said, "Dr. Criswell, I can hardly wait till the morning."

Dear reader, are you sure that you are ready for God's heaven so that when you go, your loved ones will also be able to say, "I'll see you in the morning?" Or, if your loved ones go first, you will be able to say to them with certainty, "I'll see you in the morning."

Chapter 4
The Lineage of The King

The Bible is the only religious book that provides extensive genealogical and chronological data proving its historical authenticity and reliability. This documented information in turn verifies intricately woven Biblical mysteries proving the deity and humanity of our Lord.

Genealogical records were critical to the Hebrews in Biblical times. Today, we use our genealogies to help us preserve family legacies, traditions, and culture. When the Hebrews were delivered from Egypt and finally began to settle in Canaan, Joshua divided the land by tribe. Each family received their share of property by lot. The family property became a perpetual inheritance. The Hebrew economy was a limited free enterprise system where the Hebrews could buy and sell property as we do today. However, every fifty years, the Hebrews celebrated the year of Jubilee. In each Jubilee year, the Hebrews would return to their respective property previously allotted by Joseph for their perpetual inheritance. The geographical area was tied to each land-grant that God gave to his chosen people.

You remember that the priestly tribe of the Levites did not receive a land-grant but were assigned residential property. In the Old Testament, the priestly tribe not only carried out the priestly duties but were charged with maintenance and movement of the Old Testament Tabernacle. These duties, once assigned, were passed on to later generations through their genealogical position.

There are two more critical genealogical issues in the Old Testament. The issue of the lineage of the King is of vital importance. The other issue is the lineage of both Christ to us and to our earthly progenitor Adam. It is important for us to realize that God in the Bible places the utmost importance and significance on genealogies and genealogical records. These records are critical in forming vital doctrines that relate to who Jesus is and His work of redemption.

The normal writing protocol is to develop a series of facts and then bring forth a conclusion or climax at the end. King Saul wanted to get to the bottom line after David slew Goliath. King Saul asked, "whose son is this?" In fact, King Saul asks about the sonship of David on three occasions. The bottom line is this: the God of the Bible wants us to know who Jesus is. The Christmas narratives are found in two of the four New Testament Gospels: Matthew and Luke. As a part of both Christmas narratives, we will find a genealogical record of the Lord Jesus Christ. These two records are not identical. However, both genealogical accounts are accurate and without error. Matthew records the lineage of Joseph, and Luke documents the lineage of Mary. They form a precise revelation revealing that Jesus is the Son of God, the Son of David, and the Son of man.

The Bible is not written in technical scientific language. However, the Bible is written with a precision and exactitude beyond any technical or scientific document we have available today. The Lord Himself said that not one "jot or tittle" would pass from the law. On occasion, the Bible itself uses verb tenses and the singular or plural form of nouns to make its salient points.

As you know, Charles Darwin wrote the "Origin of Species" touting the theory of evolution. Of course, Darwin's book has become the bible of the naturalists. Darwin wrote his "Origin" about 150 years ago. At that time, the formula for life protoplasm was thought to be as simple as a Jello recipe. It was thought that you could start with some water, mix in a little dirt, and let the sunshine heat it up. In a few days, that concoction would develop some pond scum containing the basic forms of life.

A few short years ago, DNA was discovered. Twenty-three chromosomes were discovered in each cell of DNA. These were compared to letters of the alphabet. Then as various proteins, amino acids, etc. were discovered, DNA components were compared to words. In a short time, DNA was thought to be as complex as a sentence. Subsequently, DNA was compared to a paragraph, then to a magazine article and onward to a book. Now we know that in one single cell of life, the information in DNA is stored as a code made up of four chemical bases: adenine (A), guanine (G), cytosine (C), and thymine (T). Human DNA consists of about three billion bases. Thus, we now know that we could compare the amount of information in DNA in a single cell to a whole library or a few thousand Bibles.

God, the creator of this universe, is the architect and engineer of DNA. The chemical building blocks within DNA abound with unmatched complexity compounded with an accuracy, precision, and exactitude that is beyond anything man can do. The Bible contains an accuracy and precision beyond the DNA necessary for life forms.

The Bible is not written in technical jargon. However, the Bible was inspired by a divine Author who used human instruments to pen the Bible with an absolute perfect precision. The word of God is perfect and precise, and additionally, the word of God is complete. We know that God has given us a perfect word and God has promised to preserve His word for us. The lineage of Jesus Christ is in a real sense a technical endeavor. We will approach our explanations and honor God and His word by simply believing and trusting every jot and every tittle of what He has written.

The New Testament opens with the first of two genealogical accounts of Christ recorded in the Gospels. Matthew's genealogy is found in **Matthew 1:1-17.** The first statement in the book of Matthew reads, **"The book of the generation of Jesus Christ, the son of David, the son of Abraham" (Matthew 1:1).** Thus, Matthew's genealogy starts with Abraham and his lineage ends with Christ.

The human author and penman of the New Testament's first gospel was Matthew, also called Levi. Matthew was one of the original twelve disciples and apostles of Jesus Christ. Before being called to follow Christ, Matthew was a publican or tax collector for the Roman Empire. Matthew's position as a tax collector would have made him an unexcelled expert genealogist. Genealogical records were a critical tool used by tax collectors. Matthew's expertise with genealogical matters by no means excludes the Holy Spirit's guidance and inspiration of his genealogical record. The names were recorded exactly as God directed.

Each gospel is written to a specific group of people and with a specific purpose. All the Gospels portray Jesus Christ as the Son of God and God the Son. All the Gospels portray various aspects of the life of Christ and end with His death, burial, and resurrection. Matthew was a publican and a Jew. Matthew wrote to the Jew with the purpose of declaring Jesus to be the son of David and the One who is eligible to sit upon the throne of David as King.

Note again, Matthew's first statement is **"The book of the generation of Jesus Christ, the son of David, the son of Abraham."** This statement sets the historical context for Matthew's genealogy and the entire narrative of Matthew's gospel.

Let us review some Old Testament history. We will start with Abraham. In **Genesis 12:2-3,** God promises Abraham, **"And I will make of thee a great nation, and I will bless thee, and make thy name great; and thou shalt be a blessing: 3And I will bless them that bless thee, and curse him that curseth thee: and in thee shall all families of the earth be blessed."** Of course, we know today, through the New Testament narrative that these promises to Abraham are ultimately fulfilled through Christ.

As we continue through the Old Testament, David as a son of Abraham receives the promises of a kingdom and throne. Note we are not covering all the promises in the Messianic Line but just hitting the highlights. Notice the promises to David written in 2 Samuel 7:13-16:

📖 **(2 Samuel 7:13-16) He shall build an house for my name, and I will stablish the throne of his kingdom for ever. ¹⁴I will be his father, and he shall be my son. If he commit iniquity, I will chasten him with the rod of men, and with the stripes of the children of men: ¹⁵But my mercy shall not depart away from him, as I took it from Saul, whom I put away before thee. ¹⁶And thine house and thy kingdom shall be established for ever before thee: thy throne shall be established for ever.**

So, God tells David that his throne will be established forever. That throne will be established through Jesus Christ. This divine promise is what we know as the Davidic Covenant. Verse 16 above declares three essential parts that make up the ongoing Davidic Covenant.

➢ First – **"thine house"**—a continued family
➢ Second – **"thy kingdom"**—a realm of political power
➢ Third – **"thy throne"**—the rulership in the kingdom of David's family

You will remember that after the children of Israel were delivered from the bondage of Egypt, they were ruled by a series of judges. When Samuel was the priest, they desired a king so they could be like other nations. God granted the request and appointed Saul king. Saul soon became unfaithful and disobedient and died in battle. David was anointed by Samuel prior to the end of Saul's reign.

David's rule established Israel as a world power. The above promises were given to David. God promised to establish David's throne forever. The ultimate fulfillment of that throne will be through our Lord Jesus Christ. The purpose of the two genealogical records in the New Testament is to prove that Jesus is eligible to take the throne of David. Jesus will take the throne of David when He returns.

However, God did not promise an unbroken line of David's successors to sit on the throne. Solomon inherited the throne from David and continued to expand Israel's wealth and power. After Solomon's death, Rehoboam succeeded his father Solomon. Rehoboam was arrogant and told the people that he would rule with a firm hand. Ten tribes would not allow Rehoboam to be king over them and defected. Thus, David's kingdom was divided into two divisions. The first was "The Kingdom of Israel" whose constituents were the 10 tribes of Israel and the second "The Kingdom of Judea" which was ruled by the descendants of David. These two kingdoms of kinfolk would each standalone for approximately fourteen generations.

After the kingdom split, the kingdom of Israel was apostate from the beginning and did not follow their God. The kingdom of Israel followed the gods of the Canaanites.

The kingdom of Judea ruled by David's heirs formed the Biblical godly line. But sad to say, the kingdom of Judea and some of the rulers on many occasions went through periods of complete apostasy. Now, we have set the historical context to discuss the genealogical records in Matthew's gospel.

In Matthew's genealogical record, there are some small "glitches" that we need to comment on. The Muslims and many within the Christian community have noted that there are three names missing from Matthew's genealogy. There is an obvious question here! "How do they know that three names are missing?" Well, these critics know because the three missing names are found in the Old Testament genealogical records. It looks as though we have a mistake or an oversight in our Bible. Did God make it? Are there scribal errors? Or maybe God directed His human authors and transcribers to omit these on purpose. Let us look.

Christians, atheists, and Muslims have noted these three missing names for centuries. When properly understood, God is interpreting His Old Testament words with His exact purpose in mind. Matthew deletes the three offspring that follow Joram (Ahaziah, Joash, and Amaziah; 1 Chron 3:11–12). Joram ruled six generations after David. Make no mistake, God orchestrated these deletions for his purposes. God left these names out of the New Testament because they were wicked idolaters. We have detailed Old Testament history to prove it.

Now, we will deal with the final "glitch" in the genealogical record of Matthew. Let us look at the promises of God that flowed down to David. As we travel through the Old Testament, we find this kingly promise to David begins with Abraham and his seed. Abraham was promised that all the families on the earth would be blessed through his seed. We can trace the promise of the kingly line from Abraham through David in the following passages. We have already noted the promise to Abraham in **Genesis 12:1-3** and **Galatians 3:16** comments and explains the Genesis passage.

The promise of this special blessing to Abraham is passed on to Isaac, Jacob, Judah etc. as we continue through the Old Testament. We have already covered the fact that David as a son of Abraham receives the promise of a kingdom and throne **(2 Sam**

7:13-16). Please note that we are not covering all the promises in the Messianic Line but just hitting the highlights.

Isaiah predicts that Christ will fulfill this covenant in the prophecies of **Isaiah 9:7 and Isaiah 11:1-5.**

Jeremiah prophesied in the days prior to the children of Israel's exile to Babylon. Jeremiah predicted the Babylonian exile with precision and witnessed the fulfilling of some of his own prophecies. Jeremiah also looks forward to the Kingdom and Kingship of our Lord in **Jeremiah 23:5-6.** In the book of Psalms there are two more prophecies that state that the kingdom of David will exist forever: **Psalms 89:3-4** and **Psalms 89:35-37.**

In the New Testament, Joseph is specifically called **"thou son of David,"** in **Matthew 1:20.** In **Luke 1:32,** Gabriel, speaking of the Christ child, says to Mary: **"the Lord God shall give unto him the throne of his father David: 33And he shall reign over the house of Jacob for ever; and of his kingdom there shall be no end."**

The Book of Matthew is the Book of the King and presents Jesus as the Son of David and King of Kings. King David in the Old Testament had two sons that need to be mentioned here. One was Solomon who became King and the other was Nathan. Thus, in Matthew we have the genealogical record of Joseph. We will find later that Luke provides us the genealogy of Mary through Nathan. Joseph was from the kingly line of Solomon. A curse by God was put on this genealogical line when Coniah sinned exceedingly. Note the following passage:

📖 **Jeremiah 22:24-30 "As I live, saith the LORD, though Coniah the son of Jehoiakim king of Judah were the signet upon my right hand, yet would I pluck thee thence; 25And I will give thee into the hand of them that seek thy life, and into the hand of them whose face thou fearest, even into the hand of Nebuchadnezzar king of Babylon, and into the hand of the Chaldeans. 26And I will cast thee out, and thy mother that bare thee, into another country, where ye were not born; and there shall ye die. 27But to the land whereunto they desire to return, thither shall they not return. 28Is this man Coniah a despised broken idol? Is he a vessel wherein is no pleasure? Wherefore are they cast out, he and his seed, and are cast into a land which they know not? 29O earth, earth, earth, hear the word of the LORD. 30Thus saith the LORD, Write ye this man childless, a man that** shall not prosper in his days: for no man of his seed shall prosper, sitting upon the throne of David, and ruling any more in Judah."

Let us review the process of the inheritance of the kingly line. In biblical times, and in the Jewish culture, the firstborn son received a double portion of the property and was the head of the family and this applied to each tribe. The firstborn of a king would inherit the throne. In the cases of David and Solomon, God establishes their right to the throne. The legal kingly line must now flow through the firstborn of Solomon.

Jeremiah 22:30 speaking of Coniah says, **"Write this man childless."** Jeremiah is stating that Coniah will not have an heir that will ascend to the throne of David. The passage is clear, **"a man that shall not prosper in his days: for no man of his seed shall prosper, sitting upon the throne of David, and ruling any more in Judah."**

Coniah had several sons. **1 Chronicles 3:17** gives a list of those sons. However, there would not be an heir from the family of Coniah who would sit on the throne of David. God has cursed the kingly line to which He has promised the throne **"for ever."** In other words, the promised line cannot take the promised throne. How will God keep His promise to David of **"thy throne shall be established for ever?"**

God solved the problem and precisely kept His word when He provided a firstborn heir through the virgin birth. The clear Biblical inference in these passages is that the next heir of David who can legally inherit David's throne must be the Lord Jesus Christ.

This explains the curse on the line of David through Joseph, the husband of Mary. It is important that you understand that without the curse, Joseph would have had a legal right to the throne of David. This is one of many astounding and glorious proofs that the Bible is the word of God!

The Book of Luke gives the genealogical record of Mary through Nathan, the other son of David. It is necessary that you remember that both Joseph and Mary were from the lineage of David approximately 28 generations later.

In summation, God promises a throne to David forever and then, God curses the kingly line of David and says none of his heirs can sit on the throne. These declarations totally contradict one another. God's word must uphold both. From a worldly perspective, both cannot happen. However, through the divine miracle of the virgin birth and the "begetting" of the Lord Jesus through the Holy

Spirit, God can and will fulfill His promises without altering one jot or tittle from His word.

We will give a more complete explanation of this when we complete this genealogical portion. It is now time to move on to the genealogy found in Luke.

Chapter 5
The Genealogy of the Son of Man Through Mary

Luke 3:23-24 And Jesus himself began to be about thirty years of age, being (as was supposed) the son of Joseph, which was the son of Heli, Which was the son of Matthat, which was the son of Levi, which was the son of Melchi, which was the son of Janna, which was the son of Joseph,..... (note emphasis)

Dr. Luke records his genealogical record in the third chapter of his gospel. Luke has been proven to be an unexcelled historian with a precise attention to detail. We must state up front, this is Mary's lineage. We will give more than ample proof of this as we develop our thoughts here. Luke uses Joseph's name instead of Mary and traces the genealogical line all the way back to Adam. There are almost 80 generations included in Luke's narrative. Yes, the higher critics have found a few "glitches" in Luke's genealogical account.

Now, you should be asking yourself this question, "why is Joseph's name in this narrative?" There are several reasons that make Joseph's name legitimate and technically correct in Luke's narrative. First and most obvious, many worthy Biblical commentators note that the normal Jewish custom was to record the names of the men and to leave out the names of the women. While there are a few women mentioned in the Biblical genealogical records, the husband is always found in the Biblical narrative. Normally Jewish genealogies leave out the names of the women.

Second, historical records indicate that Mary had two sisters and no brothers. In the time of our Lord, a father without a male heir could adopt his son-in-law, as a son, making him a legal heir. Thus, Joseph's name could rightly appear in the above context.

Third, it is the intent of the genealogical records of Christ to answer the question, "whose son is this?" From an earthly and legal perspective, Christ is the son of Joseph first, and then Mary. We intend to cover this legal perspective in more detail when we get to the chapter on Joseph. A lot of times Joseph is called the stepfather or foster father of Jesus. These terms are technically inaccurate, and we will thoroughly demonstrate this later.

The first part of **Luke 3:23** supports the doctrine of the virgin birth. Let us look at the first part of this verse again, **"And Jesus himself began to be about thirty years of age, being (as was supposed) the son of Joseph."**

Now, notice the phrase at the end of this verse, **"which was the son of Heli."** This phrase confirms that this is the lineage of Mary. Heli was Mary's father. His full name is Alexander III Helios. Mary's father was from the line of David and her mother descended from the priestly line of Levi. Alexander III Helios has multiple historical citations. We know from the Biblical account that Mary was closely related to Zacharias and Elisabeth. The historical citations prove Luke's genealogy belongs to Mary.

Thus, from the Biblical narrative we know that Joseph and Mary were distant cousins. It is quite interesting that Mary's family is well known through extra Biblical narratives. However, when it comes to Joseph, we know nothing about Jacob, the father of Joseph, except what is recorded in the Biblical record.

Note again, Joseph was the head of the household. He was listed in Luke as the son of Heli rather than Mary being listed as the daughter of Heli. It is critical for us to observe that in Luke's genealogy, Mary was also from the house and lineage of David since she descended from David's son Nathan. Again, in Matthew's genealogy, Joseph descended from David through Solomon's line which was the kingly line. The lineage of Joseph and the lineage of Mary are identical from Abraham to David. Thus, each are required to fulfill the prophecy that the Messiah would descend from Abraham and then through the house and lineage of King David. Mary's genealogical line makes Jesus physically a son of David.

Again, Mary's genealogical line is listed in the book of Luke. As Christians, we delight in reading the narratives of God using His men and women to fight His battles. The Bible comes alive when we see God's people reigning victoriously. We see the love stories, miracles, and high drama and these add spice and entertainment to our everyday lives.

But when it comes to the genealogical records, many find the tedious listings and records mundane. As we will find shortly, these lists form critical ties to the Biblical doctrines of salvation.

There is one "glitch" in Luke's genealogy. We have copied some verses for our upcoming discussion below. Their format is a standard KJV format. The problem is: there is an extra **"Cainan"** not found in the genealogical records of the Old Testament. The additional **"Cainan"** is shaded for you. Except for this extra "Cainan," Luke's chronology in this section is the same as Genesis chapter 5.

📖 **Luke 3:35-38** reads, **"Which was the son of Saruch, which was the son of Ragau, which was the son of Phalec, which was the son of Heber, which was the** son of Sala, 36Which was the son of Cainan, which was the son of Arphaxad, which was the son of Sem, which was the son of Noe, which was the son of Lamech, 37Which was the son of Mathusala, which was the son of Enoch, which was the son of Cainan, 38Which was the son of Enos, which was the son of Seth, which was the son of Adam, which was the son of God."

Also, this extra "Cainan" is not found or referenced in any of the other genealogical records or Biblical narratives. The liberal is quick to say that this is a scribal error of some type. This is not the case.

There is extra Biblical evidence for this additional "Cainan" in the **Book of Jubilees**. The **Book of Jubilees**, written about the 2nd century B.C., is an account of the Biblical history of the world from creation to Moses. Here is the citation from the **Book of Jubilees** chapter 8 and the first paragraph:

"In the twenty-ninth jubilee, in the first week, [1373 A.M.] in the beginning thereof Arpachshad took to himself a wife and her name was Rasu'eja, the daughter of Susan, the daughter of Elam, and she bare him a son in the third year in this week, [1375 A.M.] and he called his name Kainam (Cainan)."

God had the name left out of the old testament because this Cainan was an astrologer and idolater. We quote from **Jubilees** chapter 6,

"And he found a writing which former (generations) had carved on the rock, and he read what was thereon, and he transcribed it and sinned owing to it; for it contained the teaching of the Watchers in accordance with which they used to observe the omens of the sun and moon."

In the old testament this line was a Godly line until the extra Cainan comes along. The ungodly line of Cain is mentioned separately in the Genesis account. We have already noted that God removed Godless names from previous genealogical records and so we have a divine precedent for this action. We need to remember that God is the divine administrator and superintendent of the writing of every single word in the Bible.

In the new testament, God inserts the name in its appropriate place. So why was God so meticulous in inserting the second or extra "Cainan" when He left it out to start with? God required an unbroken human line to demonstrate that the humanity of Christ is completely supported by the genealogy of Luke. The Lord Jesus came as the physical "Son of man." God records for us a continuous and unbroken genealogical record tracing back to Adam.

Luke presents Christ as the "Son of man." The phrase "Son of man" is used eighty-six times in the Gospels and in Acts, and an additional twenty-six times in Luke when referring to Jesus. The favorite title of our Lord, in which He used to refer to himself, was "the Son of man." Dr. Luke puts a special emphasis on the humanity of Jesus. However, Luke does not deny the deity of Christ.

In the Old Testament, we have a legal ordinance called the law of the kinsman redeemer. The law of the kinsman redeemer is recorded in **Leviticus 25:47-55.** In Old Testament times and under the Mosaic law, a male near kinsman had the legal right to redeem a brother who sold himself into slavery because of debt. The book of Ruth beautifully illustrates the rite of the kinsman redeemer.

The Old Testament law of the kinsman redeemer reveals a critical element of our salvation. God must be both the "just and the justifier" to all that come to Christ for salvation. All sinners owe a sin debt to God. God cannot simply wipe off that debt and still be holy. That sin debt must be paid. God sent His Son into the world to be born of a woman and to become our kinsman redeemer and the kinsman redeemer of every seed of Adam. We must have a near kinsman to save us from the curse of the law. God, through His own laws, has divinely appointed a legal route for Jesus to pay our sin debt. In the New Testament, Christ is often portrayed as our kinsman-redeemer because, as our brother **(Hebrews 2:11),** He loves us and has the power to redeem us.

God's word answers God's critics in every detail. God has inserted an unbroken genealogical line from Jesus through Mary to Adam. This fulfills the legal requirement making Jesus an eligible kinsman redeemer for all men.

For us to be a Biblical candidate for salvation, Jesus must be related to Adam and in turn to us to be our kinsman redeemer. Some of the preachers from yesteryear would get in a big way of preaching and expound on the Christian's security that we possess in Christ. They would say, "if the devil were to get to me, the devil would have to come through the blood and the devil would be saved too." That is great fiery preaching, but it is not true. The devil has no kinsman redeemer. Angels have no kinsman redeemer. The devil and the angels are not the seed of Adam.

Again, for us to be a Biblical candidate for salvation, we must be kin to Adam. The following verses are clear. They demonstrate the necessity that both Christ and we be found in Adam's family tree for us to be offered salvation in Christ. Note the highlighted portions.

📖 **Romans 5:12-21 Wherefore, as by one man sin**

entered into the world, and death by sin; and so death passed upon all men, for that all have sinned: [13](For until the law sin was in the world: but sin is not imputed when there is no law. [14]Nevertheless death reigned from Adam to Moses, even over them that had not sinned after the similitude of Adam's transgression, who is the figure of him that was to come. [15]But not as the offence, so also is the free gift. For if through the offence of one many be dead, much more the grace of God, and the gift by grace, which is by one man, Jesus Christ, hath abounded unto many. [16]And not as it was by one that sinned, so is the gift: for the judgment was by one to condemnation, but the free gift is of many offences unto justification. [17]For if by one man's offence death reigned by one; much more they which receive abundance of grace and of the gift of righteousness shall reign in life by one, Jesus Christ.) [18]Therefore as by the offence of one judgment came upon all men to condemnation; even so by the righteousness of one the free gift came upon all men unto justification of life. [19]For as by one man's disobedience many were made sinners, so by the obedience of one shall many be made righteous. [20]Moreover the law entered, that the offence might abound. But where sin abounded, grace did much more abound: [21]That as sin hath reigned unto death, even so might grace reign through righteousness unto eternal life by Jesus Christ our Lord.

📖 1 Corinthians 15:22 For as in Adam all die, even so in Christ shall all be made alive.

📖 1 Corinthians 15:45-49 And so it is written, The first man Adam was made a living soul; the last Adam was made a quickening spirit. [46]Howbeit that was not first which is spiritual, but that which is natural; and afterward that which is spiritual. [47]The first man is of the earth, earthy: the second man is the Lord from heaven. [48]As is the earthy, such are they also that are earthy: and as is the heavenly, such are they also that are heavenly. [49]And as we have borne the image of the earthy, we shall also bear the image of the heavenly.

Every detail needs to be in place to make Jesus eligible to be the legal kinsman redeemer for all born into humanity. The insertion of the second Cainan ties up a loose end thus filling the last critical link in the genealogical chain.

What we have today, even in the best of Christian circles, is a failure to believe the exact precision of the word of God. God has provided His Bible with various systems of checks and balances. These systems will leave the skeptic Bible believers without excuse before God. For instance, lists of various genealogies are recorded in multiple places throughout the Bible. Many can be cross-referenced and checked.

Biblical chronologies offer another set of checks and balances. There are numerous excellent Biblical chronologists that support the precise accuracy of the chronological records in the Bible. The genealogical records support the accuracy of the chronological records and the reverse is also true.

Archbishop James Ussher, (1581, Dublin, Ire. – 1656, Reigate, Surrey, Eng.), Anglo-Irish prelate of the Anglican church, was a regimented bible commentator and a religious politician. He is the author of the history and chronology of Old Testament times entitled The Annals of the World. It is considered the standard among conservatives for its Biblical chronology. Ussher gives the date of creation as 4004 BC

Published in Latin in 1650, Ussher's *"Annals"* is an unparalleled academic chronology of both sacred and secular history. Ussher's highly regarded historical timeline has been referenced by many translations of the Bible and was included in the margins of many King James Bibles throughout the 18th, 19th, and 20th centuries.

Dr. Floyd Nolen Jones, Th.D., Ph.D., authored The Chronology of the Old Testament. Dr. Jones's book was first published in 1993 and has been reprinted at least six times. Dr. Jones has set the standard for modern Biblical chronologists and gives the date of creation as 4004 BC.

The average date of creation calculated by 29 additional chronologists from yesteryear is 4024 BC. From this data, it is easy to conclude that the earth is about 6000 years old.

The records in Genesis chapters 5 and 11 are known by many Biblical expositors as "chronogenealogies." In other words, the genealogical records must match the chronological records and they do.

Why are we discussing chronology? Conservative Christians and Jews have theorized for centuries that God would culminate and consummate his plan for man in 7000 years. The last thousand years would be the literal reign of the Messiah. The Jews are looking for their Messiah and the Christians are looking for the return of the

Lord Jesus Christ in the rapture. Both are anticipating the millennial reign of Christ.

This writer is 72 years old and was saved in the spring of 1976. In my tenure on this earth, godly men looking for the return of the Lord in their lifetime, have been buried by the multitudes. If Ussher and Jones were correct, we are living in the year of 6020 from creation. You should be asking yourself, "Where is the Lord?" Christians do not know the date of the return of the Lord. From a Biblical dispensational point of view, we are living in the age of grace. The age of grace has exceeded the duration of other dispensations by centuries. The tribulation signs have been multiplied. Israel is a nation once again.

If you are a Godly Christian, you should be wondering why the Lord has not returned. However, the Lord of Glory has a plan and will return. His return will be in His time and He will be on time. We have his promise in **Hebrews 10:37, "For yet a little while, and he that shall come will come, and will not tarry."** Would you like Jesus to return today?

Look carefully at the last two verses in the Bible, **"He which testifieth these things saith, Surely I come quickly. Amen. Even so, come, Lord Jesus. The grace of our Lord Jesus Christ be with you all. Amen" (Revelation 22:20-21).**

Can you honestly pray with John today, "Even so, come, Lord Jesus?"

Chapter 6
Mary, the Mother of Jesus–A Spiritual Profile

Mary, the mother of Jesus, is no doubt the most written about and discussed woman in our Earth's short history. And quite frankly, much of what is written is false, misleading, and many times a figment of someone's overactive imagination.

Mary is presented in the Bible as clever and quick witted with a ready response for every situation. She was an extrovert with a vivacious outgoing personality. The Bible says nothing about her physical appearance. However, there is no doubt in my mind that she was anything but drop-dead beautiful, coupled with a delightful demeanor that would turn the head and heart of any man.

Mary's lineage flows back through the tribes of Judah and Levi. As far as the tribes of Israel are concerned, Mary's heritage was comprised of the elite Jewish governmental and religious leaders. Mary's father was Alexander III Helios. Called "Heli" in Luke, he was from the Davidic line and apparently executed by none other than Herod the Great. Heli is mentioned in various historical records. If we connect the dots, Mary's family were prestigious Jewish blue-bloods, and many times were well to do.

From a worldly perspective, we may look at marriages and examine what a husband or wife would bring to the marriage. Well, Mary would bring a Godly heritage, education, and business sense. King David mourns the fact that whenever he became king he did not know how "to go in and out." There is not much emphasis put on good manners and social graces today. But Mary was no peasant girl, and she knew "how to go in and out" and had a full repertoire of social skills.

Our purpose is to look at Mary from a Biblical perspective. The Bible will speak to us from each passage in which Mary is mentioned. The passages have been organized in a chronological format and we will follow the life of Mary. We will marvel at the wondrous lady who was the mother of our Lord and Saviour Jesus Christ. Chronologically, here is the first mention of Mary in the Bible.

📖 **(Luke 1:26-38) And in the sixth month the angel Gabriel was sent from God unto a city of Galilee, named Nazareth, 27To a virgin espoused to a man whose name was Joseph, of the house of David; and the virgin's name was Mary. 28And the angel came in unto her, and said, Hail, thou that art highly** favoured, the Lord is with thee: blessed art thou among women. ²⁹And when she saw him, she was troubled at his saying, and cast in her mind what manner of salutation this should be. ³⁰And the angel said unto her, Fear not, Mary: for thou hast found favour with God. ³¹And, behold, thou shalt conceive in thy womb, and bring forth a son, and shalt call his name JESUS. ³²He shall be great, and shall be called the Son of the Highest: and the Lord God shall give unto him the throne of his father David: ³³And he shall reign over the house of Jacob for ever; and of his kingdom there shall be no end. ³⁴Then said Mary unto the angel, How shall this be, seeing I know not a man? ³⁵And the angel answered and said unto her, The Holy Ghost shall come upon thee, and the power of the Highest shall overshadow thee: therefore also that holy thing which shall be born of thee shall be called the Son of God. ³⁶And, behold, thy cousin Elisabeth, she hath also conceived a son in her old age: and this is the sixth month with her, who was called barren. ³⁷For with God nothing shall be impossible. ³⁸And Mary said, Behold the handmaid of the Lord; be it unto me according to thy word. And the angel departed from her.

Luke was the human author of this passage. Luke states that he had a perfect understanding of the events surrounding the life of Christ. He tells us that he secured his information through eyewitnesses. So, who are the eyewitnesses here?

Historically, there are two different accounts of the death of Mary. One account contends that Mary, the mother of our Lord, went to be with her Lord about eleven to thirteen years after the passion of Christ. The other account asserts that Mary lived with the apostle John until a ripe old age. Thus, it is quite possible and most probable that Dr. Luke knew Mary personally.

In any case, if you read the narratives in the first two chapters of Luke, the events center on Mary and her family. Elisabeth and Zacharias were Mary's kinfolk. The Holy Spirit is the inspiring agent behind all Scripture. However, Luke seems to be telling the Christmas story from Mary's viewpoint.

Gabriel deliver's God's message to Mary. Gabriel makes every effort to deliver God's message in a delicate and nonthreatening manner. However, the message is brief and succinct.

The Bible says that Mary was troubled as she listened to Gabriel. Mary is wide-awake. Her mind is racing and trying to make sense out of this situation. Mary does not pretend that she understands. Mary quips quickly back at Gabriel and inquires, **"How can this be, seeing I know not a man (Luke 1:34)?"** A side note here: Mary's response is in perfect agreement with the doctrine of the virgin birth.

Gabriel explains. There is no hesitation as Mary responds, **"Behold the handmaid of the Lord; be it unto me according to thy word (Luke 1:38)."** Mary has no fear and no regret. The message came straight from God to Mary via Gabriel, one of God's choice messengers, whose purpose was to minister to the heirs of salvation.

Let us speculate on what went through Mary's mind during her short conversation with Gabriel. The priestly side of Mary's family had occupied the offices of both king and priest. These were close relatives of Mary. You remember that God had put a curse on the wicked Coniah, who was from the lineage of David. That curse from God had prohibited anyone from the kingly line of David to ever sit on the throne of Israel again **(Jeremiah 22:28-30).** Mary's father had been assassinated or executed by the wicked tyrant, Herod the Great. Gabriel's message was that God was here to reestablish the line of David through Mary's child. This fulfilled a desire of Mary's heart.

Furthermore, we know that God had a remnant of true worshipers in Judea, and these worshipers were looking for the Messiah. Mary may have well been able to quote the Scriptures in Isaiah that state:

📖 **(Isaiah 9:6-7) For unto us a child is born, unto us a son is given: and the government shall be upon his shoulder: and his name shall be called Wonderful, Counsellor, The mighty God, The everlasting Father, The Prince of Peace. ⁷Of the increase of his government and peace there shall be no end, upon the throne of David, and upon his kingdom, to order it, and to establish it with judgment and with justice from henceforth even for ever. The zeal of the LORD of hosts will perform this.**

Mary is elated and filled with joy. And why not? Mary has found favor with God. That is what Gabriel said. Oh! Much more than that. Mary is "highly favored!" Mary has no sorrow, no regrets, no doubts, and no fears. Or as you will hear some say today, "no worries." In fact, as we shall shortly see, Mary is filled with joy and the Spirit of God. Mary needs to tell someone. But who is going to believe her?

Well, there is another miracle birth mother in the family. Mary will go to see Elisabeth and will tell her. Be assured, Mary will have plenty to say. Let us look at the account of Mary's visit to Elisabeth. This is one of the many passages in the Bible that reveals God's magnificent blessings on his people. Follow verse by verse as we make some comments at the appropriate verses.

📖 **(Luke 1:39) And Mary arose in those days, and went into the hill country with haste, into a city of Juda;**

We will discuss this later, but Zacharias was a sheepherder as well as a priest. Zacharias and Elisabeth lived somewhere south of Bethlehem in the hill country. Some think that the city they lived in was Hebron. Mary will travel an estimated 120 miles. She is not traveling through an unmarked wilderness but on a marked Roman road. She evidently takes no traveling companion. Mary immediately sets out to visit her cousin Elisabeth. Of course, while not living together, Mary is fully married to Joseph as per the customary marriage contract in that day. We will discuss the marriage customs and their marriage in upcoming chapters. It is Joseph's job to prepare a place for Mary. They live in the same town, Nazareth. Nazareth is your typical small town. Mary certainly knows how Joseph is progressing in the preparation of their residence. Mary, no doubt, leaves a note for Joseph letting him know that she is going to the hill country to visit Elisabeth for a few weeks. Or Mary may have just dropped by to see her husband and tell of her short departure.

📖 **(Luke 1:40-41) And entered into the house of Zacharias, and saluted Elisabeth. ⁴¹And it came to pass, that, when Elisabeth heard the salutation of Mary, the babe leaped in her womb; and Elisabeth was filled with the Holy Ghost:**

Zacharias had a special visit from the angel of God. Mary had a special visit from that same angel. Here Elisabeth is going to have a special visit from the Holy Ghost of God. Look at the narrative. The Holy Ghost reveals to Elisabeth the fullness of the divine favor of God on her cousin Mary. Just a comment here on the accuracy of the King James Bible. The Greek words for "Spirit" and "Ghost" are the same. There is a difference between a ghost and a spirit. Where appropriate the KJV translators took advantage of extra words available in English and reflected the difference between a ghost and a spirit. A ghost has a form, and a spirit has no form. The Holy Ghost was in Elisabeth. The Holy Ghost, for a few minutes, took the form of Elisabeth, just as the Holy Ghost indwells a believer today.

📖 **(Luke 1:42) And she spake out with a loud voice, and said, Blessed art thou among women, and blessed is the fruit of thy womb.**

In case you have not caught on by now, Elisabeth is going to have herself a shouting time. The old-timers would say that she is "getting happy." And why not? Elisabeth's praise and blessing are directed toward Mary and the divine babe. Just a critical doctrinal note here. Mary is highly favored and blessed. But Mary is "among" women. Mary was not sinless. Neither was Mary's conception "immaculate." The false Catholic doctrine of immaculate conception teaches that God preserved the virgin Mary from the taint of original sin from the moment she was conceived. This teaching is without evidence. Additionally, Mary was not a perpetual virgin.

Mary was born with a sinful nature, and thus sinned in the same manner as every other member of Adam's race. Mary also conceived at least 6 more times and had 4 sons named in the Bible and at least two unnamed daughters.

📖 **(Luke 1:43) And whence is this to me, that the mother of my Lord should come to me?**

Zacharias and Elisabeth were looking for and expecting the Messiah.

📖 **(Luke 1:44-45) For, lo, as soon as the voice of thy salutation sounded in mine ears, the babe leaped in my womb for joy. ⁴⁵And blessed is she that believed: for there shall be a performance of those things which were told her from the Lord.**

This passage says that the six-month-old unborn John the Baptist leaped for joy in his mother's womb. If you do not understand this, I do not either. Elisabeth says that Mary has "believed." In other words, Mary is a believer, and God's blessing is on Mary because she believed. Mary is a woman of faith, and if you are a child of God by faith, then you can expect God's blessings to be upon you. There is more. Elisabeth says to Mary that God will perform what He said He would do. Is that what she is saying? No! Elisabeth is not just saying it. Elisabeth is shouting it out! This writer has been in several services that you could call "shouting" services. I have said "amen" a lot of times but never really shouted. Just so you know, as Christians we need to believe that God is going to keep His promises. God's promises are worth shouting about.

This upcoming passage is Mary's song of praise. The ancients have given Mary's song the title of "The Magnificat." This song is patterned after Hannah's song in the Old Testament.

📖 **(Luke 1:46) And Mary said, My soul doth magnify the Lord,**

It has been pointed out that the Lord fills the heavens and the earth and technically could not be made any greater. Ah! Mary will enlarge the Lord in the eyes of all who read her song.

📖 **(Luke 1:47) "And my spirit hath rejoiced in God my Saviour.**

Mary was in the same sinful condition as everyone of us that belong to Adam's race. Here, Mary lifts her voice in praise and expresses her joy in the fact that she has a Saviour. And there is no salvation except through God. God provided His only begotten Son and Mary's Son for us that we might have everlasting life.

📖 **(Luke 1:48-49) For he hath regarded the low estate of his handmaiden: for, behold, from henceforth all generations shall call me blessed. 49For he that is mighty hath done to me great things; and holy is his name."**

Mary has a personal God. She is praising her God for what He has done for her. You need to ask and answer this question, "what is God doing for me?"

📖 **(Luke 1:50-55) And his mercy is on them that fear him from generation to generation. 51He hath shewed strength with his arm; he hath scattered the proud in the imagination of their hearts. 52He hath put down the mighty from their seats, and exalted them of low degree. 53He hath filled the hungry with good things; and the rich he hath sent empty away. 54He hath helped his servant Israel, in remembrance of his mercy; 55As he spake to our fathers, to Abraham, and to his seed for ever.**

Look carefully at Mary's praise above. Mary recognizes God's hand on His people "from generation to generation." Mary even praises the Lord for God's judgment on the prideful, haughty, and rich. You may remember that David, on several occasions, prayed for judgment on the wicked. Today, we have a false view of holiness that would permit us from asking God to bring judgment on someone. Mary's father was dead at the hands of Herod. Mary looked and longed for the day when Herod was to receive his just recompense.

So, we find that Mary shared and testified to Zacharias and Elisabeth of all that was in her heart and mind. Of course, the Holy Spirit came to direct and inspire Mary's words of praise. However, the Holy Spirit always directs inspiration using the background, experiences, and personality of the person He inspires. Mary was well schooled in the Scriptures and a true worshiper of the living God of Israel.

📖 **(Luke 1:56) And Mary abode with her about three months, and returned to her own house.**

So, Mary stays about three months and then returns to Jerusalem.

As instructed by the angel, Joseph comes to get his wife upon Mary's return. We pick up the story of Mary in the following passage.

📖 **(Luke 2:4-7) And Joseph also went up from Galilee, out of the city of Nazareth, into Judaea, unto the city of David, which is called Bethlehem; (because he was of the house and lineage of David;) 5To be taxed with Mary his espoused wife, being great with child. 6And so it was, that, while they were there, the days were accomplished that she should be delivered. 7And she brought forth her firstborn son, and wrapped him in swaddling clothes, and laid him in a manger; because there was no room for them in the inn.**

We want to feel sorry for Mary. Mary would abhor and distain our sympathy. Mary is not faint of heart.

Mary packs up with her husband and they travel up to Jerusalem and down to Bethlehem. She is carrying precious cargo. The God of heaven looks on as His Son is being carried by His mother Mary on this journey. The Heavenly Host of Angels will appear later. However, you can be sure that God has provided an unseen escort of heavenly beings to watch over the holy family.

Does Mary understand the prophecy that she is about to fulfill?

📖 **(Micah 5:2) But thou, Bethlehem Ephratah, though thou be little among the thousands of Judah, yet out of thee shall he come forth unto me that is to be ruler in Israel; whose goings forth have been from of old, from everlasting.**

Herod did not know. However, the chief priests and the scribes answered immediately. Mary was born into the priestly family. Mary certainly could have known that her child's expected birthplace was Bethlehem.

In New Testament times, basically three tribes had reoccupied Jerusalem and surrounding Judea. They were the tribes of Judah, Levi, and Benjamin. The descendants of David would be a major portion of those who occupied Judah during that era. Thus, there were several residents of Nazareth who were of the house and lineage of David. Joseph and Mary probably traveled with an entourage of those folk. In any case, there is every reason to believe that Mary is headed to Bethlehem in good spirits and in the calm assurance that God is in control.

Mary and Joseph arrive. Another chapter will cover the place where Mary gave birth and provide a little-known aspect of the place of our Lord's birth and His Nativity.

Mary brings forth her firstborn son and the next Biblical scene opens with the shepherds.

📖 **(Luke 2:16-19,) And they came with haste, and found Mary, and Joseph, and the babe lying in a manger. ¹⁷And when they had seen it, they made known abroad the saying which was told them concerning this child. ¹⁸And all they that heard it wondered at those things which were told them by the shepherds. ¹⁹But Mary kept all these things, and pondered them in her heart**

When the shepherds arrive, Mary is mentioned first in the narrative. Mary, not Joseph, is premier in the book of Luke. Joseph, not Mary, is premier in the book of Matthew. The shepherds take note of Mary first. Then, they worship the babe in a manger.

The Bible says in this passage that Mary kept these things and pondered these things in her heart. Mary is as sharp as a tack, intelligent, and brilliant. Mary makes a mental note of every detail. The word "pondered" should remind you of an ancient balance scale. The normal ancient balance scale would hold the scale in place with a three-connector rope or chain attached to the balance beam. Mary weighs this experience of the shepherds as they rehearse the scene and the sayings of the heavenly host. Mary connects these things back to the Old Testament prophecies concerning the coming Messiah and her direct experience of the visit from Gabriel.

As we continue to follow Mary through the book of Luke, we need to look at what the apostle Paul had to say about the birth of Jesus in **Galatians 4:4, "But when the fulness of the time was come, God sent forth his Son, made of a woman, made under the law."** We know that when Jesus came, He was the sinless spotless Son of God. He was beyond reproach in every area of his life. He kept the Old Testament law flawlessly. In this passage in Luke, Jesus is a baby and unable to keep the law. God has chosen two godly parents that will fulfill every Old Testament law. There will never be a time or opportunity for Jesus to receive a reproach from any man for anything.

Note the meticulous adherence to the law.

📖 **(Luke 2:21) And when eight days were accomplished for the circumcising of the child, his name was called JESUS, which was so named of the angel before he was conceived in the womb.**

The necessary fulfillment of the law continues.

📖 **(Luke 2:22-24) And when the days of her purification according to the law of Moses were accomplished, they brought him to Jerusalem, to present him to the Lord; 23(As it is written in the law of the Lord, Every male that openeth the womb shall be called holy to the Lord;) 24And to offer a sacrifice according to that which is said in the law of the Lord, A pair of turtledoves, or two young pigeons.**

The purpose of this visit to the temple by Mary and Joseph is double fold. First, they were presenting Jesus, the firstborn, to fulfill the law. You remember, the last plague in Egypt was the death of the firstborn. God spared the firstborn of the children of Israel through the sacrifice of the Passover lamb. God then laid special claim on the firstborn. In other words, the firstborn son belonged to God. Listen to **Exodus 34:20, "... All the firstborn of thy sons thou shalt redeem. And none shall appear before me empty."** Later God substituted the Levites for the firstborn. In practice, the Levites were set apart as God's special tribe to serve the Lord by performing the required ordinances of God. The firstborn of the other tribes of Israel were not set aside for the Lord's service. However, the firstborn of all the tribes were required to be presented before the Lord as an acknowledgment of God's right of claim on the firstborn. This was simply a memorial ordinance that remembered what God had done in the past, and of course, this ordinance and ceremony looks forward to what God is going to do through His Son in the future.

In the book of Exodus, the lamb was substituted and died for the firstborn at the time of the first Passover. Today, God's Lamb has died for you. God's firstborn lamb is your substitute.

The second reason for visiting the temple, was for Mary to fulfill her purification rite according to the Old Testament law of Moses. We need to note that Mary and Joseph offered turtledoves or pigeons which were the sacrifices offered by the poor. Joseph is just getting started in their marriage, and his financial means are minimal.

While Mary and Joseph were at the temple, there was an old, just, and devout prophet named Simeon who was by special revelation from God, waiting to see the Christ child. Simeon gives a brief and powerful prophecy exalting Christ. We will pick up the Biblical narrative.

📖 **(Luke 2:33-35) And Joseph and his mother marvelled at those things which were spoken of him. 34And Simeon blessed them, and said unto Mary his mother, Behold, this child is set for the fall and rising again of many in Israel; and for a sign which shall be spoken against; 35(Yea, a sword shall pierce through thy own soul also,) that the thoughts of many hearts may be revealed.**

Joseph is mentioned first here, and then Mary. Both marvel at Simeon's special prophetic message delivered especially to Joseph and Mary. This prophecy also contains an eternal warning for all generations. The eternal fate of every single person will be determined by what they do with Jesus. You will fall or rise eternally based upon your acceptance or rejection of Jesus.

Now, at this point in the narrative, Simeon turns his attention to Mary. The Son of Mary is set up **"for a sign which shall be spoken against."** If you know the Lord Jesus Christ, you love Him. This is not the case with everyone. The wicked and the profane hate Christ, and they are not silent about it. The life of the Lord Jesus Christ here on earth was filled with criticism and contradiction. Christ is the great divide. The Bible says, **"he shall be for a sanctuary; but for a stone of stumbling and rock of offence."** Many and even most will be offended by Christ. By their words, their evil and pernicious ways will be revealed to the world. In the end, you know the story, they will take Christ and hang Him on an old, rugged cross. There, the sword will pierce through the soul of Mary as predicted by Simeon.

Today, we find countless cases of wayward children who bring shame to their parents, and the sword of their rebellion pierces the souls of their father and mother. There is no rebellion in Jesus, but the actions of others who will hate her Son will bring the piercing sword to Mary's heart. Mary does not need our sympathy when she rocked the cradle to care for the Son of God. But Mary deserves our deepest compassion as she witnessed her Son die on the cross.

Luke 2:39 provides a summary of how Mary and Joseph performed the Old Testament ordinances given by Moses.

📖 **(Luke 2:39) And when they had performed all things according to the law of the Lord, they returned into Galilee, to their own city Nazareth.**

Yes, Jesus died for you, but He also lived a perfect, sinless life for you and "performed all things according to the law of the Lord."

Chronologically, it is believed by many that the Wise Men came at this point. When the Wise Men arrived, only Mary's name is mentioned. Mary and Joseph then had to flee to Egypt to protect the baby Jesus from murderous King Herod. These events are relayed to us in the gospel of **Matthew 2:1-21.** Our comments for this portion of Scripture will be reserved for another chapter herein.

Twelve years later, the family of Mary and Joseph travelled with an entourage and go up to Jerusalem for the feast of the Passover. It is a time for family, for friends, for celebration, and for worship by all Jews everywhere. They observed the feast of the Passover. On the way back and after a day's journey, Mary and Joseph found that Jesus is not among their family and acquaintances. After a three-day search, Mary and Joseph found Jesus in the temple. We will pick up the Scripture here and let it speak.

📖 **(Luke 2:46-47) And it came to pass, that after three days they found him in the temple, sitting in the midst of the doctors, both hearing them, and asking them questions. 47And all that heard him were astonished at his understanding and answers.**

Jesus has the answers. Jesus had the answers even as a child. The old well-traveled proverb is still true, "Jesus is the answer!"

📖 **(Luke 2:48) And when they saw him, they were amazed: and his mother said unto him, Son, why hast thou thus dealt with us? Behold, thy father and I have sought thee sorrowing.**

In case you are not paying close attention, Mary took the lead, and she was the one speaking to Jesus.

📖 **(Luke 2:49-51) And he said unto them, How is it that ye sought me? Wist ye not that I must be about my Father's business? 50And they understood not the saying which he spake unto them. 51And he went down with them, and came to Nazareth, and was subject unto them: but his mother kept all these sayings in her heart.**

Jesus was subject to Mary and Joseph. But it is Mary that paid attention and carefully stored all these sayings and events in her heart. Mary was a special woman. Mary watched her special Son as He grew and matured.

📖 **(Luke 2:52) And Jesus increased in wisdom and stature, and in favour with God and man.**

Chronologically, the next time the New Testament speaks of Mary, she was attending a wedding in Cana of Galilee. For our purposes here, we will just look at the first five verses and note the dialogue between Mary and her Son.

📖 **(John 2:1-5) And the third day there was a marriage in Cana of Galilee; and the mother of Jesus was there: ²And both Jesus was called, and his disciples, to the marriage. ³And when they wanted wine, the mother of Jesus saith unto him, They have no wine. ⁴Jesus saith unto her, Woman, what have I to do with thee? Mine hour is not yet come. ⁵His mother saith unto the servants, Whatsoever he saith unto you, do it.**

In the above passage, Jesus and his disciples were called, or as we would say today, "invited," to this marriage ceremony in Cana. Mary came to Jesus and simply stated, "They have no wine." Mary did not directly ask our Lord for anything in this case. Some have conjectured that Mary was the director of the wedding. After an examination of the narrative, you will note that Mary uses the word "they." So, Mary and Jesus apparently were guests at the wedding.

Jesus responded to Mary using the word "woman" and not the term "mother." Some think that Jesus was indicating to Mary that their relationship was now different and would be forever different. Granted, Jesus had left home, started His ministry, and gathered His disciples. However, a new relationship with His mother is not indicated here. The Bible certainly reveals the exact opposite.

Today, to use the address of "woman" would be offensive. However, we use the word "Lady" today as a term of endearment. This is the sense that Jesus used the term "Woman." Our Lord would never offend His mother in any way.

Jesus goes on to say to Mary, "what have I to do with thee?" You can do your own homework. You will find where this phrase or sentence is a form of rebuke and offense in other passages of the Bible. Also, most commentators find a mild rebuke from Jesus to Mary with the above comment. However, this does not fit the narrative here. Could it be that our Lord was offering this statement as a bit of playful whit with a slight tease intended?

The Lord follows this statement by saying, "mine hour is not yet come." The Lord's time would come when He truly revealed who He is through His death, burial, and resurrection. The Lord is not ready to do that on this occasion. There will be a time coming when there will be suffering and heartache for our Lord and for Mary. This is not the time. This is a wedding celebration and a joyous occasion.

No one ever walked the face of the earth who knew the humanity of our Lord as well as His mother. She was in no way rebuked or deterred in the mission of the moment. The Lord had not verbally promised to do anything to help in this situation. But Mary knew her Son, and this matter was settled to Mary's total satisfaction.

Mary turned to the servants. The Bible does not say what authority Mary has over these servants. There can be no mistaking, Mary was giving the orders. Mary evidently had a certain social standing, coupled with some natural leadership ability. Mary was not a young girl anymore. She was, in all probability, somewhere between 45 and 50 years old. Joseph was presumably dead at this point. Mary as the family matriarch assumed her position with assurance and dignity.

Mary turned to the servants and addressed them, **"Whatsoever he saith unto you, do it."** At least, part of the Nike slogan "just do it" belongs to Mary.

This is the very first miracle that Jesus performed, and this He did for his beloved mother. Think of it! Jesus performed His first miracle just to prevent an embarrassing situation at a wedding.

An interesting note here is that the water pots were described in this passage as being made of stone. A few years back, critics had a field day disparaging the Bible over the "stone" water pots. According to them, water pots were made of clay from the potter's wheel in Bible times. What an awful error in our Bible. However, this argument was easily refuted when the archaeologist's spade dug up some water pots made of stone in that region. The word of God is correct. Further explanation of this miracle does not fit the scope of this book.

We have already noted, many think the above event forever changed the social relationship of Mary from mother to woman. Not so! Let us continue in this passage

📖 **(John 2:11-12) This beginning of miracles did Jesus in Cana of Galilee, and manifested forth his glory; and his disciples believed on him. [12]After this he went down to Capernaum, he, and his mother, and his brethren, and his disciples: and they continued there not many days.**

Jesus and His disciples travelled together with Mary and His brothers. Before retirement, this writer spent a lot of time working out of town. Travel was a necessity of my occupation. In the last eight years of my career, there were about twenty-four overnight trips each year. Most of the time, they were multiple nights. These trips were always mixed with some personal time. Personal time would be shopping, sightseeing, and always eating at a special place. Many times, my wife, Pam, would travel with me. I like to spend time with my wife. Jesus liked to spend time with His mother and His brothers, and Mary especially liked to spend time with her Son.

Jesus is not walking this earth today. But Jesus has time to walk with you, and Jesus would like to walk with you. If you know Him, you need to be walking alongside Him

Just a side note. The brothers of Jesus will not readily accept His claims as Messiah. Warren Weirsbe sums up the relationship of our Lord to His brothers:

> Toward the end of Jesus' ministry, His brethren are mentioned as urging Jesus to prove His Messiahship, which they themselves doubted **(John 7:3-5).** That they were later converted is clear, for they are described in Acts as uniting with the disciples and others in 'prayer and supplication' prior to Pentecost **(Acts 1:13-14).** Paul implies that they were all married **(1 Corinthians 9:5).**

The next time we see Mary, Jesus was touring and preaching with His disciples. Mary and the brothers of Jesus came by to see Him. The Bible does not give us an exact time frame or an exact place for this episode. Let us look at the Bible:

📖 **(Matthew 12:46-50) While he yet talked to the people, behold, his mother and his brethren stood without, desiring to speak with him. ⁴⁷Then one said unto him, Behold, thy mother and thy brethren stand without, desiring to speak with thee. ⁴⁸But he answered and said unto him that told him, Who is my mother? And who are my brethren? ⁴⁹And he stretched forth his hand toward his disciples, and said, Behold my mother and my brethren! ⁵⁰For whosoever shall do the will of my Father which is in heaven, the same is my brother, and sister, and mother.**

This same scene is repeated in **Mark 3:31-35 and Luke 8:19-21.**

This would seem to be a somewhat minor incident in the life of Christ. However, a sovereign God instructed Matthew, Mark, and Luke to include this scene in their respective narratives. This was not written for Mary, or to Mary, but rather preserved for us today. The saved, born again Christian has the Lord Jesus Christ as a close relative. Thus, this was written for our admonition and for emphasizing our close personal relationship with Him. There is no doubt that Jesus found time to spend with His mother and His brethren.

Mary-is not mentioned by name in any of the three passages, and the names of his brothers are not mentioned. If we go back 150 years ago and beyond, you find a real resistance among Protestant Bible scholars and commentators to believe that Mary had children. They claim that the term "brethren" can have an extended definition and apply to cousins. You can certainly understand this belief among Catholics who believe in Mary's perpetual virginity. But why the insistence of Mary having no children by Protestants of yesteryear is a mystery. In any case, Mary had children. Let us look at the following passage.

📖 **(Mark 6:2-3) And when the sabbath day was come, he began to teach in the synagogue: and many hearing him were astonished, saying, From whence hath this man these things? And what wisdom is this which is given unto him, that even such mighty works are wrought by his hands? ³Is not this the carpenter, the son of Mary, the brother of James, and Joses, and of Juda, and Simon? And are not his sisters here with us? And they were offended at him.**

The straightforward interpretation says that Jesus is the Son of Mary. If "James, and Joses, and if Juda, and Simon... and sisters" were not of the offspring of Mary, the question does not make sense. In other words, the Bible critics claim that we know Jesus to be a carpenter, the son of Mary, and to have the afore named brothers and unnamed sisters but they belong to another mother. The passage loses any rational thought line if Jesus is the son and the others are cousins or from another wife of Joseph. Both claims are suggested by various non-believing speculators.

One more comment here. Mary was well known as the matriarch of her family.

📖 **(Matthew 13:55) Is not this the carpenter's son? Is not his mother called Mary? And his brethren, James, and Joses, and Simon, and Judas? And his sisters, are they not all with us?**

In this passage, we have the same arguments as above. Except, the brothers and sisters in this passage are siblings that are said to belong to both Joseph and Mary. Any interpretation that denies that Mary and Joseph had sons and daughters is fallacious and ludicrous. The Bible tells us how to interpret itself, **"Which things also we speak, not in the words which man's wisdom teacheth, but which the Holy Ghost teacheth; comparing spiritual things with spiritual" (1 Corinthians 2:13).** In context, the spiritual things above are words, but "**not in the words** which man's wisdom teacheth." We must compare spiritual words to spiritual words within the context of the Bible to interpret the Bible.

Finally, look at the following two verses:

📖 **(Luke 2:7) And knew her not till she had brought forth her firstborn son: and he called his name JESUS"**

📖 **(Matthew 1:25). "And she brought forth her firstborn son, and wrapped him in swaddling clothes, and laid him in a manger; because there was no room for them in the inn.**

Both Matthew and Luke make a special point of mentioning that Mary brought forth her **"firstborn"** Son. The Bible is a simple book. We do not have to be too educated to understand some things about the Bible. Here is one thing we can understand. Matthew and Luke both noted that Mary brought forth her **"firstborn"** Son because both understood that there was a second born son, and third born son etc.

Our next encounter with Mary is at the crucifixion of her Son.

📖 **(John 19:25-27) Now there stood by the cross of Jesus his mother, and his mother's sister, Mary the wife of Cleophas, and Mary Magdalene. ²⁶When Jesus therefore saw his mother, and the disciple standing by, whom he loved, he saith unto his mother, Woman, behold thy son! ²⁷Then saith he to the disciple, Behold thy mother! And from that hour that disciple took her unto his own home.**

This study about Mary should be a blessing to you. Our Bible contains a wealth of information about Mary. In many cases, it is easy for us to discern her thoughts and emotions. Now, her Son is dying an awful death. The prophesied sword of Simeon is now piercing the heart of Mary. To venture what went through Mary's mind in this situation is beyond our comprehension.

Our Lord looked on from the cross and gently addressed Mary by simply saying, **"Woman, behold thy son!"** Turning to John the disciple, **"Behold thy mother!"** The Bible continues, **"And from that hour that disciple took her unto his own home."**

At this time, circumstances had resulted in strained relationships with Mary's sons. It was apparent that John and Mary were close acquaintances. The resurrection of our Lord, His subsequent appearances, and the inauguration of the New Testament church would necessitate some special care and protection for Mary.

To many it may seem that Mary, the matriarch, kept the apron strings too tight and her brood under her feet. Well, the estranged and alienated relationships with her family do not last long. After three days and three nights, our Lord and Mary's Son came out of the grave. For forty days, the resurrected Lord was seen on multiple occasions, proving Himself to be alive by many infallible proofs. In **John 10:30-31,** John the Beloved, after the resurrection, states that Jesus did many other signs in the presence of His disciples that are not recorded in the Gospels. The Lord could have easily appeared to Mary and His brothers and sisters, or they could have been at the post-resurrection meeting mentioned in **1 Corinthians 15:7.**

The Lord ascended into heaven. Peter and the disciples gathered in the upper room for prayer, and we have a verse whose first portion is quite oft repeated, **"These all continued with one accord in prayer and supplication,"** and here we have a little phrase that's not often mentioned, **"with the women, and Mary the mother of Jesus, and with his brethren" (Acts 1:14).**

The unbelieving brothers were now believing brothers with both a physical and spiritual kinship. These brothers were not going to be believers who sit around on their blessed assurance. They became workers for the Lord and some, if not all, became spiritual blue-bloods.

James the brother of Jesus, became the leader of the church at Jerusalem (see **Acts 12:17; 15:13).** Peter ordered a special message to be sent to James after Peter's miraculous release from prison **(Acts 12:17).** Paul's documented visit to Jerusalem states that he saw only Peter, and **"James, the Lord's brother" (Galatians 1:18-19).** James made the pivotal speech at the Jerusalem meeting discussing the salvation of the Gentiles **(Acts 15:13–22).** In addition, Paul recognized James as a pillar of the church in **Galatians 2:9** and recorded visiting with James on his meeting to see Peter in **Galatians 1:9.** The Lord also directed His brother James to pen the little epistle that bears his name.

Let us not forget, that most conservative Biblical scholars deem that the writer of the epistle of Jude, who identifies himself as the "brother of James," was the brother of our Lord **(Jude 1).**

Before we close the book on Mary, let's look at this little verse found in **1 Corinthians 9:5, "Have we not power to lead about a sister, a wife, as well as other apostles, and as the brethren of the Lord, and Cephas?"** The apostle Paul is defending his apostleship in context with this verse and mentions **"the brethren of the Lord."** Apparently, the Lord's brothers were itinerant evangelists traveling from place to place with their wives.

Joseph and Mary had raised a family to be proud of. Some of the Protestant commentators of yesteryear have been terribly unkind to Mary indicating that Mary was an ignorant and backward social misfit. The Bible record reveals Mary to be a lady of class and most deserving of our respect. May I say in a moment of prideful arrogance, that I know a couple of class ladies: my wife, Pam and my daughter, Rachel.

Chapter 7
Joseph, Man of Action—A Personal Profile

(Matthew 1:18-25) Now the birth of Jesus Christ was on this wise: When as his mother Mary was espoused to Joseph, before they came together, she was found with child of the Holy Ghost. ¹⁹Then Joseph her husband, being a just man, and not willing to make her a publick example, was minded to put her away privily. ²⁰But while he thought on these things, behold, the angel of the Lord appeared unto him in a dream, saying, Joseph, thou son of David, fear not to take unto thee Mary thy wife: for that which is conceived in her is of the Holy Ghost. ²¹And she shall bring forth a son, and thou shalt call his name JESUS: for he shall save his people from their sins. ²²Now all this was done, that it might be fulfilled which was spoken of the Lord by the prophet, saying, ²³Behold, a virgin shall be with child, and shall bring forth a son, and they shall call his name Emmanuel, which being interpreted is, God with us. ²⁴Then Joseph being raised from sleep did as the angel of the Lord had bidden him, and took unto him his wife: ²⁵And knew her not till she had brought forth her firstborn son: and he called his name JESUS.

The first question in a job interview of a new applicant is this, "Tell me about yourself." Well, Joseph is not going to tell us about himself. Search through each passage where Joseph, the husband of Mary, is mentioned, and in every instance, you will find that Joseph had nothing to say.

There is great virtue in staying silent. One man said that among his favorite possessions were words that he never said. Another suggested that we should never say anything unless it improved upon silence. Some find silence to be brutally frightening. Strangely enough, silence can be an excellent method of communication. Actions always speak volumes more than words. Actions rather than words reveal what is in the heart of man. There are a lot of things that are silent about Joseph. We know that the father of Joseph was a man named Jacob. We have no idea of the age of Jacob when Joseph was born. There is nothing said about Joseph's mother. We know nothing about brothers or sisters. The Bible and history are completely silent about Joseph's family.

The Bible is totally silent about the physical features of Joseph. We know he was a Jew and of the lineage of David. The normal physical Jewish characteristics would be present. We find no description, no picture, no portrait, no photograph, no negative print, or even a faint sketch depicting the physical features of Joseph.

The Bible and history continue to remain silent about habits, pastimes, personal idiosyncrasies, and preferences of Joseph. If we think about Joseph and think about the calling of God, his marriage, and the relationship between Joseph and his firstborn Son, we would like to know more, but instead we face a silence that is deafening.

The Bible narrative utters sentences and phrases in various places that do in fact speak for and about Joseph. **Matthew 1:16** is the first mention of Joseph, **"And Jacob begat Joseph the husband of Mary, of whom was born Jesus, who is called Christ."** The Jewish marriage customs and the marriage of Mary and Joseph will be discussed in detail in the next three chapters. We have covered Joseph's genealogical record. The narrative says that Jacob begat Joseph, but the Bible in its divine accuracy does not say that Joseph begat Jesus. Thus, this portion ever so subtly and precisely supports the Biblical doctrine of the virgin birth.

Of course, when we are looking at the first sixteen verses of Matthew, we are looking at the lineage of Christ. We should not miss the fact that we are also looking at the lineage of Joseph. The lineage traces back through the kingly line of David and fourteen generations prior to that we find the father of faith and the founder of the Jewish nation—Father Abraham. The former patriarchs have supplied Joseph with a royal pedigree.

My maternal grandfather was Hiram Broyles from Greene County, Tennessee. Granddaddy Broyles was a farmer. He was tall, strong, healthy, rugged looking with coal black hair. He was an excellent manager and very prosperous. He was a steward in the Methodist Church and later in life a politician who served as County Trustee. We rotated visiting grandparents every other Sunday after church. During election season, politics was the subject of the Sunday afternoon visit. My grandfather could have easily been the forerunner of Rush Limbaugh. My grandfather's influence resides with me daily.

Today most people have no understanding of how much they are affected by their heritage. This writer was about 13 or 14 years old and played baseball at the old Bowmantown school. We were taking infield and going through our usual pregame warm-ups. The team came off the field to prepare to start the game. A middle-aged man came up to me and said, "I have no idea who you are, but you are kin to Hiram Broyles—you walk like him and move like him." We had never met. This stranger had worked with my grandfather farming and knew him well. Point being, we inherit the physical traits, the mental capacity, the emotional nature, and the personality that make us who we are internally. Externally, we inherit the reputation of our forefathers.

Our first encounter with Joseph occurs with the appearance of the angel of the Lord in a dream. The angel addresses Joseph as "thou son of David." The Bible never wastes a single word or a jot or tittle. The angel addressed Joseph as a son of David because Joseph understood his relation to his forefathers. David was a mighty man of valor and the premier warrior of the entire history of Israel. His battle exploits were unmatched. David became King and established his kingdom as a world power. David's rule brought unprecedented wealth to the nation of Israel. So, we find that King David as a great historical figure would be important to Joseph. David's relationship with God and his spiritual testimony would also be an example to Joseph. David was a man after God's own heart. He had the special blessings of God on his life. Remember, the seed of David was promised a kingship that would last forever.

The angel of the Lord is going to confirm his message and give Joseph some assurance by quoting the prophecy in **Isaiah 7:14: "Therefore the Lord himself shall give you a sign; Behold, a virgin shall conceive, and bear a son, and shall call his name Immanuel."** Mary would be fulfilling this prophecy. God is in the business of keeping and verifying His word.

In the time that Joseph lived, the subjects of history and religion were in the same book. Schooling in Joseph's day was centered around God's word, so Joseph learned about David as king and worshiper of the true God. David was part of Joseph's heritage, a hero, and a man to be replicated and imitated. Boys want to run the race, climb the highest mountain, hide in the scariest haunt, and fight the Philistines. There could be little doubt that Joseph imagined himself to be in David's shoes as he faced Goliath the giant.

Joseph's family in times past had the special grace and favor of God upon them. David's descendants forsook the God of Israel. God removed the kingship from David's line. After the wickedness of Coniah, there was a curse upon the royal seed of David, and none of Coniah's children and posterity would be eligible for the throne of David. Fourteen tedious generations had passed since the last king from David's line ruled. After Babylon, a limited number from the tribes of Judah, Levi, and Benjamin had repopulated the land of Israel. Since that time, Judea had a sordid history and little national prosperity. At times when Judea was able to rise to self-rule, members of the tribe of Levi occupied the throne. The glorious reign of David served as an unremembered relic of a day long past. Joseph was almost in exile in the little hill town of Nazareth. There had been 400 years without a revelation from God until the angel appeared to Zacharias. However, Joseph, in all probability, would not have known about this angelic visitation.

When the angel of the Lord came to Joseph, he was likely beaten down emotionally and in a state of confusion and doubt about Mary's pregnancy. Mary, no doubt, had just recently let him know of her condition and the nature of her conception. Mary would have gone directly to Joseph and let him know of her pregnancy immediately upon her return from the visit to Elisabeth. It has been well said that God is never early or never late. Thus, the angel of the Lord appeared to Joseph in a dream and saluted him, **"thou son of David."** The title, **"thou son of David"** would have certainly been uplifting to the downtrodden Joseph. But there was going to be much more than just a title. Joseph would have the desire of his heart fulfilled in the short dissertation of this angel. The angel messenger of the Lord verified Mary's account of the virgin conception.

Continuing, the angel provided us a great summary of who Jesus is. Here is a summary of what the angel said:

1. The conception of Jesus was a divine conception–of the Holy Ghost.

2. The child would be called Jesus which means, "Jehovah is salvation." The Bible goes on to say, **"for He shall save His people from their sins."** Every schooled Christian knows that the word "gospel" means "good news." "Gospel" is a combination word from the two words "God's spell." Or we would say, "God's word." The entire theme and message of the Bible is "Jesus saves." Sadly, if you were to survey Christians today, over half could not tell you that the theme of the Bible is "the redemption of mankind."

Matthew 1:22 & 23 explains that Jesus is the fulfillment of Isaiah 7:14. There can be no doubt that Joseph understood that Jesus was the Messiah and was the fulfillment of Old Testament prophecy. If Joseph did not understand that at this point, he would certainly understand it after Mary related to him the full narrative from Gabriel to her.

"Well, Joseph what do you have to say? Joseph, what do you think?" Joseph was not answering. "Joseph, what are you going to do?" The question had already been answered. Joseph immediately got up out of bed and went to get his wife. There was no argument, no discussion, and no more contemplation. Joseph did what he was told to do.

For just a moment, we will depart from the theme of this chapter. The narrative above says that Joseph "**took unto him his wife: And knew her not till she had brought forth her firstborn son: and he called his name JESUS.**" To the Catholics who religiously hold to the erroneous doctrine of the "perpetual virginity of Mary," this passage indeed teaches that Joseph and Mary consummated the marriage – "**And knew her not till.**" The passage is clear that Joseph knew her after Mary brought forth her "**firstborn**" son. The wording is exact. This passage teaches that Mary had more sons because the term "**firstborn**" is used. In fact, as we have already proved, there was at least a second born, third born, fourth born, and fifth born son. In other words, there are four additional sons besides Jesus and at least two unnamed "**daughters.**"

Another Catholic tradition holds in some circles that Joseph never married Mary. The other sons and daughters were supposedly from a former marriage. An old Joseph can be seen in some minds. This old Joseph was impotent and unable to consummate the marriage. Ignorantly, the dogma of an "old Joseph" is carried over in many cases into Protestant thought. The only Biblical basis for this thought is that Joseph apparently died before Mary. In any case, the Biblical narrative shows Joseph as a man full of energy and always moving quickly—that's a young man's quality! Now, let us look again at Joseph.

Joseph, an obscure nobody, from a virtual nowhere, had just had his stock to go up. The God of this universe has chosen Joseph to be the legal and earthly father of His only begotten (physically born) Son. In the wisdom of this world, Joseph is not much. But the wisdom of God overruled and intervened. This carpenter would have the privilege of knowing the Son of God and God in the flesh, in an intimate and personal way that no other man would ever know Him. Joseph was God's selected and assigned earthly parent, provider, personal protector, and guardian of the Lord Jesus Christ.

The Bible narrative bears proof, that this is not Joseph's first encounter with the living God. It is said of Joseph that he was a "just" man. To be just is to be righteous. Sinful man has but one path to acquire righteousness from a righteous God. That is, man must acquire righteousness through faith from God. Joseph's first mentioned ancestor was none other than Abraham. Abraham was said to be the friend of God. Abraham received his righteousness through faith. The Bible gives us this record, "**And he believed in**

the LORD; and he counted it to him for righteousness"
(Genesis 15:6). It cannot be doubted that Joseph knew and
understood that a sin sacrifice was required and that without the
shedding of blood there was no remission of sin. Joseph had
appropriated faith in Jehovah God which had been credited to his
account, and thereby God declared him a righteous and just man.
Joseph knew God.

It is my deep-seated opinion that God chose a man that He
could tailor and adapt to perfectly fit the job description of caretaker
and father of the Christ child. Joseph was a man whose intellect,
personality, and demeanor perfectly fit the job description. Although
Joseph was silent in the Biblical narrative, he was not a klutz or
backward chump. Joseph was a son of David, a child of God, and a
willing and understanding servant. Many of the excellent traits found
in Abraham and David were exhibited in Joseph. Joseph understood
responsibility and got the job done. We see here, and we will see later,
that Joseph is a man of action.

Joseph and his Heavenly Father have something in common.
They have chosen the same lady! We will shortly cover the customary
Jewish marriage technical and ceremonial process. Nazareth was a
little town with a population of two to four hundred people. Joseph
and Mary would have attended the same synagogue, social
gatherings, and religious festivals. All of Nazareth used the same
water supply. It is known today as "Mary's Spring" or "Mary's Well."
You would have to imagine that they would meet there often. Their
homes were probably less than a mile apart. We have discussed Mary,
and she was certainly the trophy of the town. We have said that Mary
could turn the head and heart of any man. It was Joseph who won her
heart.

As we have pointed out before and we will point out again,
Joseph is not the stepfather or the foster father of Jesus. These terms
tend to demean and downgrade the role of Joseph in the Biblical
narrative. Although Joseph was not the physical father of Jesus,
Joseph was 100% the legal and earthly father of Christ.

Chronologically, the next time we see Joseph after the angel
spoke to him, he travelled to Bethlehem, **"And Joseph also went
up from Galilee, out of the city of Nazareth, into Judaea,
unto the city of David, which is called Bethlehem; (because
he was of the house and lineage of David;)" (Luke 2:4).** Mary
accompanied her husband. Christmas pictures and drawings portray
Joseph and Mary traveling alone and Mary riding on a donkey.
Remember that in this time, Judea had only three tribes with a
substantial amount of people who resettled there. There is little

doubt that several from Nazareth would have to make the trip the Bethlehem. In my opinion, Joseph and Mary had a small assembly of traveling companions. Joseph dutifully made the trip with Mary as he was expected to do. That is all we know. There is no record that Joseph had anything to say.

You know the story; they arrived at Bethlehem and Mary delivered her firstborn son. What did Joseph think, and how did he feel? There is no record that Joseph had anything to say.

The heavenly host appeared to the shepherds watching over their flock. They conducted a praise and worship service. Shortly thereafter, the shepherds came to see Mary and Joseph and the Christ Child. Joseph faithfully stood by, but Joseph has nothing to say.

On the eighth day after the birth of the Christ child, Jesus was formally given His name, and the ritual of circumcision was performed. Faithfully following the law on the fortieth day, Joseph and Mary made their way to the temple to present Jesus before the Lord and to perform the purification rites for Mary. Simeon and Anna were there with their prophecies and blessings. The Bible narrative records that both Joseph and Mary marvel at the things said of Jesus. There is no record that Joseph had anything to say.

Some think that the Wise Men appeared shortly after the temple visit. For our purposes in this chapter note this portion of Scripture from Matthew.

📖 **(Matthew 2:11-15) And when they were come into the house, they saw the young child with Mary his mother, and fell down, and worshipped him: and when they had opened their treasures, they presented unto him gifts; gold, and frankincense, and myrrh. 12And being warned of God in a dream that they should not return to Herod, they departed into their own country another way. 13And when they were departed, behold, the angel of the Lord appeareth to Joseph in a dream, saying, Arise, and take the young child and his mother, and flee into Egypt, and be thou there until I bring thee word: for Herod will seek the young child to destroy him. 14When he arose, he took the young child and his mother by night, and departed into Egypt:
15And was there until the death of Herod: that it might be fulfilled which was spoken of the Lord by the prophet, saying, Out of Egypt have I called my son.**

From verse 11, it seems apparent that Joseph was not there (probably working) at the time of the Wise Men's visitation. The Wise Men seemingly arrived at twilight or early evening. They presented their gifts and night set in. That night, God appeared to the Wise Men in a dream and they departed to their own country by another road.

The same night, the angel of the Lord appeared to Joseph in a dream and instructed him to flee to Egypt. The Bible records nothing that Joseph had to say. There is no mention of complaining, questioning, rebellion, hesitation, or second guessing. I believe Jesus would have been about six weeks old at the time. Many quite erroneously speculate that Jesus was about two years old. We will deal with this matter in chapter 24 when we discuss the chronology of the Wise Men.

Joseph and Mary quickly gathered the things that they needed for travel. God had provided Joseph and Mary some financing and assets through the gifts of the Wise Men. God's instruction for Joseph was to flee to Egypt. Joseph likely did not travel to the Nile. However, some speculate that the family of Jesus fled to Alexandria where the Jewish population was over 1 million and believe the holy family remained there for a few years. The border of Egypt, at that time, was less than seventy miles away near Gaza. From Jerusalem to the border of Egypt would be a shorter distance than from Bethlehem to Nazareth. The travel time walking or traveling with one or two donkeys would be three to four days. They would be there just a few short weeks before their return.

The Bible tells us nothing about the thoughts and emotions of Joseph. Although we would like to know, there is no record that Joseph had anything to say.

The next time the Bible narrative mentions Joseph is 12 years later when their family travelled to Jerusalem for the Passover Feast which was discussed in chapter 6. You know the story. There is no record that Joseph had anything to say to Jesus when he and Mary found Him in the temple. The Bible narrative records that Jesus obediently returned to Nazareth with them and was subject to His parents.

The Biblical sequence of events documenting the actions of Joseph closes here. Additionally, as we have already documented, Joseph is referenced a few times in the gospel accounts recognizing him as the father of Jesus. Also, Joseph is known as **"the carpenter."** Jesus is specifically called **"the carpenter's son"** in **Matthew 13:55** and **"the carpenter"** in **Mark 6:3**. The indication is that Jesus operated His father's business after the death of Joseph.

Yes, we would like to know more about Joseph. Joseph was the father of at least seven children including the Lord Jesus Christ. Joseph knew the Lord. Joseph was a man of integrity and a man of action. Joseph was a man of dignity and honor. Joseph won the heart of Mary. Joseph was fully the earthly and legal father of our Lord Jesus Christ and handpicked by God for his special task. Joseph remains an example for fathers everywhere today.

Chapter 8
New Testament Jewish Marriage Customs

The Christmas story is sometimes robbed of its beauty and majesty by various Johnny-come-lately speculations and imaginations by some Biblical commentators and expositors who try to fit Jewish marriage customs into our modern-day traditions. If we properly interpret the Christmas story, we will marvel at the simple truths and doctrinal overtones found in the marriage of Joseph and Mary.

For us to understand the marriage of Mary and Joseph, we need to have a basic knowledge of Jewish marriage customs. The primary source for our review of the Jewish marriage customs will be Zola Levitt. Zola Levitt was the most beloved and well-known Messianic Jewish Bible teacher and Middle East commentator of his day. Zola's teachings were thoroughly rooted in Jewish culture and tradition. Zola Levitt Ministries was stationed in Dallas Texas and Zola sponsored a national TV broadcast. Zola's ministry was international in scope, and his doctrinal views precisely mirror those of the authors. I have reviewed literally dozens of articles and YouTube presentations on the customs of the Jewish marriage process. Zola, in my opinion, was the best. In addition, Zola's presentation of Jewish marriage customs exactly mirrors the Bible's perspectives and the numerous typology references to marriage by our Lord. These marriage customs were even followed by Zola and his father. Zola insisted that these same customs have been followed for the last 2000 years.

The Mosaic law was much too strict to allow for our modern-day dating customs. Women were exalted in the Jewish society. Christianity and Judaism have always elevated their ladies providing freedoms and opportunities unknown to other people groups, cultures, and religions throughout the world. Women could move freely in business, societal, and religious circles. Women could own property, conduct business, and generally administered all household affairs.

When a young man decided to seek a bride, Jewish societal traditions permitted the potential husband to look any place his heart desired. Ladies who were eligible and seeking a husband walked unveiled throughout the Jewish society. A suitor could meet a lady in the marketplace and follow her home. Eligible prospects might be found next door, at a synagogue meeting or a social gathering. For that matter, the young man may not have known, met, or seen the girl before, although this would be a highly unusual situation.

When the young man found a young lady that he thought would be a suitable bride, he had some preparation work to do before he could approach the bride with a marriage proposal. The suitor must have three things before he could approach the bride with the proposal.

First, the suitor must have a marriage contract. The marriage contract, called a ketubah was an elaborate and detailed document. The ketubah is a unilateral Jewish civil legal contract whereby the husband ensures to the bride that he will meet the financial obligations and other traditional marital responsibilities of the marriage.

The marriage contract would also designate the price to be paid to the father for the bride. Jewish historians are quick to point out that the suitor was not actually purchasing the bride. Call it whatever you may. If the suitor did not have the money, the suitor did not get the bride. This writer could not find the standard cost for a bride. However, the common fee was to be paid to the father based upon the labor he lost from the daughter. Jewish commentators make it plain that the purchase of a bride was not cheap. The future husband would generally be a few years older than his bride because the husband would have to generate income to cover the cost of the bride. Now, if the bride had a good and benevolent father, that father would turn around and return the bride's fee to his daughter. The price of the bride would then become part of the dowry.

This contract would provide stipulations comparable to what we would find today in a prenuptial agreement. It was possible that the bride could bring substantial assets to the marriage. Her dowry could be as simple as an old pioneer hope chest. However, if she came from an affluent family, the bride could bring money, property, animals such as sheep and goats and donkeys, and any other assets that she or her father might want to provide. In the event of divorce, the marriage contract would assure that all the assets brought to the marriage by the wife would revert to the wife. This was an excellent deterrent to divorce.

When the suitor had a suitable marriage contract drawn up, according to Zola, the other two things required were the money to purchase the bride and a flask of wine. The suitor would set up an appointment and come calling. Upon entrance into the house, the father and the suitor would meet, and the conditions of the contract would be reviewed. If everything were in order, the potential bride would be called, and an official proposal of marriage would be made by the suitor. In the process of the proposal, the suitor would pour a cup of wine for his hoped to be bride. The couple would be left alone to discuss whatever they wanted to discuss. The deliberations, if we could call it that, could be a few minutes or hours. In the end, the decision of the proposed bride was indicated by what she did with the cup. If the proposed bride pushed the cup back and did not drink of the wine, the suitor was rejected and would hit-the-door with his bride fee and useless contract in hand never to be heard from again. If the bride took the wine and toasted her suitor, the answer was "yes", and the marriage was on. Of course, the husband would respond by returning a toast to his wife.

Witnesses were called and the marriage contract was signed by the suitor and prospective bride. The witnesses formally attested to the contract. An astute suitor would no doubt have a personal, maybe somewhat intimate, present for his bride-to-be. There would be a small celebration, and the husband would leave to prepare the living quarters, house, or mansion for his wife. The husband could then return for his wife at any time.

Right here is one of the places that most contemporary Bible teachers make a huge mistake. They reason that the couple is engaged or betrothed. Not so! The couple is married, 100% positively absolutely married. The following provides infallible proof of their marriage.

1. The marriage contract has been signed by the husband before witnesses who also signed the contract, with the bride and father attesting to the marriage.
2. The husband paid for the bride up front. This was no small purchase, and the marriage contract finalized the deal.
3. The contract is a legal document binding both the husband and wife.
4. To break this contract for any reason, including infidelity or a change of heart, would require a legal divorce.
5. In the event, the husband or the wife died, the remaining partner would inherit the deceased spouse's assets.
6. After the marriage contract was signed, the bride would wear a veil, and in some cases a head band made up of coins to show that she was paid for and married.
7. They would speak of each other in terms of "my husband" or "my wife", and society would act accordingly. In other words, they were thought of as husband and wife by all acquaintances.

There are some things that we need to deal with here. Some say that in ancient times, Jewish marriages were prearranged by the parents and that the bride had little to no say in the selection of her partner. Undoubtedly this did happen in a few and rare occasions.

An example of this would be the wicked tyrant, Herod the Great, who had 9 wives. Three of those wives were daughters of the Jewish elite priestly families. In the years before Christ was born, the state of Judea was under Roman control, and there was a power struggle going on between the Jews and Rome. Herod used the Roman army to destroy Antigonos, the Hasmonean heir to the throne.

The princess Mariamne of the royal Levitical family of the Hasmoneans was used as a pawn by her mother, Queen (Salome) Alexandra, and her grandfather, Hyrcanus. In an arranged marriage Mariamne, was given to Herod the Great. Of course, this was none other than a failed attempt to keep power in Jewish hands.

Princess Mariamne was a beautiful girl with a most noble character and married Herod out of loyalty to her nation and family. History records that Herod loved her and relished his good fortune. However, Herod, full of jealousy and hungry for power, continued his cold-blooded murder of most of the members of Marriamne's family to satisfy his desire for power. Princess Mariamne was helpless to do anything to help her family.

Through political pressure, in part, by the famous Anthony and Cleopatra, Herod appointed Mariamne's brother Aristobulus, to the position of high priest. Herod loved his wife but hated her family. Herod had Aristobulus drowned at a pool party (just like we would have today) a few short weeks after he had appointed him high priest. This murder was supposed to look like an accident. However, Herod was exposed shortly after the murderous incident.

Herod was called to Rome to answer for his dastardly deed. He did not want anyone else to get his lovely wife Mariamne and gave orders to his brother-in-law to have her killed in the event he did not return.

In brief, Herod beat the charges and returned home. Salome, his sister, was jealous of the beautiful Mariamne. Salome trumped up charges of infidelity, and Herod believed his sister. Herod in turn had Mariamne tried by his personal tribunal and she was executed even though she was innocent. Herod had Mariamne embalmed, and her body was stored in the palace for seven years. Herod married seven more times, with two wives being from the priestly line of the Jews. You remember also that the Bible gives us a record of Herod's slaughter of the innocents in Matthew 2:16.

The author has read and watched well over a dozen articles and documentaries about Herod. These recorded Herod's many political and military exploits and gave glorious reviews of his architectural accomplishments. Most of these pundits stressed their disbelief in the Biblical account of the slaughter of the innocents. Herod was an arrogant, egotistical, and power crazed tyrant driven to insanity by his own desire for political position and power. The Bible is accurate as always in its account of the slaughter of the innocents by Herod. The Biblical narrative is in perfect harmony with the rest of his lifestyle. In case you have missed it, Mariamne and her family were related to Mary.

We have departed. The point is that a young lady always had the right to accept or decline a marriage proposal with one of the rare exceptions being a cruel father prostituting his daughter for financial or political gain.

It is disgraceful that so many believe that the prospective bride did not have a choice or say in the matter of choosing her own husband. From the earliest of Bible times, the woman has had a right to accept or to decline a marriage proposal. Remember Abraham sending his eldest servant to fetch a bride for Isaac? The servant presented his case and was ready to leave the next day. The family wanted the servant to stay a few days, but the servant called for a decision, and the Bible says, **"And they called Rebekah, and said unto her, Wilt thou go with this man? And she said, I will go" (Genesis 24:58).** This old and unnamed servant must have been quite a salesman. Rebecca fell in love with a man she had never seen. These verses describe a delightful insight to this romance, **"And Rebekah lifted up her eyes, and when she saw Isaac, she lighted off the camel. For she had said unto the servant, What man is this that walketh in the field to meet us? And the servant had said, It is my master: therefore she took a vail, and covered herself" (Genesis 24:64-65).** Do not miss this. Rebecca's question is rhetorical. She knew Isaac the minute she laid eyes on him. We will know Jesus when we see Him.

Some say that the parents arranged marriages and negotiated the marriage contract in Biblical times and that the groom had little to do with the marriage. Samson is an example that is pointed to. However, Zola Levitt makes no mention of the groom's parents. In New Testament times, societies were more open, and personal freedom was of paramount importance. The suitor would have to speak for himself. History records numerous young men of marriageable age as having entire armies assigned to them. New Testament times, by necessity, required boys to become men quickly.

Several Jewish marriage commentators imply that romance was not an important consideration in the Jewish marriage process.

Zola disagrees. This writer disagrees. Solomon surely disagreed in his Song. The Bible disagrees at every turn. God created romance, and it has always been important to marriage.

Some Jewish marriage commentators have said there was a year waiting period between the signing of the marriage contract and the marriage celebration and consummation. Some have said two years. All seem to think there was some flexibility in this final stage. Some have even gone so far to say that this was a testing time to find out if the bride was pregnant. This is sheer lunacy.

When the marriage contract was signed, the Jewish couple was legally married. The husband could collect his wife at any time he chose. Today, in our culture, a couple is married as soon as they take their vows and the pastor or presiding official pronounces them "man and wife." In Jewish times, the vows were in the marriage contract. In our times, when a couple pledge their vows, the couple can have a wedding celebration or leave for their honeymoon or go home or anywhere else they please; they are married. We repeat, in Jewish times, when the marriage contract was signed, the Jewish couple was legally married in the eyes of each other, their parents, their neighbors, their society, their government, and their God. The Lord Himself compared His return to the marriage customs of New Testament times. Just as the groom can collect his bride any time after the marriage contract is signed, the Lord can return and collect His bride, the church, at any time.

Zola Levitt explains the origin and significance of the Passover and demonstrates the feast in his video series entitled The Miracle of Passover. Zola also has a book with the same title. He beautifully illustrates for us how Christ is revealed in every moment of every step of the Jewish Passover feast. He calls the Passover feast "The Crown Jewel" of Biblical feasts and additionally describes this feast as the "Christian Love Story."

Throughout the Passover meal, four cups or toasts are offered as a part of the Passover celebration. The third cup or toast is described as the most beautiful and touchingly symbolic part of the entire feast. The third cup is The Cup of Redemption and is, in fact, the Passover cup that Jesus partook and offered his disciples before his crucifixion. The Passover cup exactly and exquisitely mirrors the toast that was celebrated by the bride and the groom.

Matthew 26:27–28 records the Lord raising the Cup of Redemption: **"And he took the cup, and gave thanks, and gave it to them, saying, Drink ye all of it; For this is my blood of the new testament, which is shed for many for the**

remission of sins." As you are aware, from this is derived our ordinance of the Lord's Supper.

At the third cup Zola explains the marriage customs of the Jews of Jesus' time which we have reviewed above. The marriage customs at the time of Christ were very prescriptive and precisely comparative to the redemption and salvation of the believer.

The Lord Jesus Christ came into this world, went to a rugged cross, and paid the price of redemption. Today, the Lord offers, to every sinner who will come, the cup of redemption. When a sinner says yes to the Lord, that sinner in effect is partaking of the redemption cup. The Bible is clear in declaring that the corporate church is the bride of Christ.

After the Jewish marriage contract was signed, the new husband had to return to his father's house to prepare their dwelling. The family configuration in New Testament times was more structured and tighter than today. The newly wedded couple would almost certainly live in the father's house but in a special dwelling or bridal chamber prepared by the husband. Before the husband would leave after the marriage contract was signed, he would say something like this to his wife. "Let not your heart be troubled, don't worry about a thing. I go to prepare a place for you. Ye believed in me enough to marry me. I go away now, but if I go away, I will come again and receive you to myself, that were I am there you may be also."

Think for a moment, the young husband would be preparing a place for his wife and one of his friends might drop by. The friend might ask, "when will you be done?" The young man would answer, "only my father knows." The father acting as a building inspector would protect the wife from a less than ideal dwelling put together by an overanxious husband. Here, we will quote directly from Zola Levitt's book The Miracle of Passover:

> At home the bride would keep an oil lamp and plenty of oil standing by, for her groom might well come at midnight and she had to be ready to travel, even in the dark. In fact, that was the idea; the groom would try to surprise the bride by coming at an unexpected hour. All the Jewish brides were "stolen," abducted, and they took great pleasure in the romance of it all (the Jews knew a thing or two about love!). When the bridegroom approached the house, he came with a shout.

Just as the bride waited for her husband to return, we are waiting for our Lord to return. God the Father will tell God the Son when to return. Several of the Lord's parables were set in scenes related to a wedding. We know that the next thing on God's prophetic calendar for the church is the rapture of the church. Shortly after that, God has scheduled the marriage supper of the Lamb.

As Christians today, we wait for the Lord. Although, we believe the Lord is coming, we know not when. Most of us are twiddling our thumbs and waiting patiently. We have the wrong attitude. We need to be a little bit impatient and look toward the eastern sky with an eager and expectant attitude. After all, we have been purchased with a great price **(1 Corinthians 6:20).** Our purchase price was not paid with paper currency, nor silver or gold, but with the most precious commodity that has ever been known–the blood of Christ **(1 Peter 1:18-19).** In case you have missed it, we are precious to the Lord. The Lord is looking forward to coming for you and taking believers to live with Him.

We will close with another portion from Zola's book, The Miracle of Passover. This excerpt gives us some excellent insight to the Lord's supper and the wonderful uplifting personality of one of the Lord's choice servants, Zola Levitt.

What a promise! Now you know how to get married Jewish-style! All that had to be said in order to demonstrate properly the magnificent blessing that Jesus said over the wine. **[At the Passover supper just prior to the Lord's crucifixion]** We were discussing the third cup, the one taken with the hidden bread, and now we can better understand what Jesus said when He "gave thanks." He really did toast His bride, as was the custom. Here it is: Blessed art Thou, O Lord our God, King of the universe, Creator of the fruit of the vine. That's the blessing, in all its simplicity. But what meaning it has! You see, Jesus has already said, "I am the true vine." Now He blesses "the fruit of the vine." Well, that's us! The disciples were the branches and we're His fruit. And so He drank a toast to us, the church, the fruit of the Vine, the Bride of Christ.

Upcoming, we will look at the marriage of Joseph and Mary. In summation, Mary and Joseph were completely and legally married when Mary conceived the baby Jesus through the Holy Ghost. No, they were not living together in a conjugal relationship. Their marriage made Jesus the legal Son of His earthly father and eligible for the throne of His father David. In addition, Joseph was neither a stepfather nor foster father to the Lord Jesus. Properly termed, Joseph was both the legal and earthly father of Jesus.

Chapter 9
The Marriage of Joseph and Mary

Understanding the Jewish marriage customs significantly enhances our knowledge of who we are in the Lord. We will look carefully and prescriptively at the biblical narratives leading up to the Lord's birth. Some details will be emphasized and repeated. There are two aspects of the marriage of Joseph and Mary and our Lord's birth which are almost universally misunderstood. One aspect is doctrinal and the other is practical. We will find that the Bible is correct.

Christians need to realize that Joseph and Mary were married when the Biblical narrative begins. Our previous chapter offered a seven-fold proof that Joseph and Mary were married according to the Jewish Biblical customs of their day. We will also find that the Bible narrative in the King James Version fully recognizes this.

There is a critical doctrinal issue that is at stake here. The issue: Joseph and Mary had to be married for Jesus to have a legal right to the throne of David. The Bible clearly establishes that the lineage of Christ through Joseph was given to prove that Jesus is the only possible legal heir to the throne. You remember that God put a curse on Coniah. Through Joseph and through the miracle of the virgin birth, the Lord Jesus will be legally eligible to sit on the throne of David. However, Joseph and Mary must be married to make Jesus the legal heir. We noted a group of erroneous and bogus interpretations of the lineage of Mary in Luke. Almost all Bible commentators recognize that Matthew's genealogical record of Jesus is the "legal" line descending from David. However, some Bibles fail to recognize that Joseph and Mary were legally married at the conception of Jesus. Again, they had to be married for Jesus to be the legal heir to the throne of David. Let us be clear, when Matthew opens his gospel, Mary and Joseph were already legally married, but had not consummated the marriage nor would they engage in marital relations until after the birth of Christ.

Let us look at the King James narratives. These are given for your quick review.

📖 **(Matthew 1:18-25) Now the birth of Jesus Christ was on this wise: When as his mother Mary was espoused to Joseph, before they came together, she was found with child of the Holy Ghost. ¹⁹Then Joseph her husband, being a just man, and not willing to make her a publick example, was minded to put her away privily. ²⁰But** while he thought on these things, behold, the angel of the Lord appeared unto him in a dream, saying, Joseph, thou son of David, fear not to take unto thee Mary thy wife: for that which is conceived in her is of the Holy Ghost. 21And she shall bring forth a son, and thou shalt call his name JESUS: for he shall save his people from their sins. 22Now all this was done, that it might be fulfilled which was spoken of the Lord by the prophet, saying, 23Behold, a virgin shall be with child, and shall bring forth a son, and they shall call his name Emmanuel, which being interpreted is, God with us. 24Then Joseph being raised from sleep did as the angel of the Lord had bidden him, and took unto him his wife: And knew her not till she had brought forth her firstborn son: 25and he called his name JESUS.

📖 (Luke 1:26-27) And in the sixth month the angel Gabriel was sent from God unto a city of Galilee, named Nazareth, 27To a virgin espoused to a man whose name was Joseph, of the house of David; and the virgin's name was Mary.

📖 (Luke 2:1-7) And it came to pass in those days, that there went out a decree from Caesar Augustus, that all the world should be taxed. 2(And this taxing was first made when Cyrenius was governor of Syria.) 3And all went to be taxed, every one into his own city. 4And Joseph also went up from Galilee, out of the city of Nazareth, into Judaea, unto the city of David, which is called Bethlehem; (because he was of the house and lineage of David:) 5To be taxed with Mary his espoused wife, being great with child. 6And so it was, that, while they were there, the days were accomplished that she should be delivered. 7And she brought forth her firstborn son, and wrapped him in swaddling clothes, and laid him in a manger; because there was no room for them in the inn.

The word "espoused" means wedded or married. The problem is that most Bible commentators, pastors, and teachers misinterpret the word "espoused." They interpret espoused as "engaged." The word is quite easy to understand. If you have a spouse, you are married. If I say to someone this is Pam, my spouse. That means Pam is my wife and not my date, not my fiancé, not my live-in girlfriend.

Pam is my espoused, wedded, married wife. Consider the following dictionaries and their definitions of the word "espouse."

Dictionaries and definition of "espoused"	
Dictionary	**Definition**
Merriam – Webster	Marry
dictionary.com	to marry
KJV dictionary	to marry; to wed
Free Dictionary	a. To take in marriage; marry. b. To give (a woman) in marriage.
Oxford	ARCHAIC – marry
Lexico	Archaic – Marry
Your Dictionary	To espouse means to get married.
Vocabulary.com	take in marriage
Online Etymology Dictionary	to take as spouse, marry
Dictionary.net	To take in marriage
Wordsmyth.com	to take in marriage
Wordnik.com	To take in marriage; marry; wed.

Fifteen different online dictionaries were consulted. Of course, the word "espouse" used today has the most common meaning of something like "support" as in "to support a cause." "Espouse" in some dictionaries when used in reference to marriage is considered archaic. The archaic meaning of "espouse" rendered "to marry" is in perfect accordance with the King James translation of 1611. Summing up, the unquestioned primary meaning of the archaic word "espouse" is "to marry or to wed."

Now let us look at our Bible in **Matthew 1:18-25.** The Bible says that Mary was **"espoused to Joseph, before they came together..."** The context is absolutely evident that Mary is married to Joseph in this phrase. In context, here is why.

1. In the phrase above, if Mary and Joseph were engaged, why would the phrase "before they came together" be relevant? If Joseph and Mary were not married at that time, the remark would be nonsensical.

2. "Espoused" means "married or wedded." When a "d" or "ed" is added to a word it signifies that that word is past tense.

3. The text states here that Joseph was **"her husband."** Joseph cannot be engaged and be Mary's husband at the same time.

4. The passage says that Joseph was "minded **'to put her away privily.'"** All agree that the phrase "to put her away privily" means "to divorce." Why would Joseph consider divorce if he were not married to Mary?

5. The angel of the Lord tells Joseph, **"fear not to take unto thee Mary thy wife."** We think this angel was Gabriel. The Bible does not say. In any case, his reference to Mary was this, **"fear not to take unto thee Mary thy wife."** The angel did not say, "fear not to take Mary *to be* thy wife." Mary was the wife of Joseph, and it is abundantly clear from the text.

6. The Bible says that Joseph arose and **"took unto him his wife: And knew her not till she had brought forth her firstborn son: and he called his name JESUS." (Matthew 1:25).** Joseph did not go to get Mary and take her to get married. Mary was **"his wife."**

Let us go to the book of Luke and see what Luke has to say about the marriage of Joseph and Mary. **"And in the sixth month the angel Gabriel was sent from God unto a city of Galilee, named Nazareth, To a virgin espoused to a man whose name was Joseph, of the house of David; and the virgin's name was Mary"** (Luke 1:26-27).

This passage mentions that Mary was a virgin in two different places. If they had been only engaged, there would be no point in referring to Mary as a virgin. If you are thinking ahead, you could point out that the Bible is emphasizing the doctrine of the virgin birth. You would be right. However, because Mary and Joseph are married, the virginity of Mary is mentioned and emphasized in double portion.

Joseph and Mary travel down to Bethlehem and Mary's time to deliver is at hand. We read in **Luke 2:5, "To be taxed with Mary his espoused wife, being great with child."** "Espoused" means married. The text says, **"espoused wife."**

If Joseph and Mary were not married, then we could say that Joseph and Mary did not have the sense that "nature gave a goose." We would have to ask, what were they thinking?

If they are not married at this point, Joseph and Mary made an illegitimate child of the Lord Jesus Christ and thus disqualified the Lord Jesus Christ from sitting upon the throne of David. Technically, if the conception of Mary took place at any time before the marriage of Joseph and Mary, Jesus would have had no right to the throne of David.

This writer went to biblehub.com and reviewed various old and new translations of **Luke 2:5.** There were twenty-eight Bible versions reviewed. Five versions got it right. Twenty-three versions get it wrong. Why do they get it wrong? Most new versions use a thought-for-thought sense-for-sense method of translation instead of the word-for-word translation method used by the KJV. Nineteen of the 23 erroneously translated versions failed to translate the word wife. In the phrase "espoused wife", the word "espoused" is an adjective and the word "wife" is a noun. A noun is the more important and stronger word in a sentence. The adjective is of less importance. The 19 translators in the above 19 versions make a reckless and egregious error. I contacted my beautiful and intelligent, English teacher daughter, Rachel Renée Shanks, to verify the above assessment. She quickly stated that nouns and verbs were the "beans and potatoes" of a sentence. The pseudo-translators above yielded their imaginative imitation interpretation and left the "beans" off the table and in the pot.

J. Harold Greenlee, a retired One Mission Society International missionary is the author of more than a dozen books and more than 150 articles mostly pertaining to New Testament Greek. Dr. Greenlee is a conservative Greek textual critic and journalist par excellence. Dr. Greenlee died at 96 years of age in 2012. In the Journal of Translation, Volume 8, Number 1 (2012), Dr. Greenlee writes an article entitled Short Note: *Mary, Espoused To Joseph*. This article deals with the inaccurate translation of Luke 2:5 in the modern bibles. Dr. Greenlee states, "the context of Mary and Joseph's relationship makes it clear that they were married when Mary became pregnant. Yet virtually none of the common NT versions recognizes this fact except the King James Version (KJV), which translates this Greek word as "espoused," meaning that Mary was a "spouse," a wife." He continues later in the article, "Most translations, it is clear, let the supposed lexical meaning of the Greek verb overrule the plain sense of the context rather than letting the context determine the meaning of the Greek verb." You can find this article online.

The Bibles printed in English could easily be divided into two divisions, Protestant and Catholic. It is important for us to realize that Catholic and Protestant Bibles were derived from different underlying ancient manuscripts. This is true of both the Old and New Testaments. The translators of the Protestant Bibles rejected the corrupt readings of the Catholic Bibles. Almost all new translations of the new Bibles come from revisions combining the Protestant and Catholic manuscripts. The modern translations of **Luke 2:5** perfectly document this new version corruption.

Catholics tenaciously hold to the doctrine of the "perpetual virginity of Mary." The Eastern Orthodox Church, which names Joseph's first wife as Salome, holds that Joseph was a widower and merely betrothed, but never married, to Mary, and that references to Jesus' 'brothers' are children of Joseph and Salome. While not all Catholics believe this, all Catholics do hold to the "perpetual virginity of Mary." Combination versions of the Bible can be sold to both Catholics and Protestants. The average person in the pew, and many times the pastor and priest in the pulpit, do not know the difference.

The King James Version has the precision of a surgeon's scalpel or sharpshooter's scope. In biblical narratives before Jesus was born, the noun "wife" is used three times when referring to Mary, clearly documenting that Mary was married to Joseph. The phrase "her husband" puts a double emphasis on the fact that Joseph was married to Mary. This is not hard: when a person is a husband or wife, the engagement is over. As we have said before, comparing Scripture to Scripture is a premier method of Bible study advocated by the Bible itself.

Our Bible uses the term "espoused" three times, (used two times as a verb and once as an adjective) describing the wife and husband relationship of Mary and Joseph. Many of the older Bible commentators and dictionaries note that the word "espoused" is also connected with the word "contracted." The biblical word "espoused", used in the nativity narratives, is always a descriptor of Mary. The term "espoused" was used instead of "marriage" to designate that Mary was 100% married through the contracting process. The contracting process to the Jew meant:
1. the contract price for Mary had been paid
2. the marriage contract had been signed and witnessed
3. the marriage was legal in the eyes of government, society, and God.

Thus, we find that biblical customs and the biblical narrative leave no doubt Joseph and Mary were married. This writer made every effort to simplify the translation issues in these new versions that denigrate the nativity of our Lord Jesus Christ. On a personal note, this writer is sickened and repulsed by these new version diversions that make an illegitimate child of my Saviour. When it comes to the Bible, the truth is much better than supposition, fiction, and damnable perversion.

Concluding this section: Although not the physical father, Joseph was the legal earthly father of the Lord Jesus. Joseph was a son of David through Solomon. Joseph (if he were without the curse) would have a legal right to the throne of David. Joseph and Mary were legally married at the time of the birth of Jesus. Jesus, without the fleshly connection to the line of Coniah, has no curse and possesses the legal right to the throne of David. Jesus is and will be the only one in history to be able to legally take and hold this title. Jesus' legal title to the throne of King David is through Joseph, but the physical ancestry to the Son of David is through Mary.

Christ came the first time, and they put a crown of thorns on His head. Christ will return at the second coming and take the throne of David. Then, we can proclaim Him, King of Kings and Lord of Lords. Note, it took the exact combination of the above to work this out.

Through Mary, Christ acquired His human or fleshly side from the line of David and additionally the title "Son of Man." It is through this title "Son of Man" that Jesus becomes our kinsman redeemer. Through the conception of the Holy Ghost, Christ carries the title of the Son of God. Through the birth of Jesus into the family of Joseph, Jesus has the legal right to the throne of David. The curse was removed from the kingly line through the virgin birth, and the line of David has a seed that is eligible to take the throne. Again, Jesus' legal title to the throne of King David was through Joseph, but His physical connection to David was through Mary.

Joseph and Mary combine to give Jesus the complete title "Son of David." And yes, the Lord Jesus Christ is "the Son of David and King of Kings." All of this is divinely and precisely designed because Jesus is the "only begotten." Look at the perfect architecture and craft of thought and word to precisely fit the two concepts of "the Son of David and King of Kings" and "only begotten" into a doctrinal building fitly framed together with our Lord Jesus Christ as the Chief Corner Stone. "Only begotten" provides the tie that binds, the proper connectivity and the total biblical fulfillment to the teaching of "the son of David" and "King of Kings."

Chapter 10
The Immaculate Marriage of Joseph and Mary

And no! This writer does not believe in the erroneous Catholic doctrine of the immaculate conception that teaches that Mary was born without a sin nature. Mary had a sin nature like the rest of us. Christians love the Bible. Christians love the Lord. Christians love the Christmas story. However, many pastors, teachers and Bible commentators have removed much of the simplicity and beauty of the Christmas story by their innovation, speculation, supposition, conjecture, and imagination. Quite frankly, much of this innuendo needlessly neglects the biblical narrative and dishonors our Lord.

Let us look at some of these assumptions. Some of these have already been refuted and some will be refuted herein.

1. Some think that Mary and Joseph did not get married until after the visit of the angel by Gabriel. We have already proved that this did not happen. The reason for mentioning this at this point is that at least one Bible version says that Joseph and Mary were married right after the visit by the angel. This did not happen!

2. Some think that Joseph and Mary had extended relationship problems. Finding Mary with child, Joseph did not really accept Mary. According to this scenario, the angel finally arrived right before the time to go to Bethlehem and Joseph and Mary were married at Bethlehem. This did not happen!

3. Some proclaim that Mary was viewed as an unwed mother. Depending upon the teacher or commentator, this speculative view has a variety of scenarios and variations. One commentator even says that the only reason Mary went to Bethlehem with Joseph was to avoid the brutal social disgrace that she was undergoing. Bible teachers wail about the terrible emotional trauma, crying and red eyes, that Mary went through at home without a husband. They tell about the horrendous public disgrace and the misery of social ostracization. This did not happen!

There is no biblical basis for regarding Mary as an unwed mother. We repeat. There is "no" biblical basis for viewing Mary as an unwed mother. Biblical scholars always want to define hard to understand words. For instance, let us deal with the word "no." What part of "no" do you not understand? Is it the n or the o? No means no, not, notta, zip, none, zero, not one, not any, nothing, nil, void or naught. The Greek word is όχι. We will look at every questionable passage to prove our point.

After criticism of the baseless supposition and imagination of the above, this writer will now engage in some supposition and imagination of his own. However, there will be a difference in the above suppositions. These speculations will precisely fit the biblical narrative.

We have already covered the character, personality, and intellect of Mary. We have established that she was from the Davidic and priestly lines. Mary's family was well established among the blue-bloods of society. We know nothing about the personal affluence and finances of Mary's family after her father was cruelly annihilated by the murderous hand of the power crazed Herod the Great.

If we go outside the biblical narrative, nothing is known about Joseph, his father, or his immediate family. The extra information about Joseph, found mostly within Catholic Church and Jewish commentaries, has no legitimate historical foundation.

We have previously completed a character and personality profile featuring Joseph. Briefly, we will look at Joseph and his relationship to the Nativity of our Lord. From the biblical narrative, we know that Joseph was from the lineage of David through Solomon and the kingly line. The kingly line had the promises of God pledging an earthly kingdom to David's seed forever. David's kingly seed sinned, and God put a curse on Coniah. Since the time of Coniah fourteen generations earlier, there had been no king in Jerusalem from the line of David.

We can conclude from the sacrifices offered by Joseph and Mary at the temple that Joseph had meager finances. We know not the age of Joseph, but assume he was a young man, a few years older than Mary. Joseph was a carpenter and just getting started in life when the account of the Nativity of our Lord begins. Joseph may have been an apprentice at the time he married Mary. However, carpentry was a skilled trade, and if Joseph were endowed with natural skill and ability, he could make an excellent living for his family.

What we do know about Joseph is that he wooed and won the heart of Mary. Nazareth has been described as the original small town. Isolated in the country about thirteen miles from the Sea of Galilee, the population is estimated at about four hundred. Joseph did not marry a stranger. In such a small town as Nazareth, Joseph no doubt chose the cream of the crop. Those who speculate that Joseph was an old broken-down man have no basis for their speculation. This speculation is dramatically out of context with the biblical narrative.

We know from history that Mary certainly had some beautiful women in her family, and we assume she was well featured, and intelligent, with a vibrant personality. Mary could turn the head and heart of any man. She chose Joseph clearly indicating that Joseph would have been an excellent prospect for marriage.

There could be no doubt of their love for one another. God, in His wisdom, had knit their hearts together. Joseph may have been poor, but he came up with the assets for the contract price of Mary to purchase his bride. Thus, Joseph and Mary were married. Joseph was working on their living quarters when Gabriel appeared to Mary.

Gabriel made his visit to Mary and announced the process and circumstances to be accomplished through the Nativity of our Saviour. Mary left quickly for the hill country to visit with Elisabeth who was also experiencing a miracle pregnancy. There is no doubt in this writer's mind that Mary knew Joseph's construction progress of their quarters. Mary, as a courtesy to her husband and being especially attentive of social protocol, dropped a note to her husband or stopped by for a short visit to tell Joseph of her visit to Elisabeth. The biblical narrative is clear. Mary visited for three months and returned home. These three months were a time of rejoicing and relaxation for Mary. There could be no reason for any social stigma or concerns that you would find in an unwed mother situation. Mary was not an unwed mother; she was married.

Mary had three months to think, contemplate and formulate the next steps in dealing with her husband. The Lord was watching. The Lord was guiding. When Mary returned home, she either went directly to see her husband, Joseph, or dropped Joseph a note asking for him to come and see her.

Let us stop a minute. Most people seem to think that Mary developed a baby bump and a rumor started. The news of her pregnancy traveled through the gossip chain back to Joseph. This writer has a son, John David Shanks. He is the pastor of Beulah Baptist Church in Kingsport, TN. I called my son and asked, "how did Joseph find out that Mary was pregnant?" He responded that he never thought about it but guessed that Mary told him. The next call was to my daughter Rachel Renée Shanks. Same answer. We can safely say, that in any culture, when a woman finds out she is expecting, she tells her husband first.

Again, Mary and Elisabeth had time to think and talk about Mary's situation. Old Zacharias did not have much to say about the subject! (That's a joke.) Mary no doubt had been impressed to take the proper steps by the Lord. Joseph and Mary met maybe late in the evening after work. Mary explained her situation. At about three months into her pregnancy, Mary would possibly display her small baby bump to Joseph. With the modest dress and loose robe type of apparel of that day, no one in the public would have expected Mary's pregnancy.

Joseph loved his wife. Joseph certainly did not understand. Joseph probably left bewildered and sick with an upset stomach. To Joseph's credit, there is no indication that he flew off the handle. Search the entire Gospel narrative and you will find that Joseph had nothing to say—not one word, nor one iota of one syllable of speech. Joseph left brokenhearted.

Joseph returned home. He probably spent several hours pondering the situation. If Joseph were to accuse Mary of infidelity, that would become a public issue and embarrassment to both Mary and him. The Bible plainly says that Joseph was a just man. The only way for a man to be righteous or just is for God to justify him and forgive him of his sins. Joseph was a man who knew and trusted the God of the Bible. He concluded that he would divorce her privately, showing his love and concern for Mary. This was exactly the right decision. The biblical narrative recounting Joseph's thoughts and actions indicates back-to-back occurrences. Joseph found out that Mary is pregnant. He made his decision. He continued to think about and ponder his situation. Joseph, emotionally exhausted, finally slipped off to sleep. The angel of the Lord appeared. We will pick up the Bible narrative here.

📖 **(Matthew 1:20-24) But while he thought on these things, behold, the angel of the Lord appeared unto him in a dream, saying, Joseph, thou son of David, fear not to take unto thee Mary thy wife: for that which is conceived in her is of the Holy Ghost. 21And she shall bring forth a son, and thou shalt call his name JESUS: for he shall save his people from their sins. 22Now all this was done, that it might be fulfilled which was spoken of the Lord by the prophet, saying, 23Behold, a virgin shall be with child, and shall bring forth a son, and they shall call his name Emmanuel, which being interpreted is, God with us. 24Then Joseph being raised from sleep did as the angel of the Lord had bidden him, and took unto him his wife:**

The angel of the Lord delivered his message verifying Mary's story, and assured Joseph of Mary's truthfulness and faithfulness. Joseph, **"being raised from sleep did as the angel of the Lord had bidden him, and took unto him his wife."** It seems to me that most people miss this. Joseph got up and went to fetch his bride!

Maybe you will permit some additional speculation and imagination. If both Joseph and Mary dwelled in the town of

Nazareth proper, the distance between Joseph's house and Mary's house would have been less than thirty minutes walking time.

It is apparent from the biblical narrative that Joseph acted immediately. He walked to Mary's house and knocked on the door. Mary opened the door so fast that her action startled Joseph. Mary may have said something like, "I was just expecting you!" There was probably not much said. There would be plenty of time to talk and to sort things out later. Mary had her bags packed beside the door, motioned to the bags, and they both headed to Joseph's house.

The Bible only gives us the title of the angel of the Lord in the Nativity passage in Matthew. We suspect that the angel was none other than the well-traveled and often used Gabriel. In this writer's mind, Gabriel hung around and watched over the situation until Joseph and Mary got home. Joseph was happy. Mary was happy. And God the Father looked on completely satisfied and pleased with His chosen couple.

In the next few days, there can be no doubt that Joseph and Mary discussed and rehearsed numerous times the accounts of the angelic visits. Their understanding of what was happening to them may have been somewhat limited especially compared to the knowledge we have today looking back at their situation. However, Joseph and Mary understood that Mary was carrying the promised Messiah and Saviour. They also knew that God was going to restore the kingly line of David and that their Son would one day sit on the throne of David. Joseph and Mary had the hand of God on them. They were blessed. They were looking forward to the future with anticipation, great expectations, and hope.

Remember, Joseph and Mary were 100% married and Joseph had the right to take his bride at any time. Although the Bible does not specifically say, it is possible and probable that Joseph and Mary lived together about six months before the birth of Jesus.

Here, speculation and imagination end. Our speculation fits the biblical narrative. We need to repeat our special emphasis here: there is no biblical or legitimate historical record that Mary ever received any ridicule or ostracization due to her pregnancy with Jesus.

Chapter 11
Jesus–The Son of Joseph

And no! We do not believe that Jesus was the physically born or begotten son of Joseph. There have always been the heathens, infidels, skeptics, atheists, agnostics, and unbelievers who have denied the doctrine of the virgin birth. In so doing, they picture Mary as an unwed mother and commonly suggest that the conception of Mary was due to a Roman soldier stationed in a nearby town. There will be no attempt to answer any of these critics. However, we will cover the doctrine of the virgin birth in some detail.

In this chapter, we will address the recent Johnny-come-lately Christian critics who teach that Jesus' enemies often questioned His parentage. This is no small issue. Dr. J Harold Greenlee in the previously mentioned article says, "If it had been discovered that Mary was pregnant and was not married to Joseph—the idea of a miraculous birth would have been considered nonsense or worse—Mary would have lived under a cloud for life, and Jesus would have had no possibility of becoming a rabbi. Almost certainly, no one except Mary and Joseph ever had any thought other than that Jesus was the legitimate son of Mary and Joseph."

Greenlee is right. Several articles were reviewed by this writer. In the Jews prescriptive culture, individuals of questionable parentage were ostracized outcasts and not allowed to enter the temple. The Lord Himself asked, **"Which of you convinceth me of sin?" (John 8:46).** If the Jews thought for one second that Jesus was illegitimate, their reply would have been, "you were born in sin."

We will make every effort to look at every passage that is relevant to the parentage of Jesus. We will find that the reputation of Joseph, Mary, and Jesus was above reproach.

📖 **(Luke 3:23) And Jesus himself began to be about thirty years of age, being (as was supposed) the son of Joseph, which was the son of Heli,**

This verse says that it was customary for the Jews in the time of Christ to **"suppose"** or think Jesus was the son of Joseph. This writer has never heard this verse mentioned in a Bible lesson or sermon. Just think about this. The Jews thought Jesus was the son of Joseph. The language here is straightforward and plain. Upfront, this verse refutes all these speculators that read into the Bible the ridiculous interpretations that claim that the parentage of Jesus was ever questioned.

📕 (Matthew 13:53-57) **And it came to pass, that when Jesus had finished these parables, he departed thence. ⁵⁴And when he was come into his own country, he taught them in their synagogue, insomuch that they were astonished, and said, Whence hath this man this wisdom, and these mighty works? ⁵⁵Is not this the carpenter's son? Is not his mother called Mary? And his brethren, James, and Joses, and Simon, and Judas? ⁵⁶And his sisters, are they not all with us? Whence then hath this man all these things? ⁵⁷And they were offended in him. But Jesus said unto them, A prophet is not without honour, save in his own country, and in his own house.**

Jesus is in his own country. This was early in the ministry of Jesus. However, Jesus had performed several miracles, and He was recognized as a prophet. This passage identifies Jesus as the carpenter's son and the son of Mary. Of course, the answers to their questions are rhetorical. This passage in no way questions the parentage of Jesus. Instead, this passage confirms the parentage of Jesus. Jesus is the son of the carpenter and Mary.

📕 (Mark 6:2-3) **And when the sabbath day was come, he began to teach in the synagogue: and many hearing him were astonished, saying, From whence hath this man these things? And what wisdom is this which is given unto him, that even such mighty works are wrought by his hands? ³Is not this the carpenter, the son of Mary, the brother of James, and Joses, and of Juda, and Simon? And are not his sisters here with us? And they were offended at him.**

This appears to be Mark's account of the same event we reviewed in Matthew. Look at the phrase, **"Is not this the carpenter, the son of Mary...?"** Some commentators speculate that because Jesus was not said to be the son of Joseph in this passage, that the parentage of Jesus was being questioned. Really?

In this passage, Jesus, is called **"the carpenter."** Joseph is evidently dead. Jesus is the carpenter and the head of the household at this point. The critics specifically note the family link connecting Jesus and his brothers and sisters, **"The brother of James, and Joses, and of Juda, and Simon? And are not his sisters here with us?"** With the family connection made to the brothers and sisters, no question of the illegitimate birth of Jesus can be reasonably implied. Note the wording. Mary and the brothers and sisters of Jesus were at the synagogue, and that is the reason they were mentioned. The synagogue crowd was offended because the carpenter whom they knew from their town had become a prophet of God. All anyone must do to get this right is to compare Scripture to Scripture.

📖 **(Luke 4:21-22) And he began to say unto them, This day is this scripture fulfilled in your ears. ²²And all bare him witness, and wondered at the gracious words which proceeded out of his mouth. And they said, Is not this Joseph's son?**

This is Luke's version of the same event mentioned in Matthew and Mark. Here, the people of Nazareth simply verify that they positively thought that Joseph was the father of Jesus. The question is rhetorical. The asking of rhetorical questions was an often-used mode of expression in that day as it is today.

📖 **(John 6:40-42) And this is the will of him that sent me, that every one which seeth the Son, and believeth on him, may have everlasting life: and I will raise him up at the last day. ⁴¹The Jews then murmured at him, because he said, I am the bread which came down from heaven. ⁴²And they said, Is not this Jesus, the son of Joseph, whose father and mother we know? How is it then that he saith, I came down from heaven?**

One nationally known blueblood pastor and commentator uses the above passage as a reference and makes the following comment about the above passage: "Jesus' enemies often questioned His parentage." This pastor's comment is utterly ridiculous and fallacious, totally reversing what the Bible is clearly saying. This is an incorrect Bible interpretation. And no doubt, this interpretation is wrought through some type of doctrinal prejudice or bias.

Again, the question is rhetorical and has an obvious answer before the question is asked. Look at the passage again. The Jews plainly said, **"whose father and mother we know."** To say that the parentage of Jesus is being questioned is unsubstantiated.

If we consider the four previous passages, we note the rhetorical questioning mode of the day was a common recurrence. If we were trying to make the same point today, we would say, "Who does he think he is?" In each of these passages, Jesus is in His hometown, and every person in the little town of Nazareth knew Him. The Lord immediately recognized the problem when He said, **"and A prophet is not without honour, save in his own country, and in his own house."**

This writer was in Washington DC over 20 years ago for a training session. Attending were some of my coworkers and members of our executive board, and they were grouped after a session break. A young lady coworker addressed and stated something very close to this, "Mr. Shanks, I have called and made reservations at Houstons in Georgetown at such and such time, is that all right?" I looked at her and the others nonchalantly and headed back to my room. There was no answer from me. There was no answer needed. Everyone in the group knew that Houstons was my favorite and nothing more needed to be said. In the above passages, the answer was rhetorical. No response was needed because the answer was clear. That is exactly what the gospel writers meant to convey in the passages above. Read on.

📖 **(John 1:45-46) Philip findeth Nathanael, and saith unto him, We have found him, of whom Moses in the law, and the prophets, did write, Jesus of Nazareth, the son of Joseph. And Nathanael said unto him, Can there any good thing come out of Nazareth? Philip saith unto him, Come and see.**

Philip sums up our position. Philip emphatically declared that he had found the Messiah, and that the Messiah was Jesus of Nazareth, the son of Joseph.

There is one other verse some Bible commentators use to question the parentage of Jesus, **"Ye do the deeds of your father. Then said they to him, We be not born of fornication; we have one Father, even God" (John 8:41).** These commentators claim that this statement insinuates Jesus was "born of fornication." If we look at this verse by itself, it appears that this might be what the enemies of Christ are insinuating. But, if we look at the passage in context, they are plainly defending themselves, just exactly as the sentence states. Jesus is speaking at the start of this passage.

📖 **(John 8:37-45) I know that ye are Abraham's seed; but ye seek to kill me, because my word hath no place in you. 38I speak that which I have seen with my Father: and ye do that which ye have seen with your father. 39They answered and said unto him, Abraham is our father. Jesus saith unto them, If ye were Abraham's children, ye would do the works of Abraham. 40But now ye seek to kill me, a man that hath told you the truth, which I have heard of God: this did not Abraham. 41Ye do the deeds of your father. Then said they to him, We be not born of fornication; we have one Father, even God. 42Jesus** said unto them, If God were your Father, ye would love me: for I proceeded forth and came from God; neither came I of myself, but he sent me. ⁴³Why do ye not understand my speech? Even because ye cannot hear my word. ⁴⁴Ye are of your father the devil, and the lusts of your father ye will do. He was a murderer from the beginning, and abode not in the truth, because there is no truth in him. When he speaketh a lie, he speaketh of his own: for he is a liar, and the father of it. ⁴⁵And because I tell you the truth, ye believe me not.

This passage opens by Jesus saying to the Jews who are gathered with Him that He knows these Jews were "Abraham's seed." Jesus talks about His heavenly Father. Jesus also in this passage, is referring to the Jews spiritual father, the devil. The old Methodist Adam Clarke says this in his comment on **John 8:41** where he explains what the Jews are saying to Jesus, "We be not born of fornication – We are not a mixed, spurious breed – our tribes and families have been kept distinct – we are descended from Abraham by his legal wife Sarah; and we are no idolaters."

The issue is this: the Jews believe that because they are physically born into the Jewish family (Abraham's seed), they are automatically born into God's family. The Jews think their physical pedigree makes them a child of God. They were not questioning the parentage of Jesus. The Lord provoked their response by questioning the spiritual heritage of the Jews. Jesus said to them, **"If ye were Abraham's seed?"** The Jews were just adamantly defending themselves against Jesus accusation. If they thought that Jesus was a child of fornication, they would have pointed directly to Jesus and told him so. They did not. The Lord was doing everything He could to convince them that they needed a "new" birth.

Was the Lord concerned about the reputation of Joseph and Mary? The answer is yes. Joseph and Mary would have their trials and hurdles to cross as they served the Lord. The fabrication that Mary was thought to be an unwed mother when she carried Jesus seems to be a recent concoction brewed up by some overly spiritual Christians. Once started, there was monkey see monkey do scholarship. This writer checked nearly two dozen older commentaries, and there was no suggestion of any Jewish stigma on Joseph, Mary or Jesus concerning the paternity of Jesus. There is no biblical evidence that the paternity of Jesus was ever questioned. Few Bible commentators recognize the accuracy and precision of the word of God. The word of God was not intended to be a technical manual.

However, the word of God is always technically correct with an exactitude comparable to DNA and mathematical formulas and equations.

Few realize the importance of this issue. There are family and legal issues at stake. We will start by establishing the relationship between Joseph and Jesus. Joseph was not the foster father or stepfather of Jesus. Joseph was not a substitute father, nor did he step into the place of another father. Joseph can properly be called the "earthly" father of Jesus or the "legal" father of Jesus. In no wise, are we stating that he was the physical father of Jesus. Joseph was the **earthly and legal father of Jesus:**

1. Jesus was conceived after Joseph and Mary were married.
2. Jesus was born after Joseph and Mary were married. Both one and two were necessary components to qualify Jesus as the legal heir for the throne of David.
3. As we have just proved, the Jews always regarded Jesus as the son of Joseph.
4. Joseph from the very beginning provided food, clothing, training, guidance, and fatherly companionship for Jesus.
5. The Bible narrative recognizes and entitles Joseph as both the father and parent of Jesus.

Jesus was the son of Joseph:

1. Jesus was conceived after Joseph and Mary were married.
2. Jesus was born after Joseph and Mary were married. Both one and two were necessary components to qualify Jesus as the legal heir for the throne of David.
3. Jesus was subject to Joseph (and Mary). **Reference: Luke 2:51, "And he went down with them, and came to Nazareth, and was subject unto them: but his mother kept all these sayings in her heart."**
4. Joseph and Mary both regarded Jesus as their son.
5. As we have thoroughly proved, society regarded Jesus as the son of Joseph.
6. This relates to numbers 1 and 2 in this section. The Bible itself has promised that Jesus will sit on the throne of David. To be legally entitled to the throne of David, Jesus had to be the legal heir of Joseph. And of course, Jesus was not the seed of Joseph. We covered this before.

The previous chapter entitled "The Immaculate Marriage of Joseph and Mary" is this writer's feeble attempt of some dry wit parody of the Catholic doctrine of "the immaculate conception." However, God set out His plan to keep the patrimony of Jesus above all reproach. There are still more barbs on this hook, and we will set them in the upcoming chapters. Jesus was the legal and earthly son of Joseph.

Chapter 12
Old Testament Prophecies of The Virgin Birth

The atheist, agnostic, unbeliever, pagan, and skeptic have a right to say that they do not believe in the virgin birth. However, neither the pagan nor the Christian has any basis to say that the Bible does not teach the virgin birth.

The teaching of the virgin birth starts in the book of Genesis. You remember the garden story about how Adam and Eve sinned and fell. For our purposes let us look at **Genesis 3:13-15.**

📖 **(Genesis 3:13-15) And the LORD God said unto the woman, What is this that thou hast done? And the woman said, The serpent beguiled me, and I did eat. ¹⁴And the LORD God said unto the serpent, Because thou hast done this, thou art cursed above all cattle, and above every beast of the field; upon thy belly shalt thou go, and dust shalt thou eat all the days of thy life: ¹⁵And I will put enmity between thee and the woman, and between thy seed and her seed; it shall bruise thy head, and thou shalt bruise his heel.**

Every person that has ever been born is from the seed of a man. The reference to **"her seed"** has been hailed throughout New Testament times to refer to the virgin birth. The Lord God Himself prefigures the virgin birth through the prophesy of the promised seed of a woman in **Genesis 3:15**. Here is what the Methodist theologian and Bible scholar of yesteryear, Adam Clarke had to say about **Genesis 3:15:**

He; who? The seed of the woman; the person is to come by the woman, and by her alone, without the concurrence of man. Therefore the address is not to Adam and Eve, but to Eve alone; and it was in consequence of this purpose of God that Jesus Christ was born of a virgin; this, and this alone, is what is implied in the promise of the seed of the woman bruising the head of the serpent. Jesus Christ died to put away sin by the sacrifice of himself, and to destroy him who had the power of death, that is, the devil. Thus he bruises his head – destroys his power and lordship over mankind, turning them from the power of Satan unto God; (Reference Acts 26:18). And Satan bruises his heel – God so ordered it, that the salvation of man could only be brought about by the death of Christ; and even the spiritual seed of our blessed Lord have the heel often bruised, as they suffer persecution, temptation, etc., which may be all that is intended by this part of the prophecy.

Let us listen to another Methodist, the famous evangelist John Wesley, as he comments on the phrase "her seed" and its prophecy concerning Christ.

Notice is here given them of three things concerning Christ. (1) His incarnation, that he should be the seed of the woman. (2) His sufferings and death, pointed to Satan's bruising his heel, that is, his human nature. (3) His victory over Satan thereby. Satan had now trampled upon the woman, and insulted over her; but the seed of the woman should be raised up in the fulness of time to avenge her quarrel, and to trample upon him, to spoil him, to lead him captive, and to triumph over him, Col 2:15.

Beginning in **Genesis chapter 3**, God is working for one purpose; God is setting things up to bring the promised seed into this world. On December 31, 1961, W. A. Criswell, pastor of First Baptist Church in Dallas, Texas, spent several hours walking his congregation through the Bible's grand narrative, tracing the "scarlet thread through the Bible." Today, The Scarlet Thread Through the Bible is an excellent book detailing critical portions of God's word, showing how God preserved the promised seed throughout the Old Testament.

To those who do not think the virgin birth is important, the first prophecy of hundreds of prophecies contains a definite allusion to the virgin birth. If you have a chain reference Bible, **Genesis 3:15** provides the first reference in the chain concerning Christ. If we look at the Old Testament as one drama linked together by various scenes, the Old Testament is about the devil's seed fighting the godly seed in effort to prevent the promised seed from coming to this earth.

The prophet Isaiah prophesied in some rough and tough times. Judah was being assaulted from a confederate group in the north. Wicked Ahaz was the king of Judah. Isaiah came to Ahaz with a message of deliverance. The LORD instructed Ahaz to ask for a sign. Ahaz ignorantly refused and responded with a foolish, pious answer, **"I will not ask, neither will I tempt the LORD."** Isaiah proceeded to proclaim a prophecy of deliverance, and the first part is recorded in **Isaiah 7:14, "Therefore the Lord himself shall give you a sign; Behold, a virgin shall conceive, and bear a son, and shall call his name Immanuel."** Wicked Ahaz will be temporarily delivered, but he will not see God's prophesied sign of deliverance.

However, God has let us see this sign thru His word. And yes, we know that sign of deliverance to be Jesus, the virgin born Son of God, who will deliver us. Isaiah predicted this prophecy over 700 years before the birth of Christ.

There are Bible commentators who say that the prophecy in Isaiah 7:14 has a twofold fulfillment. That is—the prophecy was fulfilled in Isaiah's time, and then a final consummating prophecy was fulfilled through Mary and the virgin birth. Many times, prophecies in the Bible do have a twofold fulfillment. This is not the case here. There is only one virgin that ever conceived and that was Mary; and, the ultimate fulfillment of this prophecy is found in the Son of Mary, the only begotten Son of God.

The liberals have ferociously attacked **Isaiah 7:14** claiming that the Hebrew word "almah" should be translated "young woman" instead of "virgin." It would take a week to read all the arguments.

This writer reviewed this verse in twenty-eight English translations and twenty-five of the twenty-eight used the word virgin in **Isaiah 7:14**. Even the error riddled Septuagint (Old Testament Hebrew translated into Greek) uses "parthenos" which means "virgin." The King James translators were without question the most qualified group of Bible translators ever assembled, and they use the word "virgin" in **Isaiah 7:14.**

This is not that hard. In fact, it is simple—if you believe the Bible. Matthew, the gospel writer, by direct inspiration correctly interprets the **Isaiah 7:14** reading to mean "virgin." The New Testament Greek word is "parthenos" which always means "virgin." You may remember that the Parthenon, a marble temple built in the fifth century B.C., during the ancient Greek Empire was dedicated to the Greek goddess Athena. Athena whose name means virgin (derived from the word "Parthenon") was a virgin goddess. Even Greek mythology confirms our definition.

Before we close this chapter, let us look at another prophecy that is often quoted during Christmas.

📖 **(Isaiah 9:6-7) For unto us a child is born, unto us a son is given: and the government shall be upon his shoulder: and his name shall be called Wonderful, Counsellor, The mighty God, The everlasting Father, The Prince of Peace. ⁷Of the increase of his government and peace there shall be no end, upon the throne of David, and upon his kingdom, to order it, and to establish it with judgment and with justice from henceforth even for ever. The zeal of the LORD of hosts will perform this.**

In these two verses, there is no mention of the promised

"seed" or of the "virgin" birth. However, the Bible says, **"For unto us a child is born, unto us a son is given."** His name shall be called **"The mighty God."** The only specific technical way that this Son can be called "The mighty God" is for this Son to be the Son of God.

Note this little verse found in **Acts 20:28, "Take heed therefore unto yourselves, and to all the flock, over the which the Holy Ghost hath made you overseers, to feed the church of God, which he hath purchased with his own blood."** This verse says that God purchased the church with His own blood. All true born-again Christians believe in the blood atonement. The blood of goats and bulls could never atone for sin. The blood from any of Adam's race could never atone for sin.

The blood that ran through the veins of Jesus was the blood of God. The blood of God can atone for sin. The blood of God is sinless blood. The blood of God is divine blood. The blood of God is holy blood. The blood of God is precious blood. And yes, the blood of God is atoning blood.

A personal word: there is no hope for a wicked sinful and vile creature like me except through the blood of Jesus. There is no goodness, no merit, nor works within me or any man that can atone for sin. However, the old song says, and this is my testimony, "My hope is built on nothing less, than Jesus' blood and righteousness."

In the Old Testament, on numerous occasions the Bible talks about the "seed" of the various patriarchs: Abraham, Isaac, Jacob, and David. Although references to "seed" do not refer to the virgin birth, many times their ultimate fulfillment is through the "promised seed" and the virgin born Son of God.

Chapter 13
The Essential Doctrine of the Virgin Birth

Since early New Testament times, apostates have showered constant and vicious attacks on critical Christian doctrines. These foundational doctrines include the word of God, creation, the person of Christ, the blood atonement, the judgment of God, the resurrection, and our topic for this chapter—the virgin birth. One of the great mysteries of the virgin birth is the great amount of misinformation and disinformation about the virgin birth and much of these untruths flow from church circles. The next three chapters will be dedicated to expounding the biblical truths of the virgin birth.

The Ebionites evolved about the time of the destruction of the Jewish Temple in Jerusalem (AD 70). The Ebionites were Jews who were relocated in various provinces surrounding Israel. The Ebionites were faithful followers of the law. They believed the Old Testament and recognized Jesus as the Messiah. However, The Ebionites snubbed the virgin birth of Jesus, and taught that Jesus was the biological son of Joseph and Mary. The Ebionites believed in Jesus as the Messiah because He kept the Jewish Law.

The University of Dayton is a Catholic research institution. They published the following: "Perpetual Virginity: Dogmatic Status and Meaning." While this writer adamantly disagrees with their theology, an excellent brief history of their distorted view, and numerous references are provided for us in the following article:

> This doctrine underwent a period of discussion until the late fourth century when general consensus emerged. The earliest witness to the perpetual virginity of Mary seems to appear in the apocryphal Protogospel of James (circa 150). Tertullian (d, circa 220) denied the virginity of Mary after Jesus' birth. Origen (d 254), by contrast, taught Mary's perpetual virginity. In the East, St. Athanasius strongly defended Mary's virginity after the birth of Jesus. Shortly after, St.Basil the Great (d, circa 380) accepted Mary's perpetual virginity and claimed that it reflected the general sense of believers, though he did not consider it to be a dogma. Around the same time in the West, Jovinian and Helvidius denied the perpetual virginity while Ambrose (d. 397), Jerome (d. 420) and Augustine (d. 430) staunchly defended it.

Augustine of Hippo may be considered the premier proto-Catholic. Many Catholics and Protestants believe that Augustine was arguably the most brilliant mind and influential theologian since the apostle Paul. Augustine is the father of the hyper-Calvinistic views of double predestination. Augustine's views were simply restated and popularized by John Calvin in the Reformation period. Augustine's theological dogma was a stirred and shaken cocktail of Gnostic, pagan religion and ancient mystic philosophy served in a Christian chalice. Listed below are some of his damnable and heretical views:

1. **Double predestination (God decides who will be lost or saved)**
2. **Man lost his freewill in the Edenic fall (monergism)**
3. **A true believer cannot be assured of salvation**
4. **Everything was created in an instant and other creation heresies**
5. **God commands impossibilities and demands helpless man to stop sinning**
6. **The supreme authority of the Roman church**
7. **Non-Biblical view of time**
8. **Purgatory**
9. **Prayers for the dead**
10. **A perverted view of the doctrine of original sin**
11. **The damnation of unbaptized infants and adults**
12. **Sex is sinful even within marriage**
13. **Replacement theology (the church replaced Israel)**
14. **Apocrypha is included in the Scriptures**
15. **Eucharist is necessary for salvation**
16. **Church could bestow an official "saint" title**
17. **Politically advocated for the punishment of religious heretics**
18. **Pro Jewish at times and contra Jewish at times**
19. **The perpetual virginity of Mary**
20. **Mary never committed sin**
21. **Advocated worship and prayer to and through Mary**

Augustine was no doubt a brilliant man. In his brilliance, Augustine mated the learning of the world with the Bible and produced his own demented view of God. Pay special attention to the last three on the list. These were Augustine's apostate teachings about Mary. The Catholics maintain the wrong view of Mary, and their heresy starts with the perpetual virginity of Mary. Well, maybe Augustine was not as brilliant as some of these super spiritual thinkers pretend him to be. If we listed the things that Augustine was right about, the list would be much shorter. Augustine's political backing and encouragement for the punishment of religious heretics has helped to bring untold pain, suffering, and death to the thousands and even millions of traditional, conservative, and

Orthodox Christians. Augustine is the true father of the damnable doctrine of Calvinism which perverts the love of God and emasculates evangelism.

The unbelieving Protestants and the heathens claim that Mary was never a virgin, and each generation has produced its critics and cynics refuting the virgin birth. Newfound more intense attacks on the virgin birth were generated during the Age of Enlightenment. The Enlightenment was a late seventeenth and eighteenth-century intellectual movement emphasizing reason, individualism, skepticism, naturalism, and science. Christians ignorantly reacted by trying to interpret the Bible in the light of new scientific thought. The mission of the liberals is to demote Christ of all supernatural power, deity, and authority.

Skeptic and unbelieving Protestant theologians wanted to paint the gospel as a myth. Early in the twentieth century (1932), the Formgeschichte critics, whose two German founders were Rudolf Bultmann and Martin Dibelius, invented the term "theologumenon" to describe the virgin birth. Dibelius, explained the term "theologumenon" to mean a theological theory that had nothing to do with historical events. This is like a little boy marking on a sheet of paper and making up words.

About the same time in America, the blatant liberal Harry Emerson Fosdick was a Baptist who took the pastorate at the First Presbyterian Church in New York City. On May 21, 1922, he delivered his famous sermon "Shall the Fundamentalists Win?" Fosdick insisted that Christians could disagree with those who believe the virgin birth to be historically true. Of course, his sermon was a total denial of the virgin birth. Fosdick divided the church into two factions. One faction was labeled as "fundamentalists;" these were Christians who believe the virgin birth to be historical fact. The other faction was labeled as "enlightened"; these were Christians who no longer oblige themselves to believe the Bible to be historically correct and abandon the "biological" miracle of the virgin birth, but still consider themselves to be Christians.

Ancient heresies concerning Mary have been enhanced in the last century by the Catholic Church. The elevated position of Mary in the Roman Catholic Church is unknown to scripture and the early church. Papal encyclicals have bestowed new titles and exalted Mary to Godhood status. Encyclicals are papal circular letters usually addressed to the Catholic church leaders and congregations. These letters contain the pope's views on church teachings and doctrine. Many times, they do not reflect the church's official sanctioned doctrine, but shape church thought and teaching. Here is a listing of the doctrinal errors concerning Mary. Every effort has been made to use exact phraseology from Catholic writings and yet, maintain brevity. Note again, many of these are new claims of the last century or so.

☒ Roman Catholicism teaches today that Mary is the Mother of God and is also labeled the Mother of our Head.

☒ Catholicism insists upon The Immaculate Conception of Mary which means that she was conceived in Anne her mother without the stain of original sin.

☒ Adding to the above, Catholicism claims Mary is full of grace, therefore free of original sin and kept from all actual sin and thus free from any personal or inherited blemish.

☒ Catholicism asserts that Mary is perpetually a virgin. That is: Mary was a virgin not only before but during and after the birth of Jesus.

☒ The Catholics have also crowned and entitled Mary "Queen of Heaven."

☒ Catholicism claims Mary was bodily assumed into heaven where she now reigns with Christ. A papal encyclical says, "Mary now glorified in body and soul reigns together with her Son." This can be compared and paralleled to the bodily resurrection of Christ.

☒ Although not officially sanctioned, Catholicism has given to Mary the title of Mediatrix of all graces and teaches that it was an answer to Mary's all-powerful prayers that the Divine Redeemer's Spirit was given to the newly born church and by her intercession obtains from Him (Jesus) abundant streams of grace to all the members of the mystical body.

☒ Another title not yet officially sanctioned, but still given to Mary, is that she is Co-redemptrix with Jesus. This has papal affirmation through encyclical teaching by stating, "Mary offered Jesus to the Father for all the children of man who are defiled by Adam's unfortunate fall and by bearing her immeasurable sorrows she has supplied what was lacking in the suffering of Christ for His body, the church."

You should have discerned by now that the Catholics are systematically paralleling Mary to Christ in Catholic theology. These are efforts to elevate and exalt Mary to the position of full Godhood.

It would be easy to provide detailed rebuttals to each false conjecture above with a multitude of scripture. This book has already provided sufficient scriptural detail to bury the above error-filled speculations. We have seen that Mary herself acknowledged God as her Saviour. Mary needed a Saviour because she was a sinner and, therefore, could not be God. Mary could not have been a perpetual virgin, because we have established that she traveled with a full brood of children that were conceived through normal relations.

On December 24, 2016, the <u>Washington Post</u> published an article entitled "Megachurch pastor ignites debate after suggesting that Christianity doesn't hinge on Jesus' birth." The article stated, "The pastor of one of America's largest megachurches stirred up Christmas controversy after preaching that the story of Jesus' virgin birth is not crucial to the Christian faith." Andy Stanley, the son of Charles Stanley, was the pastor. In his December 4, 2016 sermon at North Point Community Church, which draws 36,000 attendees across six locations in suburban Atlanta, Stanley said "Christianity doesn't hinge on the truth or even the stories around the birth of Jesus."

Stanley, no doubt, has vigor and enthusiasm to build his mega church empire, but Stanley is blatantly ignorant about the word of God.

If the virgin birth is not true:

1. There is no incarnation. The incarnation of Jesus the Christ is the defining doctrine of the Bible. The incarnation is taught from Genesis to Revelation. All other religions require man to work himself to God. God became man and came to us. See **John 1:14**.
2. The Bible is not true. The Old Testament prophecies concerning the virgin birth and the New Testament narratives are found to be lies.
3. Man cannot be saved. The Bible says that, "salvation is of the Lord." If Jesus were not virgin born, He would not be Lord.
4. Jesus could not be "born of woman." See **Galatians 4:4-5.**
5. Jesus was misnamed. Jesus means "Jehovah saves" or "Jehovah is salvation."
6. Mary was a liar and that is being kind.
7. Jesus was not the "last Adam." Thus, the doctrine of the "new birth" would be senseless and we would still be "in Adam" without any hope of salvation. See **1 Corinthians chapter 15.**
8. John 3:16, the most quoted verse in the Bible, is not true. Unbelievers have re-defined "only begotten" to mean "unique, one-of-a-kind." Jesus is the unique and one-of-a-kind son, but that is not what "only begotten" means. **John 1:14** says, **"And the Word was made flesh, and dwelt among us, (and we beheld his glory, the glory as of the only begotten of the Father,) full of grace and**

truth." The parenthesis always adds explanatory and definitive information. Note **"made flesh"** is defined as **"only begotten."** In other words, Jesus was the only physically born son of God. If the virgin birth did not occur, Jesus is not the "only begotten" Son of God.

9. The blood running through the veins of Jesus was not the blood of God. See **Acts 20:28.**

10. Jesus is not Lord and not the Messiah

Mary had a divine calling and had many supernatural events to occur in her life. However, and in contrast, Mary was human. Most of the years of her life were simply filled with normal day to day occurrences, work, and social interactions as experienced by all today.

The atheist, agnostic, unbeliever, pagan, and skeptic have a right to say that they do not believe in the virgin birth. However, neither the pagan nor the Christian has any ground to say that the Bible does not teach the virgin birth. Born again Christians believe in the virgin birth.

You may be reading this book and do not know that if you were to die today heaven would be your home. Jesus told Nicodemus, a ruler of the Jews and a religious teacher, **"Except a man be born again, he cannot see the kingdom of God."** Nicodemus wanted to know more about the new birth.

Let me ask you. Do you know you are a sinner? Would you like your sins forgiven? Are you tired of your sins and tired of yourself? Would you like to be different on the inside and get rid of your guilt and shame? Would you like Jesus to change your life? If your answer is yes, you are a candidate for the new birth.

Jesus can come into your life and change you and make you a new person! That is what the new birth is all about! Jesus can and will forgive you of your sins, change your desires, and help you to be what God wants you to be.

You cannot change yourself. You will never be able to change yourself. If you want Jesus to change you, then you must place your faith in Christ.

You may ask, "What do I need to do to have a new birth?" Jesus told Nicodemus how to have the new birth in **John 3:16** which says, **"For God so loved the world, that he gave his only begotten Son, that whosoever believeth in him should not perish, but have everlasting life."** Jesus loves you. Jesus wants to save you and change your life.

Paul told the jailer: **"Believe on the Lord Jesus Christ and thou shall be saved."** To be saved is simple. Jesus died for you on the cross to pay your sin debt. They buried Him in a borrowed tomb and put guards at the door of a dead man. But on the third day, He arose from the grave.

You are saved through faith. Biblical faith is believing and trusting in Jesus. It is as if Jesus were knocking on your door. But you must open the door and let Him in. The Bible plainly says, in **John 1:12, "But as many as received him, to them gave he power to become the sons of God, even to them that believe on his name:"** You receive Christ by simply believing on His name. You can be changed and have a new life today. You can know that your sins are forgiven and be assured of a home in heaven.

You may ask, "How much faith does it take?" **Romans 10:13 says, "For whosoever shall call upon the name of the Lord shall be saved."** Invite the Lord into your life and He will save you.

You can pray this prayer to receive Christ: Dear Jesus: "I am a sinner and need to be saved. Come into my life, change me, and help me to be all that you would have me to be. I believe you died for me, I repent and turn from all of my sins, and I am placing my faith in you right now. Thank you, Jesus, for saving me." The exact words are not important. When you trust Christ as your Saviour, you are saved. Contact us and let us know of your decision, and we will send you some free information to help you get started in your walk with the Lord.

Chapter 14
The New Testament Doctrine of the Virgin Birth

The defining doctrine of the Bible is the incarnation of the Lord Jesus Christ. This writer was curious and googled the definition of the "virgin birth." Merriam Webster's dictionary defines the "virgin birth" as "the theological doctrine that Jesus was miraculously begotten of God and born of a virgin mother." This is particularly amazing in that Merriam Webster's definition is much better, more concise, and more accurate than those from biblical scholars, commentators, and Bible dictionaries.

The doctrine of the virgin birth is exclusive to Christianity. Liberals have constantly promoted the pseudo-tenet that the Christian doctrine of the virgin birth imitates pagan and Jewish myths that credit virginal conception to folklore heroes. However, there has been some recent and excellent scholarly research investigating the possible proof to these pagan comparisons. There was no proof found. To any skeptic who wishes to make this claim, you may safely ask for a legitimate reference: country, library, book, chapter, page, and paragraph. Here is an example sometimes mentioned: Buddha was said to be born when a white elephant entered the side of his mother while she was asleep, and she conceived. This is some loony lunacy that could not even acquire the status of a good fairytale. Yes, there are other ridiculous and foolish fables that are equated to the virgin birth. Bottom line, there is no basis found in antiquity for any legitimate comparison or parallel to the Christian doctrine of the virgin birth.

The virgin birth is intricately woven throughout the fabric of the Bible. The word of God is unbelievably amazing as it wraps and winds the doctrine of a virgin birth through the work and person of Christ. The virgin birth is the subject of explicit mention on occasion. Much more often, the virgin birth is referenced, implied, or connected to various doctrinal teachings throughout the New Testament. Listed below are a few critical connections to the virgin birth:

1. The incarnation of Christ
2. Jesus, the personal name of Christ, means "Jehovah saves" or "Jehovah is salvation"
3. The divinity of Christ: Christ was and is Immanuel or "God with us"
4. The eternality of Christ
5. The names of Christ

6. The titles of Christ
7. The prophecies about Christ
8. The genealogical records of Christ
9. The blood of Christ
10. The man from, or of heaven
11. The only begotten Son
12. The Son of God – **John declares: "the Word was God" in John 1:14, "And the Word was made flesh, and dwelt among us, (and we beheld his glory, the glory as of the only begotten of the Father,) full of grace and truth."** Note: **"made"** and **"begotten"** are the same Greek word.
13. God sent forth His Son **"made of a woman."** See **Galatians 4:4.** From a human standpoint, Jesus was **"made of a woman"** not a man and a woman.
14. The last Adam or the second man

Let us scan the New Testament for scriptures that doctrinally relate to the virgin birth.

📖 **(Matthew 1:16) And Jacob begat Joseph the husband of Mary, of whom was born Jesus, who is called Christ.**

Of course, **Matthew 1:1-16** is the listing of the genealogy of Christ through Joseph. The word "begat" is used 39 times in this passage. Jacob begat Joseph but Joseph did not "begat" Christ. Joseph was the husband of Mary, and Mary birthed Jesus. Note the highlighted portions in **Matthew 1:18 to 25: [emphasis mine]**

📖 **(Matthew 1:18-25) Now the birth of Jesus Christ was on this wise: When as his mother Mary was espoused to Joseph, before they came together, she was found with child of the Holy Ghost. 19Then Joseph her husband, being a just man, and not willing to make her a publick example, was minded to put her away privily. 20But while he thought on these things, behold, the angel of the Lord appeared unto him in a dream, saying, Joseph, thou son of David, fear not to take unto thee Mary thy wife: for that which is conceived in her is of the Holy Ghost. 21And she shall bring forth a son, and thou shalt call his name JESUS: for he shall save his people from their sins. 22Now all this was done, that it might be fulfilled which was spoken of the Lord by the prophet, saying, 23Behold, a virgin shall be with child, and shall bring** forth a son, and they shall call his name **Emmanuel, which being interpreted is, God with us**. ²⁴Then Joseph being raised from sleep did as the angel of the Lord had bidden him, and took unto him his wife: ₂₅**And knew her not till she had brought forth her firstborn son**: and he called his name **JESUS**.

The following phrases emphatically reference the virgin birth.

➢ **Jesus Christ**
➢ **before they came together**
➢ **with child of the Holy Ghost.**
➢ **that which is conceived in her is of the Holy Ghost**
➢ **thou shalt call his name JESUS**
➢ **a virgin shall be with child**
➢ **Emmanuel**
➢ **God with us**
➢ **And knew her not till she had brought forth her firstborn son**
➢ **Jesus**

In the above portion of Scripture, there are two occasions which plainly state that Joseph did not have conjugal relations with his wife before Jesus was born. The word virgin is used on one occasion in relation to Mary. The divine conception through the Holy Ghost is mentioned twice. The name Jesus is mentioned three times. Jesus means "Jehovah saves." The biblical names of Jesus are always descriptive and definitive. In other words, the clear teaching of the Bible is that Jehovah of the Old Testament is none other than Jesus in the New Testament. Emmanuel is defined as "God with us" teaching us that Jesus is God on two occasions (2 + 1 + 3 + 2 + 2 = 10). Thus, the doctrine of the virgin birth is specifically taught or referenced 10 times in the above passage.

📖 **(Luke 1:26-38) And in the sixth month the angel Gabriel was sent from God unto a city of Galilee, named Nazareth, ²⁷To a virgin espoused to a man whose name was Joseph, of the house of David; and the virgin's name was Mary. ²⁸And the angel came in unto her, and said, Hail, thou that art highly favoured, the Lord is with thee: blessed art thou among women. ²⁹And when she saw him, she was troubled at his saying, and cast in her mind what manner of salutation this should be. ³⁰And the angel said unto her, Fear not, Mary: for thou hast found favour with God. ³¹And, behold, thou shalt conceive** in thy womb, and bring forth a son, and shalt call his name JESUS. ³²He shall be great, and shall be called the Son of the Highest: and the Lord God shall give unto him the throne of his father David: ³³And he shall reign over the house of Jacob for ever; and of his kingdom there shall be no end. ³⁴Then said Mary unto the angel, How shall this be, seeing I know not a man? ³⁵And the angel answered and said unto her, The Holy Ghost shall come upon thee, and the power of the Highest shall overshadow thee: therefore also that holy thing which shall be born of thee shall be called the Son of God. ³⁶And, behold, thy cousin Elisabeth, she hath also conceived a son in her old age: and this is the sixth month with her, who was called barren. ³⁷For with God nothing shall be impossible. ³⁸And Mary said, Behold the handmaid of the Lord; be it unto me according to thy word. And the angel departed from her.

Again, we will look at the highlighted selected phrases that relate to the virgin birth.

➢ **To a virgin**
➢ **virgin's name was Mary**
➢ **shalt call his name JESUS**
➢ **the Son of the Highest**
➢ **I know not a man**
➢ **The Holy Ghost shall come upon thee**
➢ **the power of the Highest shall overshadow thee**
➢ **holy thing**
➢ **Son of God**

In the above passage, we note 9 phrases that either explicitly teach the virgin birth or allude to the virgin birth. Now, the baby Jesus is described as a **"holy thing."** That certainly cannot be said about any other baby! There is no doubt that you have seen a considerable share of babies that were a holy terror!

Also note the phrase **"Son of God."** Jesus is given the title of the Son of God forty-five times in the New Testament. The biblical title of "the Son of God" is made viable through the virgin birth. Jesus is **"the Son of God,"** but the saved are called **"the sons of God."** There are various heretical groups in Christendom that claim that Jesus is a Son of God through adoption because He led a righteous life. This is completely spurious without any Biblical doctrinal support.

The Bible critics, detractors, and subtracters have often tried to reject the virgin birth because many of the New Testament writers did not mention the virgin birth. These critics need to be answered. In his gospel, Mark starts immediately with, **Mark 1:1, "The beginning of the gospel of Jesus Christ, the Son of God."** As we have already stated, Jesus is the Son of God through the virgin birth. The Heavenly Father claimed the Lord Jesus as His Son at the beginning of His adult ministry. Note **Mark 1:11, "And there came a voice from heaven, saying, Thou art my beloved Son, in whom I am well pleased."** Again, to be the legitimate Son of God, it was necessary for Jesus to be born of a virgin. Mark attributes the title the **"Son of God"** to Jesus in two more instances.

So far, we have looked at the first three Gospels: Matthew, Mark, and Luke. We need to see if we think that John believes in the virgin birth. Note the following passages from the Bible written by John the disciple.

- (John 1:1-3) **In the beginning was the Word, and the Word was with God, and the Word was God. ²The same was in the beginning with God. ³All things were made by him; and without him was not any thing made that was made.**
- (John 1:14) **And the Word was made flesh, and dwelt among us, (and we beheld his glory, the glory as of the only begotten of the Father,) full of grace and truth.**
- (John 3:16) **For God so loved the world, that he gave his only begotten Son, that whosoever believeth in him should not perish, but have everlasting life.**
- (John 3:18) **He that believeth on him is not condemned: but he that believeth not is condemned already, because he hath not believed in the name of the only begotten Son of God.**
- (1 John 4:9) **In this was manifested the love of God toward us, because that God sent his only begotten Son into the world, that we might live through him.**

John is often called the beloved disciple. It is quite evident that John had a closer earthly relationship with Jesus than any of the other disciples. John opens his gospel by talking about the Creator God that made all things. John designates this Creator God with the titles of "the Word" and "God." In a few short sentences later, John tells us about "the Word." According to verse fourteen the Word was "made flesh" defined as "the only begotten of the Father." We have previously established that the term "only begotten" refers to the physical birth of Jesus. The only way Jesus can be the only begotten of the Father is to be virgin born.

There is another critical doctrinal issue found in the first chapter of the Gospel of John. John, the beloved disciple says, that the "Word was God." In other words, John is teaching that Jesus is the "Son of God" and "God the Son." John is declaring the full divinity of Christ.

Notice that the virgin birth also assumes the eternal preexistence and divine sonship of Jesus. To put it another way, Jesus was the Son of God before the incarnation. Jesus is exclusively and distinctly the God-Man and the only one qualified and eligible to be our Saviour.

The detractors and rejecters of our Saviour claim that Jesus was not really God, but Jesus was "a god." Specifically, the Jehovah's Witnesses claim that Jesus was a little god who was created. Others who deny the Bible assert that Jesus can be the son of God through adoption and still not be fully God. Frankly, these must be blind or ignorant of the word of God. When Jesus claimed God to be his Father, the Jews sought to kill him. Listen to **John 10:33, "The Jews answered him, saying, For a good work we stone thee not; but for blasphemy; and because that thou, being a man, makest thyself God."** The Jews clearly understood that if you claimed to be the Son of God, you were also claiming to be God. As previously noted, the man Jesus could not have been God unless He was born of a virgin.

The deity of the virgin born Lord Jesus Christ is a continuous and frequent theme of the New Testament. To give due diligence to this theme could easily fill another book. The following are some additional passages that teach Jesus is God: **Hebrews 1:8, Titus 2:13, Romans 9:5, 1 John 5:20, John 20:28, Colossians 2:9, John 5:23, John 10:33, Mark 10:18, Mark 2:5-10.** In addition, Jesus is proven to be God when He is One with the Father: **John 10:30, John 12:45, John 14:7-10, John 17:10.**

There are thirteen epistles authored by Paul in the New Testament: **Romans, 1 Corinthians, 2 Corinthians, Galatians, Ephesians, Philippians, Colossians, 1 Thessalonians, 2 Thessalonians, 1 Timothy, 2 Timothy, Titus and Philemon.** Paul attributes to Jesus the mantra of **"the Son of God"** in eight instances. In addition, in **Galatians 4:4,** Paul says, **"But when the fulness of the time was come, God sent forth his Son, made of a woman, made under the law."** In other words, the man Jesus was physically "made of woman" and not made of a man and a woman, a clear allusion to the virgin birth.

Let us look again at some additional quotes from the apostle

Paul.

📖 **(Philippians 2:5-7) Let this mind be in you, which was also in Christ Jesus: ⁶Who, being in the form of God, thought it not robbery to be equal with God: ⁷But made himself of no reputation, and took upon him the form of a servant, and was made in the likeness of men.**

And again.

📖 **(Colossians 1:14-17) In whom we have redemption through his blood, even the forgiveness of sins: ¹⁵Who is the image of the invisible God, the firstborn of every creature: ¹⁶For by him were all things created, that are in heaven, and that are in earth, visible and invisible, whether they be thrones, or dominions, or principalities, or powers: all things were created by him, and for him: ¹⁷And he is before all things, and by him all things consist."**

Quite simply, both references point to the pre-existence of Christ, and both clearly impart the doctrinal teaching that Jesus was both divine and human. In other words, Jesus was the God-Man. In order for Jesus to be pre-existent and to be the God-Man, the virgin birth is a necessity.

The pre-existence of Christ is interlinked with the deity of Christ and the virgin birth. Note the following verses that teach the pre-existence of Christ: **Micah 5:2, Isaiah 9:6, 1 John 1:1-4, Hebrews 1:2-10, Revelation 1:8.** We will look at one more verse that is a particular favorite of this writer and plainly exhibits the eternal preexistence of the Lord Jesus Christ. **"I am he that liveth, and was dead; and, behold, I am alive for evermore, Amen; and have the keys of hell and of death" (Revelation 1:18).**

Our purpose here was just to look at the direct references of the deity and pre-existence of Christ. The deity of Christ covers a much wider territory than covered here. His deity can be proven through His fulfillment of prophecies and accomplishment of miracles. The ultimate proof of His deity is the resurrection.

The titles "the last Adam," "the second man," and "the Lord from heaven" were all assigned to Jesus by the apostle Paul in **1 Corinthians 15.**

📖 **(1 Corinthians 15:45-47) And so it is written, The first man Adam was made a living soul; the last Adam was made a quickening spirit. ⁴⁶Howbeit that was not first which is spiritual, but that which is natural; and afterward that which is spiritual. ⁴⁷The first man is of** the earth, earthy: the second man is the Lord from heaven"

In **Romans chapter 5**, the apostle Paul again compares Adam, the first man, to the Lord Jesus Christ, the second man or second Adam from heaven. The following statement would be a simple summary of the comparisons made by Paul in these passages: All in Adam sin, which reigns unto death; all in Christ receive grace which reigns unto eternal life. The doctrine of the virgin birth stamps a seal of approval on the titles of "the last Adam," "the second man," and "the Lord from heaven." These three titles would be null and void if the virgin birth were not true. The epistles of the apostle Paul verify his understanding and realization of the virgin birth.

The unchallenged leader and sometimes unappointed mouthpiece of our Lord's disciples was Simon Peter. Peter demonstrated that he understood the virgin birth when he recognized the divinity of Christ. Note, **"Simon Peter, a servant and an apostle of Jesus Christ, to them that have obtained like precious faith with us through the righteousness of God and our Saviour Jesus Christ:" (2 Peter 1:1).**

James, the physical half-brother of our Lord, recognized Jesus in the doctrine of a virgin birth when he identified Jesus as **"the Lord of glory." "My brethren, have not the faith of our Lord Jesus Christ, the Lord of glory, with respect of persons" (James 2:1).**

Now, we will see what Jude, the younger brother of James, and another half-brother of the Lord Jesus Christ had to say about his older half-brother. **Jude 1:4** comments on apostasy in the church, **"For there are certain men crept in unawares, who were before of old ordained to this condemnation, ungodly men, turning the grace of our God into lasciviousness, and denying the only Lord God, and our Lord Jesus Christ."** Jude said that his half-brother, Jesus, is **"the only Lord God and our Lord Jesus Christ."**

There is one last critical element in doctrinal teaching that relates to the virgin birth. Luke was the inspired writer of the book of Acts, and he stated, **"Take heed therefore unto yourselves, and to all the flock, over the which the Holy Ghost hath made you overseers, to feed the church of God, which he hath purchased with his own blood" (Acts 20:28).** Note carefully, the blood that flowed through the veins of Jesus was the pure, holy, sinless, precious, and incorruptible blood of God.

In case you are not keeping count, we have referenced all the inspired writers of the New Testament: Matthew, Mark, Luke, John,

Paul, Peter, James, Jude and the human author of the book of Hebrews. Also, we have listed a total of ninety-eight references that directly affirm the virgin birth or doctrinal truths that would not be valid without the fact of the virgin birth.

The doctrine of the virgin birth of Jesus has been a foundation stone of orthodox Christian theology since the New Testament era. The Apostle's Creed and numerous ancient church patriarchs affirmed their belief in the virgin birth.

The virgin birth shows us that our redeemer is wholly a man; yet Jesus was without sin and the sin nature passed down to Adam's seed. The supernatural birth presents Jesus as fully God and fully man.

The virgin birth demonstrates God's power and His love for fallen man. It is God who acted first and initiated salvation for his fallen creatures. God planned for our salvation before the foundation of the world. The Bible says that "in due time Christ died for the ungodly." We repeat, God took the initiative and worked out His redemptive blueprint for us. Properly understood, this teaching proves the divine authorship and authority of the word of God.

In summation:

☑ Mary and Joseph believed in the virgin birth
☑ Matthew, Mark, Luke, and John believed in the virgin birth
☑ Peter and Paul believed in the virgin birth
☑ James and Jude, the physical half-brothers of Christ believed in the virgin birth
☑ The writer of the Hebrews believed in the virgin birth
☑ The demons believed in the virgin birth (missed this above) see **Mark 1:24**

Chapter 15
The Mystery of the Virgin Birth

The term "mystery" is frequently mentioned in the Bible. A Bible mystery is a Biblical teaching that was previously hidden and then plainly revealed by the word of God. "Mystery," in its singular and plural forms, is mentioned 26 times in the New Testament. Thus, the word of God in many cases delays the discovery of certain spiritual truths until God is ready to open His revelation to His people.

If we look carefully at the Biblical narrative, it seems very apparent that the virgin birth was not made known until after the resurrection of our Lord. Most people have never thought about this. However, consideration of this matter is worthy of our attention. The Bible is the only religious book in the world that tells us how to interpret itself. We will begin by establishing three principles of Bible interpretation.

➤ Compare Scripture to Scripture—**1 Corinthians 2:13, "Which things also we speak, not in the words which man's wisdom teacheth, but which the Holy Ghost teacheth; comparing spiritual things with spiritual."**

➤ Scripture relates to other Scripture—**2 Peter 1:20, "Knowing this first, that no prophecy of the scripture is of any private interpretation."**

➤ Every word is critical—**Matthew 4:4, "But he answered and said, It is written, Man shall not live by bread alone, but by every word that proceedeth out of the mouth of God."**

The biblical foundation for this chapter has been laid in the previous chapters dealing with the virgin birth and the personalities of Mary and Joseph. The following scriptural evidence is offered to support the revelation of the virgin birth *after* the resurrection of Christ.

Luke 3:23, "And Jesus himself began to be about thirty years of age, being (as was supposed) the son of Joseph..." The Bible is plain and straightforward in this instance. Jesus was thought to be the son of Joseph during the time of His ministry on earth. The biblical timing and placement of this Scripture is critical to its proper interpretation. Jesus was an adult. The date was given as the fifteenth year of Tiberius Caesar. Jesus had been announced and baptized by John the Baptist. Jesus had started His ministry. When He was thirty years old, the public believed Jesus to be the son of Joseph.

The angelic announcement of the virgin birth in the Gospel of Matthew was to Joseph alone. There is no biblical evidence that anyone else was informed, nor is there specific mention of the virgin birth to any other person at any other place in the gospel of Matthew.

In the Gospel of Luke, the messenger Gabriel delivered his communication to Mary exclusively. Mary left immediately to see her cousin Elisabeth. Elisabeth, by revelation of God, recognized Mary as **"the mother of my Lord."** And these two ladies had a shouting spell. There is certainly no doubt in my mind that the Lord has recorded these scenes, and we will get a chance to see them. Thus, from the biblical narrative, the virgin birth was revealed to Joseph, Mary, and Elisabeth. Although, not specifically mentioned, it is probable that Zacharias was also cognizant of Mary's situation. This would limit the awareness of the virgin birth to both husband and wife couples who were aware of divine and angelic intervention into their lives. These couples may have been given specific instruction to stay silent about their heavenly visits, or they may have been led by the Spirit of God to remain silent. May I say, without any intent to be sacrilegious or critical, that many religious testimonies would have been better said if they had not been said at all. We all need to learn to keep quiet more.

Previous chapters have analyzed every passage in which some have erroneously questioned the parentage of Jesus or directed a slur at the virgin birth. We found that the public reputation of Joseph, Mary, and Jesus was above reproach. To restate the matter, there was no affront made to Mary or Jesus about the virgin birth. Additionally, there was no question about the parentage of Jesus. Those that adhere to these positions are mistaken and misguided because:

➤ They remove the text from the context.
➤ The questions asked about the parentage of Jesus are clearly rhetorical. Rhetorical questions are used frequently in the Bible. The Lord God asked many of these. For instance, God asked Job, "Where were you?" To Abraham and Jeremiah, the Lord asked, "Is there anything too hard for the Lord?"
➤ On occasion, many fail to understand the rhetorical question mode of speaking and completely reverse the meaning.
➤ They ignore the context of the entire passage in the word of God.
➤ On two different occasions, the Bible records Mary noted certain instances and stored them in her heart. In one instance, the Bible uses the word "pondered" and in another instance it was said that Mary "kept all these sayings in her

heart." Joseph and Mary kept the virgin birth in and close to their hearts.

Additionally, there is a complete misunderstanding of societal issues of that day, human nature of that day and this day, and the long memory of mankind. Let us do some supposition and speculation. Just picture a beautiful teenage girl, a senior in high school. We will call her Mary. Mary is an honor-roll student, faithful in church, and has a reputation that is above reproach. She is considered as a model for her peers and excels in church and social interactions. Mary is the darling favorite of her father and mother, her pastor, her teachers, and her coach. She is engaged to be married after high school. Mary turns up pregnant. Her story is that an angel appeared to her and that her conception is a miracle and a gift from God. Who is going to believe her?

? What about Mary's fiancé?

? What about Mary's father?

? What about Mary's mother?

? What about Mary's teachers?

? What about Mary's coach?

? What about Mary's Sunday school teacher?

? What about Mary's pastor?

If the virgin birth had not been kept undisclosed until after the resurrection, the results would have been devastating and entirely untenable for the family to handle. If Mary and Joseph had made the virgin birth public, all credibility would have immediately been lost. God's chosen couple would have been the objects of unrelenting ridicule. The ministry of Jesus would never have been recognized as legitimate.

The Jews were an arrogant and stiff-necked people. Jewish writers of yesteryear believed that God created the earth for the Jew. The Gentiles were created to be subservient to the Jew. However, during the time of Christ, Judea was ruled by a client king and assistant governors appointed by Rome. The arrogant and corrupt Jewish leaders had forgotten their past and lived with an unrealistic view of the present. To illustrate, when Jesus told the Jews that the truth would make them free, the Jews responded that they were never in bondage to any man. Before Moses, the Jew was in bondage to Egypt. After Moses, the nation of Israel was split into two kingdoms and were carried away into Syria and Babylon. As we have previously stated, the Jews were ruled by Rome in the time of Christ. The times would have allowed no tolerance, nor benefit of the doubt, if the parentage of Jesus were ever in question.

Things have not changed. Rahab is found in the lineage of David and Christ, but we speak of her as "Rahab the harlot." Jacob was a prince with God, but we remember Jacob as the one who supplanted his brother two times. Thomas proclaimed Jesus to be his Lord and God, but today we call him "doubting Thomas."

If the parentage of Jesus were suspect in any manner, no tongue in cheek insinuations would have ever been made. The haughty and arrogant Jew would cast their indictments and accusations straight into the teeth of Jesus without mincing words. If any questionable circumstance existed in the eyes of the Jew, Jesus would be deemed ineligible to be the master or rabbi.

There is one other aspect that needs to be discussed. Jesus had a minimum of six siblings (four boys mentioned by name and at least two unnamed sisters). If these children had been aware of the virgin birth, think of the family havoc. It would have quickly leaked out, and we would be right back in the situation above.

The previously cited and quoted Dr. J. Harold Greenlee gives us some interesting insight.

If it had been discovered that Mary was pregnant and was not married to Joseph—the idea of a miraculous birth would have been considered nonsense or worse—Mary would have lived under a cloud for life, and Jesus would have had no possibility of becoming a rabbi. Almost certainly, no one except Mary and Joseph ever had any thought other than that Jesus was the legitimate son of Mary and Joseph. Is it possible that the miraculous secret was finally divulged by Mary during the ten days of prayer before Pentecost, to keep the knowledge of the virgin birth from dying with her forever? Only then could such a miracle have been believable.

We stated in previous chapters that each divinely inspired writer of the New Testament records truths that are direct references or divine allusions that confirm their adherence to and belief in the virgin birth.

There seems to be a lack of understanding or a complete forgetfulness of the relationship that the New Testament biblical writers had with the Lord, the family of Jesus, and with one another. Since the Age of Enlightenment, we have had apostate Christian teachers and expositors who have crept into our church leadership and seminaries. They have denied the traditional authorship of the New Testament Gospels: Matthew, Mark, Luke, and John. These same Bible critics take the position that the Gospels were not written until many years after the ministry of Christ. In addition, when discussing the New Testament writers, some Bible commentators

repeat one another with statements such as these:
- ✓ Mark writes his gospel from Peter's point of view.
- ✓ Luke includes almost all of Mark's gospel in his narrative.
- ✓ Matthew uses Mark as a source for much of his information.

What we find today is "monkey see, monkey do" expositions and commentaries. Biblical traditionalists and conservatives unanimously agree that all of the books of the New Testament, with the exception of the book of the Revelation, was completed before the destruction of the temple at Jerusalem in 70 A.D.; that is forty years after the passion of our Lord. Conservatives believe that Matthew was written as soon as eight years after our Lord's crucifixion. Mark came shortly thereafter. Revelation is the last New Testament book written. John, the beloved disciple, and firsthand witness, wrote the book of Revelation in about 95 or 96 A.D.

Before we get back to our point, permit a short illustration. This writer worked in the employment and training business for twenty-five years. My company of employment assisted with training people and helping them secure employment after training. Throughout my career, the same complaint was constantly made by job applicants: "In order to get a job, you have to know somebody." My response was always the same, "that's the way it's supposed to be!" People who get up off their blessed assurance, who go somewhere, get out and do something, and get to know people get a job. Come to think about it, my only hope of heaven is knowing the Lord Jesus Christ by faith.

The New Testament writers knew each other. The gospel writers of Matthew and John were disciples of the Lord Jesus Christ. Matthew and John knew one another intimately. John, at Calvary, was even assigned the duty of taking care of our Lord's mother.

Many believe that Mark mentions himself, in his gospel as the one who fled away naked in the garden of Gethsemane when our Lord was arrested. In any case, it is positively evident from the book of Acts that Mark knew the entire cadre of our Lord's disciples, especially Peter, Mary and our Lord's brothers (James and Jude), the apostle Paul, and Luke who was the nephew of Barnabas. Remember that Peter was imprisoned by Herod and miraculously delivered by the angel. Peter came to where the disciples were gathered praying. Note **Acts 12:12, "And when he had considered the thing, he came to the house of Mary the mother of John, whose surname was Mark; where many were gathered together praying."**

What can we say about Peter? Well, we can easily and accurately infer that Peter intimately knew all the other writers in the

New Testament.

Let us look at James and Jude, the two brothers of our Lord and writers of their respective epistles. If Jude were with James at the conference in Jerusalem where the salvation of the Gentiles was on the agenda, then both of our Lord's brethren would have made acquaintance with all the writers of the New Testament. The possible exception is Luke, but James and Jude could and probably did cross paths with Luke in other venues.

It is entirely possible and most probable that every New Testament writer was intimately acquainted with every other New Testament writer.

Today we have new fly-by-night Bible critics from the Enlightenment folklore scriptural society who wish to deny and cast doubt on the inspiration of the Holy Scriptures. The New Testament writers lived during the time of Christ, and they knew each other. The apostle Paul adamantly presented our case here in **Acts 26:26** when he stated, **"this thing was not done in a corner."** The New Testament writers had ample sources of material because they lived in New Testament times. They were either eyewitnesses or collected their material directly from eyewitnesses. God chose each writer to record specific events and occurrences with the exact words that the Holy Spirit inspired.

There is a new and recent Bible criticism. Some critics say the disciples could not read and write. In several debate situations reviewed by this writer on YouTube, legitimate apologists failed to give legitimate answers. Matthew was a tax collector requiring excellent reading and math skills. Luke was a doctor. Peter and John were in business together and both wrote books of the Bible. Paul's credentials are well known. The family of Mark was a family of wealth and means and could in no wise be illiterate. Jude and James wrote books of the Bible. The "illiterate disciples" argument is fiction and is a pure willing ignorance of our inspired word by Bible hating scholars. This is sheer speculation with no legitimate evidence. The biblical narrative and historical accounts document literate and sophisticated Roman and Jewish societies.

We do not know the specifics and details of Mary's revelation of the virgin birth to the New Testament Church. However, we do know that when the virgin birth was revealed, the news of the virgin birth would have traveled quickly to each writer of the New Testament and in turn throughout all Christianity.

The New Testament canon was compiled with lightning speed, and New Testament writers knew one another. From a human perspective, this served as a system of checks and balances. If a New

Testament writer were inaccurate in the reported details or occurrences, the writer would have been quickly reproved and corrected. We find no such instance. We can be assured today that we have the New Testament passed down to us through competent writers who had first-hand details and resources along with the supernatural, guided inspiration of the Holy Ghost. The Bible is right. The Bible is correct in every detail. The Bible is the word of God. The Bible is quick, powerful, sharper than any two-edged sword, and can secure the souls of men.

Chapter 16
The Mysterious Chronology of the Birth Date of Jesus

We wish to discuss the chronology of the approximate birth date of Jesus. God did not give us the exact date. This is a mystery when we consider the number of events dated in the Bible.

To examine this, we must look at the beginning of the public ministry of our Lord. The date for the start of the ministry of Jesus is found in **Luke 3:1, "Now in the fifteenth year of the reign of Tiberius Caesar, Pontius Pilate being governor of Judaea, and Herod being tetrarch of Galilee, and his brother Philip tetrarch of Ituraea and of the region of Trachonitis, and Lysanias the tetrarch of Abilene,..."** The Bible wants to ensure there is no mistake and thus the Bible lists four government rulers in six geographical areas who ruled concurrently. Historical information is available for us to trace this date.

Next, we need to couple the above date with the age of Jesus at the start of his ministry. **Luke 3:23** says **"And Jesus himself began to be about thirty years of age, being (as was supposed) the son of Joseph, which was the son of Heli,"** The Bible clearly states that Jesus started his ministry at about thirty years of age in the 15th year of Tiberius Caesar. Tiberius Caesar began his sole reign in September, of 14 A.D. However, Tiberius was co-regent with Augustus Caesar approximately 2 years before that time. Commentators who pay attention to biblical dating schemes recognize that the 14th year is based upon the co-regency of Tiberius with Augustus. Thus, the start of Tiberius Caesar's reign is about 12 A.D. The Bible is always precise. The date given is the "15th year of the reign of Tiberius Caesar."

Most Bible commentators believe that Jesus was born in 4 BC. If Tiberius Caesar started his reign in 12 A.D. and Jesus started His ministry the fifteenth year of Tiberius Caesar, then that would bring us to 27 A.D. Pontius Pilate, Herod the Tetrarch, and Philip the Tetrarch, according to the recorded historical accounts, are all rulers of their regions in 27 A.D. Now let us do some math and see if everything works. 27 A.D. + 4 BC = 31 years. Well, we are close. There is no "zero" year. Thus, we must subtract one year bringing Jesus to thirty years old. Tradition has long held that the ministry of Jesus was about 3 to 3½ years long. We will come back to this later in this chapter.

Josephus, the Jewish historian who worked for Rome,

documents that Herod's death was preceded by a lunar eclipse and followed by Passover. "A partial eclipse best observed from the west coast of Africa, took place on March 13, 4 BC about 29 days before Passover." (Josephus, Antiquities, 17.6.4) Also, the encyclopedia Britannica verifies the death of Herod as occurring before the Passover of 4 BC.

Philip Schaff (1819-1893) is an excellent biblical commentator. Schaff wrote a detailed eight-volume work entitled: History Of The Christian Church. Schaff states in a separate article entitled: *The Founder of Christianity*: "Jesus Christ came into the world under Caesar Augustus, the first Roman emperor, before the death of king Herod the Great, four years before the traditional date of our Dionysian era."

If Jesus were born in 4 BC, He would have had to be born in January or February. This writer believes that it could be possible that Jesus was born in the last quarter of 5 BC. Philip Schaff quoted above supports a December 25 birthdate of our Lord in his History of The Christian Church. If we go back any further, Jesus would have to have been about thirty-one years old when he started his ministry. Thus, it is highly probable that Jesus was born in the last quarter in the year 5 BC or in January or February of 4 BC. This writer believes the date was 4 BC. In any case, the Wise Men could not have visited Jesus at two years old or even one-year-old because Herod was dead. Wicked Herod could not have issued his order for the slaughter of innocents when Jesus was 2 years old, because he was dead.

There are numerous prognosticators that have conjured various theories about the birthday of our Lord. Some look to the stars and the chronological alignments of the consolations, planets etc. Other astronomers combine the Old Testament feasts with their heavenly findings. Quite frankly, those who have taken on these endeavors have contributed a massive amount of work in efforts to discern the birthdate of Jesus. Their work is impressive. Computer simulations are available to duplicate the alignment of stars and constellations for any day in history and from any point on earth.

There are a few astronomers that have researched and discovered other eclipses that occurred relatively near the birth of Christ. Several argue that Josephus had the wrong date. These eclipse finders have done their homework and make some excellent cases for their birthdates.

Others research Zacharias and his priestly order Abija and try to guess when Elisabeth conceived. From there, calculations are made of when the virgin birth could have possibly occurred. Several birthdate prognosticators failed to understand that the priestly order not only served twice a year but also served during the feast weeks. Thus, bogus calculations were submitted for the service of Zacharias.

While these birthday searchers have put in countless hours and efforts, their calculated birthdates are outliers. In other words, their dates are historically impossible. The birthday seekers feel as though they have an accurate date and are quick to point out that history could be wrong.

With all these speculations, how do we know what is right? The first consideration is to make sure we honor the biblical narrative trusting every jot and tittle in the word of God. God has dated a multitude of biblical events knowing that this information would be preserved for us to verify His word. The above information has historical attestation that can be cross referenced for verification. The Bible left us the cross-reference information naming specific rulers in precise geographical locations at a specific time.

To honor the biblical narrative, we start with the Bible. The Bible does not give us the birthdate of Jesus. However, the Bible does give us the year that Christ started His ministry. In addition, we know that Herod died in 4 BC before Passover. We have already researched the dates. So next, we need to discern if there could be any variation in the standard historical dates.

When historical data is researched, we find definite dates given for the Roman Caesars and Herod the client king of Judea, and the subsequent puppet rulers and governors. If ruling periods and dates are triangulated through chronological data and there are no discrepancies, then historical data would appear to be right. That is the case with the death of Herod and the reign of Tiberius Caesar.

Let us do some more Bible research. Our Lord was in the habit of keeping the various feasts. The Biblical account of the first Passover that Jesus attended is found in John chapter 2. Note the following Biblical record:

📖 **(John 2:13-21) And the Jews' passover was at hand, and Jesus went up to Jerusalem, ¹⁴And found in the temple those that sold oxen and sheep and doves, and the changers of money sitting: ¹⁵And when he had made a scourge of small cords, he drove them all out of the temple, and the sheep, and the oxen; and poured out the changers' money, and overthrew the tables; ¹⁶And said unto them that sold doves, Take these things hence; make not my Father's house an house of merchandise. ¹⁷And his disciples remembered that it was written, The zeal of thine house hath eaten me up. ¹⁸Then answered the Jews** and said unto him, What sign shewest thou unto us, seeing that thou doest these things? ¹⁹Jesus answered and said unto them, Destroy this temple, and in three days I will raise it up. ²⁰Then said the Jews, Forty and six years was this temple in building, and wilt thou rear it up in three days? ²¹But he spake of the temple of his body.

Of course, Jesus was in no small dispute in this account. When the Jews asked for a sign Jesus stated, **"Destroy this temple, and in three days I will raise it up."** The Jews quickly respond, **"Forty and six years was this temple in building, and will thou rear it up in three days?"** Their testimony is noteworthy. The temple at that time was still under construction and was not finished until 62 or 64 A.D. It is well attested that Herod the Great started construction on the temple in the eighteenth year of his reign which equates to 20 B.C. Calculating from 20 B.C. to the 46th year of construction puts us at 27 A.D. If you are doing the math on this: (20 + 27 = 47), then we must subtract 1 because there is no zero year which puts us in the 46th year of the temple construction). Thus, we find Jesus was in Jerusalem in 27 A.D. for the observance of the first Passover of His ministry.

Jesus announced His ministry in Luke 4:18-19 where Jesus quoted from **Isaiah 61:1–2a.** Jesus heralded the purpose of His ministry, **"he hath sent me to heal the brokenhearted, to preach deliverance to the captives, and recovering of sight to the blind, to set at liberty them that are bruised, To preach the acceptable year of the Lord."** Dr. Floyd Nolan Jones says, "This portion of Scripture is an undeniable offer of Jubilee." Dr. Jones also documents that AD 27 was the Year of Jubilee. (Reference: The Chronology of the Old Testament by Dr. Floyd Nolan Jones, page 219)

Various commentators list the possible years of Jesus' death from 27 AD to 33 AD. However, traditionally the most widely accepted date for Jesus' crucifixion is AD 30. which perfectly matches the above scenario.

In addition, Dr. Floyd Nolan Jones, in his previously mentioned Chronology offers some excellent insight to help us to nail down an AD 30 date for the crucifixion of Christ.

The 40 years of Judea's iniquity and its association to the siege of Jerusalem in Ezekiel 4:4-7 is herewith offered as a double reference prophecy with its second fulfillment being the span from the crucifixion to the ending of the sacrifice system by Titus' A.D. 70 destruction of the temple and its altar. Moreover, Titus began the siege of Jerusalem on 14 Nissan A.D. 70. Are we to actually believe it is mere coincidence that this was 40 years to the very day from a 14 Nissan A.D. 30 crucifixion?"

If we were to calculate the probability of these two dates being a random occurrence using a minimum parameter, the law of odds would be 1 in 5,329,000. God had a guiding hand in this occurrence.

In summation, the Bible verifies ancient history, and tradition leads us to a solid conclusion that Jesus was born early in 4 BC or late in 5 BC. In this writer's opinion, it appears the most likely months for the birth of Jesus would be December of 5 BC, or January and February of 4 BC. To those who want an exact birthdate for Jesus, we can provide no definite date. To those who have established a definite date that lies outside the above parameters, they are wrong.

Conservative commentators are quick to deny and downgrade December 25. Others who use December 25 as the birthday of Christ have made some compelling arguments. However, in the end, the Bible gives us no clear revelation. Despite all the study and good intentions, efforts to nail down the precise birthday of Jesus appear to be nothing more than speculation.

Chapter 17
The Mystery of No Room for Jesus

Luke 2:1-7, And it came to pass in those days, that there went out a decree from Caesar Augustus, that all the world should be taxed. ²(And this taxing was first made when Cyrenius was governor of Syria.) ³And all went to be taxed, every one into his own city. ⁴And Joseph also went up from Galilee, out of the city of Nazareth, into Judaea, unto the city of David, which is called Bethlehem; (because he was of the house and lineage of David:) ⁵To be taxed with Mary his espoused wife, being great with child. ⁶And so it was, that, while they were there, the days were accomplished that she should be delivered. ⁷And she brought forth her firstborn son, and wrapped him in swaddling clothes, and laid him in a manger; because there was no room for them in the inn.

The first Christmas there was no room for the Lord Jesus in the inn. I am afraid that today for many there will be no room for Jesus.

It is not by chance or mere circumstance that there was no room for the Lord Jesus. It was prophetic that for all His lifetime and throughout the history of this cruel world, there never has been nor will there ever be room for the Lord Jesus in this world's system.

The Lord Jesus was born in a stable. He died outside the city of Jerusalem, not even inside the city, but outside the city of Jerusalem, crucified between two thieves. When the Lord Jesus was buried, He was buried in a borrowed tomb. There has never been room for the Lord Jesus Christ.

The prophet Isaiah says this about the Lord Jesus in **Isaiah 53:3, "He is despised and rejected of men."** There is no room for Jesus. You should not think for one moment that the world system has improved. Do not think that this world today has somehow become more like the church. The church has become more like the world.

There has never been room for the Lord Jesus Christ. And why? Why was there no room when Mary and Joseph came to that inn in Bethlehem? Well, you say, "The innkeeper did not know." He did not know that this one, this baby was to be born the King of Eternity. He did not know. That is correct. He did not know. But ignorance is no excuse. The shepherds knew. The Wise Men knew. Mary and Joseph knew. Anna and Simeon knew. God speaks to those who want to know. Ignorance is never an excuse for not honoring the King of Kings.

There are many people in this world today who are ignorant of just who the Lord Jesus is, but God will hold them accountable for their ignorance. Because if you will seek Him, you will find Him.

I believe that others did not know simply because they were just so careless that day. For instance, that innkeeper, whose inn was filled with people, was lining his pockets with cash. It was a good time of the year for him. When Caesar said all the world was going to be taxed, that was a goldmine for him.

Many today are not interested in Jesus. When the news and the newspapers report on the holiday season they ask, "What is the shopping season like? Are we buying more this year or less this year? What are retail sales doing?" For many people, the jingle bells we sing about are the jingle bells of the cash register.

There may have been in the innkeeper's heart just a little coldness, a little callousness. The Bible says in **(Luke 2:5)** that Mary was great with child. She was about to have her baby.

Would you say to a young man and his wife who is about to give birth to a child, "We do not have any room for you?" You say, "Maybe he really did not have any room." Well, there was at least one room he could have given. That was his own. He could have given his own room. There was room.

There is an old story about a man who came to a hotel, and the man behind the desk said, "We just don't have any room sir." "Well," the man said, "I want to ask you a question. If the President of the United States were coming would you have a room for him?" "Well," the clerk said, "yes." The man replied, "He's not coming. I'll take that room."

There's always room if we want to make room. Yet there was no room for the Lord Jesus Christ. Many of us today are just calloused, indifferent, careless, greedy, or we are ignorant. But these are not legitimate excuses for not having room for the Lord Jesus, the King of Kings.

You must feel sorry for Mary. We do not know how old Mary was, the Bible does not tell us, but she was young. I would say perhaps eighteen or nineteen. This was her first baby. She was away from home. She was away from her family and away from her mother.

There was no doctor there, or even a mid-wife so far as we can tell from the Bible story. There were no sanitary conditions. How would you like to give birth to a baby, your first baby, without a doctor and in a stable for animals?

And poor Joseph. Have you ever thought about Joseph, how helpless he must have felt? How ashamed he must have felt that he could not provide better for Mary? There they are in this stable. A place where the animals were kept, and the little baby was laid there in a manger.

But this was not by accident; it was not by incident, that this happened. All of this was engineered by Almighty God. The fact that Jesus Christ would be born in Bethlehem was prophesied centuries before by the prophet Micah.

📖 **(Micah 5:2) But thou, Bethlehem Ephratah, though thou be little among the thousands of Judah, yet out of thee shall he come forth unto me that is to be ruler in Israel; whose goings forth have been from of old, from everlasting.**

All of this was in the plan of God down to the smallest detail. Caesar said, "All of the world is to be registered and taxed." Each one had to go to his own home city or his own hometown. God moved a multitude of people in this taxing, so that one verse of Scripture might be fulfilled! This was no accident. All of this was in the plan of God. This is a prophecy of the fact that the world never has had room for the Lord Jesus Christ.

Dr. John R. Rice has a book called I Love Christmas. In his book he points out that the world never has had room for the Lord Jesus Christ. This world has always begrudged everything that Jesus had. He points out that in Bethlehem, they begrudged Him a place to be born. He had nowhere to lay His head. He points out that Herod begrudged Jesus His kingly title. Herod sought to slay Him.

Nazareth begrudged Him His fame, they were offended, and they said, "Is not this the carpenter's son?" The Pharisees begrudged the Lord Jesus the power that was His and said, "This man only cast out demons by the prince of demons, Beelzebub." They begrudged the Lord Jesus, His right to His Father's house, and when He cleansed the temple, they said, "By what authority do you do this?"

The chief priests begrudged the Lord Jesus the Sabbath when He healed the sick and a man with a withered hand on the Sabbath day. They begrudged Him His own day of which He was Lord.

They begrudged Him the worship that He received, even of harlots and publicans and they snapped at Him and said, "This man receiveth sinners and eateth with them." They begrudged Him times of happiness and joy that He had. Every feast that He went to, they said that He was a winebibber and a glutton.

They begrudged Jesus the worship of a fallen woman, Mary, who washed His feet with her tears and wiped them dry with her hair. They criticized Him for this.

Judas begrudged Him an opened box of expensive ointment, and said, "Why this waste?" The Pharisees even begrudged the cries of the little children as they said, "Hosanna in the highest." They scoffed when children worshiped Him.

They begrudged Him even an hour of prayer in the Garden of Gethsemane. When He prayed, the sweat was as drops of blood upon His brow. They came in to disturb the Lord Jesus, even in the hour of prayer, with sticks, staves, and swords, to bind Him and carry Him away.

The soldiers begrudged His very garments and stripped Him naked when they crucified Him. They begrudged Him His title, "King of the Jews," and asked Pilot to change that title. When He was on the cross dying, they begrudged Him even a drink of clear water and gave Him vinegar and gall to drink.

They even begrudged the peace of death; they put a spear in His side when He hung upon that cross. Men begrudged everything that the Lord Jesus Christ had upon this earth, and today they still do.

Today, they begrudge Him and His miracles. The so-called Bible scholars begrudge His bodily resurrection. They argue about the inspiration of His words. They try to strip the Lord Jesus Christ of His deity. There is nothing that this world hates more than the fact that there is only one Saviour of the world, and His name is Jesus Christ.

This world never has, and never will have, room for the Lord Jesus Christ. Do not get the idea that if you honor Jesus, this world will honor you.

There are several things that need to be pointed out about the subject of no room for Jesus.

First, there is no room for Jesus in this world's government. There is no room for Jesus in the worldly system of things as they are today. The bible says, in **Psalms 2:2-3, "The kings of the earth set themselves, and the rulers take counsel together, against the LORD, and against his anointed, saying, 3Let us break their bands asunder, and cast away their cords from us."** The rulers of this world, the kings, the high monarchs, never have room for the Lord Jesus Christ. King Herod sought to slay the baby Jesus. The world never has room for the Lord Jesus Christ.

The Jews of that day, when it was time for Jesus' crucifixion, were faced with a decision. Pilot said, "Shall I crucify your king?"

They said, "We have no king but Caesar." What irony that they would choose the cruel leadership of Rome to murder the Lord. No room for Jesus, but room for Caesar. The governments of this world have not changed. We have secularized our society to the point that not only are we neutral, but we have a hostility toward the things of God.

The Bible says, **"He came unto His own, and His own received Him not."** There is no room for Jesus in the governments of this world.

Second, there is no room for the Lord Jesus in the educational institutions of our world. Go to today's universities. Go to today's public schools, and you will find there is room for evolution. There is room for humanism. You will find there is room for a study of the world's religions. There is room for criticism of the Bible, but there is no room for the Lord Jesus Christ. In our public schools today, rather than developing character, we are developing characters. Today we cannot post the Ten Commandments on the classroom walls, but we have resource officers in the halls. In some schools, our students are required to pass through metal detectors to get into the classrooms, because a student might be armed with some weapon, and still there is no room for the Lord Jesus Christ. We have engineered ourselves as a society to the point that there is no room for the Lord Jesus Christ in education. Without a knowledge of Jesus, all education is just splendid ignorance. Education without salvation is damnation.

General Omar Bradley once said, "We're living in a time when our achievements, our knowledge of science, has gone far beyond our power to control it." We have too many men of science, and too few men of God. We have brought about brilliance without wisdom, and power without conscience. We are living in a time of nuclear giants, and spiritual pygmies. There is no room for the Lord Jesus Christ. Jeremiah prophesied this in **Jeremiah 4:22, "For my people is foolish, they have not known me; they are sottish children, and they have none understanding: they are wise to do evil, but to do good they have no knowledge."** There is room for everything but Jesus.

There is no room for Jesus in this world's religion. How many churches today are truly preaching the full deity of the Lord Jesus Christ? How many are preaching the virgin birth of the Lord Jesus Christ? How many are preaching the blood atonement of the Lord Jesus Christ? It was to a religious world that the Lord Jesus is speaking to in **Revelation 3:20,** when He says, **"Behold I stand at the door and knock, if any man will hear my voice and open the door, I will come in to him."** The picture is Jesus Christ on the outside of a Laodocean church, knocking at the door, asking to be let into the church that bears His name. There is no room for Jesus!

May I say next, that really there is little room for the Lord Jesus in Christmas? How many this Christmas season, honestly, will honor the King of Kings and the Lord of Lords? Do you know who stands to make the most profit this Christmas? The distillers—yes, the distillers. The most beautiful ads you will see on television this season will be the beer commercials. That horse drawn sleigh being driven through the snow; isn't that a beautiful ad? The distillers today are looking forward to Christmas. Someone who does not ordinarily drink will drink at a Christmas party, and what will they say? They will say, "Well after all, it's Christmas." You see, it is an excuse for drunkenness.

There is a new industry today, obscene Christmas cards. Think about that.

What about the churches? Did you know at Christmas time in churches there is generally a letdown in attendance? There is generally a letdown in offerings, and generally a letdown in evangelism. Who are the heroes of Christmas today? Tiny Tim, Rudolph, and a jolly red-faced man with a beard? Those are the heroes, fictitious characters. Oh! There are some who will make much of the babe in the manger. Why they love to sing "Silent Night" in the bar rooms! The giddy crowd will dance around a manger. But there is no celebration of the full deity of Christ, no celebration of His lordship, no celebration of His blood atonement, nothing about His saving power is celebrated. There is no room for the Lord Jesus even in Christmas.

The true Christmas tree is a cross. **1 Peter 2:24** tells us, that Jesus **"his own self bare our sins in his own body on the tree, that we, being dead to sins, should live unto righteousness: by whose stripes ye were healed."** Jesus was born to die. There was no room for the Lord Jesus when He came the first time. There's truly little real room for the Lord Jesus today in government, in education, in religion, or even in the celebration.

Here is the point. Those of us who name the name of Jesus and are saved, must make room for the Lord Jesus in our hearts and in our lives.

If you want to find the Lord Jesus this Christmas, if Christmas is not all that you feel that it ought to be, if you are trying to be happy and find satisfaction in your gifts, toys, and parties, and they don't quite get there, let me tell you how to find Him.

If you would like to find Jesus Christ this Christmas, you will find Him. But you will find Him where you will always find Him, despised, and rejected of men, on the outside, not on the inside. In **Hebrews 13:12-13** the Bible says, **"Wherefore Jesus also, that he might sanctify the people with his own blood, suffered without the gate. ¹³Let us go forth therefore unto him without the camp, bearing his reproach."** What is this saying? It says that when Jesus Christ was crucified, they did not even have the decency to crucify Him inside the city. He was crucified outside the city, as some say on a garbage dump, outside the city. If you visit the Holy Land, you will find Calvary still outside the city walls, standing there by a bus station. In Jesus' time it was a garbage heap, the place of crucifixion—and that is where the Lord Jesus died—right next to the road because the Romans wanted to make a public example of those they executed.

Do not get the idea that He died, as the song says, on "a green hill far, far away." No, no! He died in a place of humiliation and shame. The Bible says in Hebrews 13:12-13, if you would find Him, you are going to have to go outside, where the Lord Jesus is. If you want to find the Lord Jesus, do not go to the inn; go to the stable. If you want to find the Lord Jesus, do not go inside the city; go outside the city. If you want to find Him, He will be outside of the world's system. Do not look for Him inside this world's system, you will always find Him outside.

Now, when you find Him to fellowship with Him there, here is what you are going to discover. You will discover that the world which had no room for Jesus will now have no room for you. Do not get the idea that if you live for the Lord Jesus, you are going to be loved and flattered and praised. In the book of John, Jesus said:

📖 **(John 15:18-20) If the world hate you, ye know that it hated me before it hated you. ¹⁹If ye were of the world, the world would love his own: but because ye are not of the world, but I have chosen you out of the world, therefore the world hateth you. ²⁰Remember the word that I said unto you, The servant is not greater than his lord. If they have persecuted me, they will also persecute you; if they have kept my saying, they will keep yours also.**

The world that has no room for Jesus, will have no room for you if you follow Jesus. Let me make this clear and plain, you cannot go outside the camp without bearing His reproach. That is what the Bible says in the book of Hebrews. Jesus died outside the city, and the Bible says, "let us go outside the city with Him." And when we go outside to fellowship with the Lord Jesus Christ, then we go out to bare His reproach. This vile world is not a friend of grace, and it will be no friend of yours. The Bible says that friendship with this world is warfare with God.

Yes, when you go outside to find the Lord Jesus, you are going to bare the reproach of the Lord Jesus. However, once you are out there, you are going to find it is not bad; it is wonderful. If you are sick and tired of this rat race, if you are sick and tired of what is happening in the inn, if you are sick and tired of the materialism, the blasphemy, the coarseness, and the crudeness, and the crowd in the inn, just go on out to the stable. There is plenty of room out there. Jesus is out there. His presence will turn that stable into a palace and will turn that manger into a throne. If you know sweet fellowship with the Lord Jesus: do not ever, do not ever, do not *ever* feel sorry for yourself because you are an outsider. Because the outsiders are the insiders. They are there with the King of Kings and the Lord of Lords.

As Christians we must also remember that we can have no room in our hearts for a world that had no room for Him. How can we claim to be followers of the Lord Jesus Christ and still make room for a world system that nailed Jesus to the cross? The worldly Christian is a traitor to heaven's King.

There is one more thing. The writer of the book of Hebrews said, when we go outside to bare His reproach, the Bible says we will see Him and fellowship with Him. Then it gives this explanation, **"For here we have no continuing city, but we seek one to come."** This world has no room for the Lord Jesus. It has no room for us. But we have a wonderful promise: it is not always going to be that way.

Have you ever read where our Lord Jesus taught us to pray this: **"Thy kingdom come, Thy will be done in earth, as it is in heaven"? (Matthew 6:10).** Would our Lord have taught us to pray that prayer if it would not have been answered? Have you ever read where Jesus said in the Beatitudes, **"Blessed are the meek: for they shall inherit the earth"? (Matthew 5:5).** Have you ever read where the Bible says, **"The earth shall be filled with the knowledge of the glory of the LORD, as the waters cover the sea," (Habakkuk 2:14)** and Jesus shall reign? What did the angels say? **"His name shall be called Jesus" (Matthew 1:21).** And He is going to rule **"over the house of Jacob forever; and of his kingdom there shall be no end" (Luke 1:33).** One day those little baby feet that were scratched and prickled with straw in the manger will be those nail pierced feet that are going to touch on the Mount of Olives when He comes again, and those swaddling clothes will be exchanged for a robe woven on looms of light, that crown of thorns will be replaced by a royal diadem, and that wilted reed that they put in His hand will become a scepter of iron. Those bloody nails will be removed and in His right hand will be power, majesty, and glory. When He was here the first time, He was despised and rejected of men. When He was here the first time, He stood before Pilate. When He comes again, Pilate will stand before Him. When He came the first time, He came as a baby. When He comes again, He comes as a King. When He came the first time, He was rejected, but our Lord says, **"As I live, saith the Lord, every knee shall bow to me, and every tongue shall confess to God."** There is coming a time when every politician on Capitol Hill and all the wise men in the Pentagon will bow their knee and say, "He is Lord." There is coming a time when every Christ-rejecting, Christ-denying sinner will say, "He is Lord." There is coming a time when every liberal, Bible-doubting preacher will say, "He is Lord."

There is no room for Him now, but one of these days they will say, "Make room for the King." He is on His way. One day there will be plenty of room for Jesus, and for all who follow Him. **"The kingdoms of this world are become the kingdoms of our Lord, and of his Christ; and he shall reign for ever and ever."** Room for Jesus? Is there room in your heart for Him? Have you received Him? **"He came unto His own and His own received Him not, but as many as received Him to them gave He the power to become the sons of God."** There was no room for Him when He came the first time. There is still no room for Him today. But you can make room for the Lord Jesus in your heart.

Do you want to find Him? Just go outside the gate. He is still there. And, oh, what a fellowship you will have with Him.

Chapter 18
The Mystery of the Child That Was Born to Die

📖 (Luke 2:10-11) "And the angel said unto them, Fear not: for, behold, I bring you good tidings of great joy, which shall be to all people. {11} For unto you is born this day in the city of David a Saviour, which is Christ the Lord."

📖 (Matthew 1:21) "And she shall bring forth a son, and thou shalt call his name JESUS: for he shall save his people from their sins."

Do you remember the excitement and expectation when your first child was born? Every child that is born into a loving God-fearing family today is a child with many hopes and dreams. The anticipation and aspiration for a bright and fulfilling future are always in the forefront in the mind of every parent that loves their child. Your child was born to live. But not so with our blessed Saviour, Jesus was born to die. This is a mystery to the natural man but should be no mystery to the Christian today.

When we glance at the story of the birth of Jesus, things seem to be in disarray. Ah! It is not so. Do you not think that the God of this universe would not make the best preparation for His only begotten son? Mary and Joseph may not have always understood the mysterious ways of God, but you may be assured that God was working his perfect plan.

You see, many people do not see Jesus as a suffering Saviour. Many do not see Him as a sin sacrifice. Many do not look at Jesus' death as our sin substitute. These people are too refined and cultured to accept the doctrine of the blood atonement, but Jesus came to die for your sins and my sins.

It could be said of Jesus that He was a born teacher, philosopher, or humanitarian. So He was. Jesus excelled all others in these fields. However, Jesus was born to die. When Jesus came to this earth, He knew his destiny was the cross. Let us look at some proof passages.

📖 (John 2:1-4) And the third day there was a marriage in Cana of Galilee; and the mother of Jesus was there: ²And both Jesus was called, and his disciples, to the marriage. ³And when they wanted wine, the mother of Jesus saith unto him, They have no wine.

⁴Jesus saith unto her, Woman, what have I to do with thee? mine hour is not yet come.

Three times John says about Jesus that His hour had not yet come. What hour did Jesus refer too? The hour of Christ was the hour He would go and die on the cross. Let us look at a text that illustrates this. In **John 12:23**, Jesus on the day that He would be arrested said: **"...The hour is come, that the Son of man should be glorified."** Again, the hour of Christ is when He will go to the cross and die for the sins of all mankind. Everything about the birth of Christ points to the fact that Jesus came to this earth to die. In **Luke 2:7** the Bible says, **"And she brought forth her firstborn son, and wrapped him in swaddling clothes, and laid him in a manger; because there was no room for them in the inn."** Then in **Luke 2:12** it says, **"And this shall be a sign unto you; Ye shall find the babe wrapped in swaddling clothes, lying in a manger."**

When the Lord Jesus was born, he was human and thus wrapped in the traditional clothing for that day. What exactly are swaddling clothes? To swaddle means to wrap. Swaddling clothes were narrow bands of linen cloth. When a child was born during the time of Christ swaddling clothes were used.

Immediately after birth, they would anoint the baby with oil and rub salt into the baby's skin to toughen it. They thought that this would be beneficial and help prevent infection to the newborn.

Then the baby would be wrapped in swaddling clothes from its shoulders to its feet with its arms and legs extended straight. The belief during that time was that this would make the arms and legs strong and give the child a good foundation. Dake's Study Bible says that this is the exact same process used to wrap a body for burial.

It was the same process and material used to wrap the body of Jesus for burial. The Bible says in **Matthew 27:59, "And when Joseph had taken the body, he wrapped it in a clean linen cloth..."**

The lesson is simple. The death of Jesus is all wrapped up in the birth of Jesus. God planned every detail in the birth, life, and death of Jesus before the foundation of the world. The birth of Jesus did not take God by surprise. God uses every opportunity to present the gospel to us, and we need to use every opportunity to present the gospel to others. Christmas gives us a golden opportunity to present the gospel to others.

God also likes to brag on his Son. Jesus is the beloved Son in whom God is well pleased. God is well pleased with the work of His Son, and His work was to go the cross and die for sinners.

There are four ways that the death of Jesus is illustrated through his birth.

The first illustration is that of the swaddling clothes. We have already discussed these, and we will discuss them more later.

Now, let us look at the first prophecy and the first promise of Christ in the Bible. It is found in the book of **Genesis:**

📖 **(Genesis 3:14-15) And the LORD God said unto the serpent, Because thou hast done this, thou art cursed above all cattle, and above every beast of the field; upon thy belly shalt thou go, and dust shalt thou eat all the days of thy life: ¹⁵And I will put enmity between thee and the woman, and between thy seed and her seed; it shall bruise thy head, and thou shalt bruise his heel.**

Here we have the first prophecy and promise of the coming of Christ. This Seed, the Seed of the Messiah, was to be different from all other children. The Seed of Jesus that was promised was to be **"her seed"** The seed of the woman. In **Galatians 4:4** the Bible says, **"But when the fulness of the time was come, God sent forth his Son, made of a woman, made under the law..."**

This is also the beginning of the doctrine of the virgin birth. A heel bruise was to be delivered to the seed of a woman and a head bruise to the serpent. The heel bruise took place at Calvary. Jesus suffered and died on the cross. The devil had his moment but on the third day "up from the grave He arose a mighty victor over His foes." We serve a risen Saviour. He is alive today. When Jesus Christ came out of the tomb, He delivered the head blow to Satan. Satan is a defeated foe.

In Genesis, we have the first prediction of the birth of the Saviour, and the prophecy points toward His death as well. Jesus was born to die.

Next, Jesus was born in a stable and not just any stable, and His birth was announced to Shepherds and not just any shepherds. Look at **Luke 2:8-16:**

📖 **(Luke 2:8-16) And there were in the same country shepherds abiding in the field, keeping watch over their flock by night. ⁹And, lo, the angel of the Lord came upon them, and the glory of the Lord shone round about them: and they were sore afraid. ¹⁰And the angel said unto them, Fear not: for, behold, I bring you good tidings of great joy, which shall be to all people. ¹¹For unto you is born this day in the city** of David a Saviour, which is Christ the Lord. [12]And this shall be a sign unto you; Ye shall find the babe wrapped in swaddling clothes, lying in a manger. [13]And suddenly there was with the angel a multitude of the heavenly host praising God, and saying, [14]Glory to God in the highest, and on earth peace, good will toward men. [15]And it came to pass, as the angels were gone away from them into heaven, the shepherds said one to another, Let us now go even unto Bethlehem, and see this thing which is come to pass, which the Lord hath made known unto us. [16]And they came with haste, and found Mary, and Joseph, and the babe lying in a manger.

Nowhere in the Bible is the word stable used, but you find a manger in a stable. The question is where was Jesus born? It is traditionally believed that Jesus was born in Manger Square in Bethlehem (pictured below). A church is built there over a cave (one of the many) that were used as stables in Bethlehem. On the next page you will also see a picture of the cave under the Church of the Nativity. The spot with the star around it is said to be the place where Jesus was born.

Manger Square, Bethlehem, Israel

The Grotto of the Nativity at the Church of the Nativity in Bethlehem. A star marks the place believed to be the birthplace of Jesus Christ

How did this tradition come to be? This tradition is carried out because Helena, the mother of Constantine built a church over this site, The Church of the Nativity.

But is this really the place where Jesus was born, or does the Bible give us a different picture? Sometimes customs and traditions can twist the truth of the word of God, and it is not with any malice, but because of a lack of understanding.

In **Micah 5:2** the Bible says, **"But thou, Bethlehem Ephratah, though thou be little among the thousands of Judah, yet out of thee shall he come forth unto me that is to be ruler in Israel; whose goings forth have been from of old, from everlasting."**

In **Micah 4:8** it says, **"And thou, O tower of the flock, the strong hold of the daughter of Zion, unto thee shall it come, even the first dominion; the kingdom shall come to the daughter of Jerusalem."**

At the time that these prophecies were written the Jews are praying for a Messiah. They were praying for a King. They were praying for a deliverer. The Prophet Micah said there would be a King coming to the daughter of Jerusalem.

This prophecy brings about two questions: Where will the King of the Kingdom arrive? What point of identification do we have for where this deliverer is going to come?

Again, in Micah 4:8 the Bible says, **"And thou, O tower of the flock, the strong hold of the daughter of Zion, unto thee shall it come, even the first dominion; the kingdom shall come to the daughter of Jerusalem."**

Micah 4:8 says this deliverer, this king, is going to come to the Tower of the Flock. The Tower of the Flock is located across the valley from Rachel's tomb in Bethlehem. If you were to go to Bethlehem today (after you entered Bethlehem), Rachel's tomb would be located on the right. It is still there; you can visit it and find pictures online.

Now if you went into the fields across from Rachel's tomb you would come to the Shepherd's Field, the place where the birth of Jesus was announced to the shepherds. From the Shepherd's Field, if you went right, you would come to the field of Boaz. The threshing floor of Boaz is still there, and you can go and see it.

The first time the Tower of the Flock is mentioned in the Bible is in the account of Rachel, who died after giving birth to Benjamin, the youngest son of Jacob. We read about this in **Genesis:**

📖 **(Genesis 35:16-21) And they journeyed from Bethel; and there was but a little way to come to Ephrath: and Rachel travailed, and she had hard labour. ¹⁷And it came to pass, when she was in hard labour, that the midwife said unto her, Fear not; thou shalt have this son also. ¹⁸And it came to pass, as her soul was in departing, (for she died) that she called his name Benoni: but his father called him Benjamin. ¹⁹And Rachel died, and was buried in the way to Ephrath, which is Bethlehem. ²⁰And Jacob set a pillar upon her grave: that is the pillar of Rachel's grave unto this day. ²¹And Israel journeyed, and spread his tent beyond the tower of Edar.**

Now, as we said, Rachel's tomb is located at the entrance to Bethlehem. Amazingly, the location mentioned here was marked out for the future fulfillment of prophecy. In Hebrew, the term "Tower of Edar" is "Migdal Eder." The literal meaning of "Migdal Eder" is "Tower of the Flock."

This is the place where Jesus Christ was born, as described by Luke's Christmas story. Again, the Bible says, in **Genesis 35:21, "And Israel journeyed, and spread his tent beyond the tower of Edar."** So, what happened? Rachel died giving birth to

Benjamin. Jacob, or Israel, moved down the road a short distance. He did not want to live in view of his wife's grave, so he journeyed down the road from Rachel's tomb and pitched his tent beyond the Tower of Edar. The Tower of Edar was a Jebusite tower. It was a military tower when it was first built. But when David and his armies defeated the Jebusites they converted this tower. Not only did David defeat the Jebusites but he had a vision of a house for God. He wanted to build a temple. God was not going to allow him to do so, because David had been a man of war.

In that temple daily sacrifices had to be offered. And because of the required daily sacrifices, hundreds of lambs had to be raised. Before Jesus came and died on the cross, all sacrifices were temporary. There had to be a blood sacrifice to cover every sin. All of this points to Jesus coming as the Lamb of God to die for the sins of the world. Jesus was born to die.

The Jebusites are defeated and this Jebusite tower in Bethlehem became the Tower of Edar. Edar means flock so, it is the Tower of the Flock (pictured on the next page).

Now this tower is a three-floor tower. When it was a Jebusite tower, it was a military tower. The top floor was a lookout, and they would have had soldiers there keeping watch. The middle floor was used for soldier's quarters. The bottom floor of the tower was a stable for horses and animals.

Once the Jebusites were defeated, it was converted to the Tower of the Flock. The top floor was where shepherds were keeping watch over their flocks. The second floor served as living quarters for the shepherds. The first floor was a delivery room for delivering sacrificial lambs.

The Tower of the Flock in Shepherd's Field was no ordinary place. This was the place where lambs were raised for use in temple ministry as well as for Passover. You will recall that Passover lambs had to be one year old, without spot or blemish.

The Messianic Jewish 19th century scholar, Alfred Edershiem, highlights this in his book, <u>The Life and Times of Jesus the Messiah.</u> He says this:

> This Migdal Eder was not the watchtower for the ordinary flocks which pastured on the barren sheep ground beyond Bethlehem, but lay close to the town, on the road to Jerusalem. A passage in the Mishnah *(The Mishnah is the first major written collection of the Jewish oral traditions known as the "Oral Torah" that was written after the destruction of the second temple when the Jewish Rabbis were afraid that their oral traditions would die out.)* leads

to the conclusion, that the flocks, which pastured there *(at Migdal Eder)*, were destined for Temple sacrifices, and, accordingly, that the shepherds, who watched over them, were not ordinary shepherds.

These shepherds were Levitical shepherds and priests who specialized in raising sacrificial lambs. These priestly shepherds kept watch over their flock of sheep day and night from the Tower of the Flock. When a lamb was ready to give birth, she would be brought into the bottom floor of the Tower of the Flock or Migdal Eder, and there she would give birth. Any lamb that was to be offered as a sacrifice had to be without blemish and without spot. These priestly shepherds did not want the sacrificial sheep to get dirty, stepped on,

A watchtower, Shepherd's Field, Bethlehem (circa. 1934)

or bruised out in the field.

After a lamb was born, these priestly shepherds would inspect the newborn lamb to look for any defects. They would determine if he were worthy to be a sacrifice. Does this sound familiar? Then they would wrap the newborn lamb in swaddling clothes!

Now let's look back at the book of **Luke 2:8, "And there were in the same country shepherds abiding in the field,**

keeping watch over their flock (notice it does not say flocks) **keeping watch over their flock by night.**"

The Bible is a very exact book, and it says they were keeping watch over **their flock.** The Bible says **their flock,** because it was *the flock* to be set aside to be offered sacrificially.

Unlike the portrayal we see in movies and cartoons, the place where Jesus was born was not a normal stable with donkeys, chickens, and cows. This stable was set aside for only lambs. But not just any lambs. These were lambs consecrated for holy use. These lambs were born to die. Jesus was born to die.

Where else would we expect the Lamb of God to come into the world, but in the very place that the Passover lambs were born? Again the Bible says in **Luke 2:4, "And Joseph also went up from Galilee, out of the city of Nazareth, into Judaea, unto the city of David, which is called Bethlehem; (because he was of the house and lineage of David:)." In Luke 2:6** the Bible says, **"And so, it was, that, while they were there, the days were accomplished that she should be delivered." In Galatians 4:4** the Bible says, **"But when the fulness of the time was come, God sent forth his Son, made of a woman, made under the law,"**

God had a plan, God had a purpose, and God had a timetable for when His son would be born into this world. None of this happened by accident, nor was it by mere coincidence, that this happened. All of this was engineered by Almighty God.

As noted in a previous chapter, Caesar Augustus decreed, that all the world must be registered and taxed. Each had to go to his own home city and to his own hometown. Millions of people were moving about in the Roman Empire so that God could fulfill the one verse of the Prophecy of Micah that says Jesus would be born in Bethlehem.

To qualify as the Lamb of God that would be led to the slaughter, as Isaiah 53 says, Jesus had to be born at the place that all the other lambs for sacrifice were born. Jesus was born to die.

Now imagine that you are one of these priestly shepherds. Surely you would know the prophecy of Migdal Eder and Bethlehem. This is where you would spend most of your days. If the Magi from the east knew of the prophecies **(Matthew 2:6),** then certainly the temple shepherds did. Then one night, as they were out with the lambs of God, a heavenly host appears. In **Luke 2:10-12**: the Bible says:

📖 **(Luke 2:10-12) And the angel said unto them, Fear not: for, behold, I bring you good tidings of great joy, which shall be to all people. ¹¹For unto you is born this day in the city of David a Saviour, which is Christ the Lord. ¹²And this shall be a sign unto you; Ye shall find the babe wrapped in swaddling clothes, lying in a manger.**

An analytical re-creation of how the Tower of the Flock may have looked

Now, these shepherds were in the Shepherd's Field in Bethlehem. After the angel appeared to them, they went back to Migdal Eder—the Tower of the Flock. The question is: How did they know to go there? Jesus could have been anywhere in Bethlehem. If you visit Shepherd's Field in Bethlehem, you will find that there are many stables and mangers there. How did they know where to go?

First, they knew the prophecy of **Micah 4:8,** that the restoration of Israel's royal authority would come from Migdal Eder; and they knew from **Micah 5:2,** that it was not merely Bethlehem, but Bethlehem Ephrathah, the town of David, the home of Boaz, just over the hill from Rachel's tomb was where the Messiah would be born.

The shepherds knew exactly which manger to go to, even though there were certainly dozens, if not more, in the area. It was the one of which the prophet Micah spoke, the Tower of the Flock.

Now there is one more thing that we need to see. In **Luke 1:5** the Bible says, **"There was in the days of Herod, the king of Judaea, a certain priest named Zacharias, of the course of Abia..."**

In the Old Testament when the priests had become numerous, David divided the whole body into twenty-four classes or "courses," which were appointed to do service in weekly rotation, and each of the courses had to attend the temple twice in the year for a week each time. All the courses served on the feast days.

My friend Dr. Ralph Sexton Jr. has been to Israel more than fifty times. He has studied with the rabbis in Israel. The Rabbis in Israel will tell you, and have told him, that Zacharias, the father of John the Baptist, served in the temple twice a year and the three feast periods. He was of the course of Abaia. For the rest of the year he served as a temple shepherd watching over these sacrificial sheep in the Shepherd's Field.

It is reasonable to assume that John the Baptist spent some time with his father out there with those sheep. I imagine he would watch his father look those sheep over when they were born, and Zacharias would say, "this one looks good; he's without spot and without blemish. Let us wrap him in swaddling clothes; let us not let him get bruised and blemished. Let us set him aside and keep him up until the eighth day, and then we will put him in the flock to be offered as a sacrifice." These sacrificial sheep had to be watched over for a whole year. Zacharias would have done this time and time again.

Now let us fast forward to **John 1:29.** John the Baptist was in the Jordan River at Bethabara baptizing. Now, John was a grown man and saw Jesus walking down the road. This same John who grew up in the Shepherd's Field watching his father grade those sacrificial sheep, said when he saw Jesus, **"Behold the Lamb of God, which taketh away the sin of the world."** Jesus was without spot and without blemish. Jesus was born to die. There was no-one more qualified than John the Baptist to identify Jesus as the Lamb of God. Jesus was born in the place where the sacrificial sheep were born, because Jesus was born to die.

The Christmas story is the story of a Child born, the only begotten Son of God. Born, then going to the cross to die for you, rising on the third day, and now offering you eternal life. Today, if you are lost, it is my prayer that the Holy Spirit will pierce your heart and that you will come to Christ for salvation.

If you are a Christian, now is the time for you to go and share with your lost loved ones and friends about the Baby born in the manger who was born to die for them. If you have family and friends who are lost, you should pray that they will come to the saving knowledge of Jesus Christ.

Christian, as we said earlier, you were born to live. When you were born again you were born to live for Jesus. Are you living for Him today?

Chapter 19
Mary's Lamb

1 Corinthians 5:7, "…For even Christ our passover is sacrificed for us:"

We have a little nursery rhyme that we sing: "Mary had a little lamb, his fleece was white as snow." And indeed, Mary, the Virgin Mary, had a little Lamb. His fleece was white as snow. He was God's sinless and spotless Lamb. In the Bible, a lamb depicts the Lord Jesus Christ.

Passover is about a lamb; that Lamb's name is Jesus. The Old Testament feast of Passover was a picture, prophecy, portrait, and an afore glimpse of God's Lamb, who would one day come into the world.

We are going to look at the Old Testament ceremony of Passover. Then we are going to look at the New Testament Passover. It is not only the Jews who are commanded to keep the Passover, Christians are commanded to keep the Passover as well.

Note **1 Corinthians 5:8, "Therefore let us keep the feast.…"** And there are two things that we need to see in this study of the Passover. We need to think first about Moses' symbolic lamb; and then, we need to think about Mary's saving lamb.

First, let us think a little bit about Moses' symbolic Lamb. Now, let us look in **Exodus** for just a moment.

📖 **(Exodus 12:1-4) And the LORD spake unto Moses and Aaron in the land of Egypt, saying, ²This month shall be unto you the beginning of months: it shall be the first month of the year to you. ³Speak ye unto all the congregation of Israel, saying, In the tenth day of this month they shall take to them every man a lamb, according to the house of their fathers, a lamb for an house: ⁴And if the household be too little for the lamb, let him and his neighbour next unto his house take it according to the number of the souls; every man according to his eating shall make your count for the lamb.**

This passage took place when the Jews were slaves in the land of Egypt. They were getting ready to be delivered from this land of bondage. Egypt illustrates a condition of sin, darkness, and slavery.

Pharaoh, the hard taskmaster, represents Satan himself, who keeps the children of God in bondage. So, here is a picture of how God was going to deliver his people from the land of Egypt. Do you know what the symbol of ancient Egypt was? It was a serpent, a snake.

The King of Egypt wore a coiled serpent emblem on his crown. This insignia of a coiled, venomous serpent would be sported on their staffs, on their scepters, and by their throne.

God was getting ready to destroy the power of Egypt. God is getting ready to deliver His people, and He is going to defeat the serpent. Do you know what He is going to use to defeat that snake?

A little lamb. A lamb is possibly the weakest and gentlest of all the animals. Think about a lamb: a lamb cannot run, it is slow, and its little legs cannot move long distances. A poor lamb cannot outrun anything except the tortoise.

A lamb has no fangs or poison like a serpent. A lamb has no huge teeth like a lion. A lamb has no claws to shred and rip. A lamb is a defenseless animal, so gentle, so meek. A lamb seems to say, "If you are hungry, eat me. If you are cold, shear me; take my wool and get warm."

In **Exodus 12**, God was getting ready to take His people out of Egypt's land of slavery. There are several things that we need to see about Moses' lamb.

First, we need to see that it was a special lamb. Let us look again at **Exodus 12:5, "Your lamb shall be without blemish, a male of the first year: ye shall take it out from the sheep, or from the goats:"**

This special lamb had to be absolutely and totally perfect, without spot and without blemish. It pictured the sinless, spotless character of the Lord Jesus.

This lamb was a prophetic portrait of the Lord Jesus Christ Himself, who was without sin. Jesus never, ever committed even one sin. He was a spotless Lamb. He was a special Lamb.

This Lamb was to be a male and a firstling of the flock. This spotless lamb represents Jesus, the Son of the living God.

Next, they examined the lamb. As a matter of fact, according to this scripture, they would keep the lamb up for four days from the tenth to the thirteenth day for inspection.

Then the priests would scrutinize the lamb carefully and check its mouth and examine the eyelids. They would meticulously inspect the lamb. It had to be a special lamb.

The special lamb was then a slain lamb. Look in **Exodus 12:6, "And ye shall keep it up until the fourteenth day of the** same month: and the whole assembly of the congregation of Israel shall kill it in the evening."

The lamb had to die at a specific and prescribed time. Note **Leviticus 23:5, "In the fourteenth day of the first month at even is the LORD'S Passover..."**

This lamb was to die in the evening at the specified time, not in the morning but the evening. The lamb was slain. Again, it pictures the Lord Jesus Christ, the Lamb of God, who would one day die for our sins.

The liberals and modernists today do not like the idea of the blood of the Lamb. They do not like the idea of a blood sacrifice. They call it a "slaughterhouse religion." But, let me remind you, **Hebrews 9:22 says, "Without shedding of blood there is no remission of sins."**

This lamb was slain. The liberal makes much of the life of Christ and little of the death of Christ. But we are not saved by learning lessons from the life of Christ; we are saved by receiving life through the death of Christ. It is the death of Christ that saves us.

This lamb was a special lamb. This lamb was a slain lamb. Therefore, this lamb became a saving lamb. The blood of this lamb was caught in a basin. **Exodus 12:7** provides further instructions: **"And they shall take of the blood, and strike it on the two side posts and on the upper door post of the houses, wherein they shall eat it."**

📖 **(Exodus 12:22-23) And ye shall take a bunch of hyssop, and dip it in the blood that is in the bason, and strike the lintel and the two side posts with the blood that is in the bason; and none of you shall go out at the door of his house until the morning. ²³For the LORD will pass through to smite the Egyptians; and when he seeth the blood upon the lintel, and on the two side posts, the LORD will pass over the door, and will not suffer the destroyer to come in unto your houses to smite you.**

This lamb was a saving lamb. They were to take the blood, and nothing else but the blood. If they had set a live lamb by the door, it would have done no good. Had they written beautiful poetry and posted it on the doorpost, it would have done no good. Had they encrusted the doorposts with rubies, and diamonds, and emeralds, and gems, it would have done no good. For God said, "When I see the blood, I will pass over you."

The angel of God's wrath, the angel of God's vengeance, the angel of God's justice, was passing through the land. People could enter the house of safety only one way: they walked in under the blood.

They walked in, every one of them, underneath the blood. The only place there was no blood was on the bottom sill of the door. No one can trample the blood of Jesus with dirty feet and go to Heaven.

The lamb's blood on the side and on the top of the doorpost symbolized a covering for our atonement, a satisfaction for the holy fires of the wrath of Almighty God. This lamb was a saving lamb.

This lamb was a special lamb, a slain lamb, a saving lamb, and next a shared lamb.

Exodus 12:8, "And they shall eat the flesh in that night, roast with fire," The fire speaks of God's wrath. Jesus, God's Lamb took God's wrath for you. Jesus, God's Lamb, suffered the full fury of the wrath of God. Jesus, God's Lamb, suffered our hell on the cross that we might be saved.

📖 **Exodus 12:8-11, "And they shall eat the flesh in that night, roast with fire and unleavened bread; and with bitter herbs they shall eat it. ⁹Eat not of it raw, nor sodden at all with water, but roast with fire; his head with his legs, and with the purtenance thereof. ¹⁰And ye shall let nothing of it remain until the morning; and that which remaineth of it until the morning ye shall burn with fire. ¹¹And thus shall ye eat it; with your loins girded, your shoes on your feet, and your staff in your hand; and ye shall eat it in haste: it is the LORD'S passover.**

Can you imagine that scene? Here is the blood on the doorpost and on the lentil. Then, they take the body of that lamb and begin to kindle fires. Can you imagine what the Egyptians must have thought?

Can you imagine the aroma that went over the land of Egypt as a quarter of a million lambs are being roasted at one time? And then, they begin to feed on the lamb. All of them and their families take this lamb that has saved them, and now they feed on the lamb.

For the lamb that saved them was the lamb that would strengthen them. Every one of them, when they walked out of Egypt, walked out with a lamb on the inside. The Bible says, **"Christ in you, the hope of glory" (Colossians 1:27).**

The saving lamb was the strengthening lamb. Now, a bunch of slaves were becoming a nation, and they were fellowshipping together by feeding on a lamb.

God made a nation out of a group of slaves. Moses' lamb was a special lamb, a slain lamb, a saving lamb, and a shared lamb. The Lamb of God was Moses' lamb in picture, type, and prophecy.

Now let us look at the next part of this chapter and think not only of Moses's lamb, but of Mary's saving, sacrificial Lamb. The Lamb of God was the New Testament fulfillment of the Old Testament prototype. Jeremiah, the prophet, had taught that something better was to come. Jeremiah is looking to the future: **Jeremiah 31:31, "Behold, the days come, saith the LORD, that I will make a new covenant with the house of Israel, and with the house of Judah:**

Notice the phrase "new covenant." Do you know what the word covenant means? It means "testament." This is talking about the New Testament. God said, "You have an Old Testament, but I'm going to give you a New Testament." Note:

📖 **(Jeremiah 31:32-34) Not according to the covenant that I made with their fathers in the day that I took them by the hand to bring them out of the land of Egypt; which my covenant they brake, although I was an husband unto them, saith the LORD: 33But this shall be the covenant that I will make with the house of Israel; After those days, saith the LORD, I will put my law in their inward parts, and write it in their hearts; and will be their God, and they shall be my people. 34And they shall teach no more every man his neighbour, and every man his brother, saying, Know the LORD: for they shall all know me, from the least of them unto the greatest of them, saith the LORD: for I will forgive their iniquity, and I will remember their sin no more.**

God was saying, "It's going to be a spiritual religion, not one of the letter, but one of the spirit. This new covenant was not one of the law, but a law that now is written in the heart and one of intimate knowledge.

You will not have to be taught about the Lord. You will know the Lord. Your sins will be forgiven. This is something new, not like what happened to you when you came out of Egypt in the land of the Passover."

Do you remember that they were to keep this feast of the Passover as a memorial, a perpetual feast?

That is the reason our Jewish friends today keep the Passover. Every April, they keep the Passover. But now, something began to happen in those Old Testament days in the time of Moses. They began to learn how to keep the Passover.

In New Testament times, one day John the Baptist, was baptizing down by the Jordan River. When he saw Jesus, he said in **John 1:29: "Behold the Lamb of God, which taketh away the sin of the world."**

God's Lamb has now come. Mary's Lamb was born of a virgin. John knew him. The Holy Spirit said, "That's the One. That is the One that the centuries have been yearning for. That is the Lamb of God." Let me tell you about that Lamb.

He was a special lamb. There was never another like this One. Jesus Christ was the sinless, spotless, virgin-born, male child of Almighty God, the Son of the Highest.

In the previous chapter we learned that there were certain Old Testament priests that were shepherd priests who specialized in raising sacrificial sheep in the shepherd's field in Bethlehem.

Those lambs were bred by those priestly shepherds as Passover lambs. They were incredibly special lambs. They were raised to be without spot or without blemish.

Now remember, Jesus was born in Bethlehem, and those little lambs for Passover were born in Bethlehem. Jesus was born right out there in the field of Boaz. He was born in the Tower of the Flock in the birthing room where those sacrificial sheep were born.

Four days before Passover, they would begin to bring those lambs into the city, through the sheep gate. Those lambs would be coming to the Temple Mount. At the same time on Palm Sunday when those Passover lambs would be coming in through that sheep gate into the city, out of the field of Bethlehem. On that same Sunday, Jesus Christ comes into the city, riding upon a donkey. The same time as those Passover lambs are being brought in for inspection, God's Lamb is coming into the city.

Then, the priest would begin to examine those lambs and look at those lambs. For four days, they would examine those lambs to make certain they are perfect.

Have you ever wondered why the gospel story spends so much time on the last four days of the life of Christ?

The gospels of Matthew, Mark, Luke, and John are not long books. But if you study your Bible, you will find out how much time is given to that last week, and especially the last four days of that last week.

Jesus was being examined by the Sadducees, Pharisees, and civil rulers on the Temple Mount. They were examining Jesus trying to find a flaw and trying to find a fault. But they had to admit, **"Never man spake like this man"** (John 7:46).

Jesus said, in **John 8:46, "Which of you convinceth me of sin?"** They could lie about Him; they could slander Him, but not one could accuse Him of sin, not one! Even Pilate had to say, **"I find no fault in him" (John 19:6).** God's perfect Lamb was examined there.

This Lamb was a special Lamb. Next, this lamb was a slain lamb. The Lord Jesus Christ took Himself, by the will of God, to that place called "Calvary." Remember that the Jewish day begins at sundown at about 6 p.m. That same night, Jesus said, "Go into the city to prepare, we must eat the Passover."

So, the disciples went to that place. They prepared a Passover meal. Jesus broke the bread and said, **"This is my body, which is broken for you" (1 Corinthians 11:24).**

Then, the Bible tells us in Luke chapter 22, after the supper, Jesus took the cup and said, **"This cup is the new testament in my blood" (Luke 22:20).**

Jeremiah said there was the old covenant with the old Passover. Now, Jesus said, "Here is a New Testament, a new covenant, not with the blood of Moses's lamb, but with the blood of Mary's Lamb. This is the new covenant in My blood"

Then, He went to Gethsemane that night of agony. By 9 a.m., He was on His way to be crucified. Jesus took the cross, to "Mount Calvary," also called "Golgotha." It was a part of Mount Moriah. Do you know where Mount Moriah was? In **Genesis**, God had told Abraham to sacrifice his son in a place God said, **"I will tell thee of" (Genesis 22:2),** not just any place but "in a place I will show you."

The very place that God told Abraham to sacrifice his son was Mount Moriah. Now, as Abraham and Isaac were going up that hill Isaac said to Abraham, his father, **"Behold the fire and the wood: but where is the lamb for a burnt offering" (Genesis 22:7).** Abraham said to Isaac, **"God will provide himself a lamb for a burnt offering" (Genesis 22:8);** it is not that God will provide a sacrifice for Himself, but God will provide Himself a sacrifice.

God will be the sacrifice. **"God was in Christ, reconciling the world unto himself" (2 Corinthians 5:19).**

Notice carefully that the place where Abraham was to have sacrificed Isaac is the place where God the Father provided Himself a sacrifice. On that same mountain is where God's Lamb, God's Passover, the Lord Jesus was sacrificed.

It all begins to come together. He, Jesus, was the special Lamb. He, Jesus, was the slain Lamb. He was that One that was crucified. And, while Jesus was there on one end of Mount Moriah, on the Temple Mount, the Levites and the priests were on the other end of Mount Moriah.

Remember, they were to sacrifice the lamb in the afternoon. When did Jesus die? It was three o'clock in the afternoon. At three o'clock in the afternoon, those Levitical priests had sharpened their lethal knives.

Those lambs had been examined. They were perfect and spotless lambs. And, without a whimper, they were lying there. The Levitical priest took their chin and with that razor-sharp knife he cut their throat, and the blood spilled out.

At the same time, Jesus bowed His head in agony, and He said, **"It is finished" (John 19:30).** It is paid in full. It is done.

Levites, you can go home now. Priests, you can go home now. Priestly shepherds, you can retire now. We do not need you anymore. That is the Old Testament. That is the old covenant. That is finished. It is done.

Christ, our Passover, was sacrificed for us. He died in the right place, at the right time, for the right reason, and He is God's saving Lamb.

God says to every one of us, when that blood is applied to our hearts and our lives, and when He sees the blood, He will pass over you. Every man, woman, boy, or girl is under the judgment of God and needs God to pass over His judgment on us.

Without the blood of the Lamb you will not escape that judgment. Your sin will be pardoned in Christ or punished in Hell, but it will not be passed over apart from the blood of Jesus Christ. He is God's saving Lamb.

In the Old Testament, they took that blood, and they took hyssop, which is a common weed that just grew out of the wall; they took hyssop, and they applied the blood to the doorposts.

Jeremiah said, this new covenant is going to be in the heart, not on some door, but in the heart. What does that hyssop represent? It was so common and so easily available. What does it represent? It represents the fact that the blood was applied by faith. The hyssop represents faith that applies the blood to our hearts.

The Bible says:

📖 **(Romans 10:9–10) That if thou shalt confess with thy mouth the Lord Jesus, and shalt believe in thine heart that God hath raised him from the dead, thou shalt be saved. For with the heart man believeth unto** righteousness; and with the mouth confession is made unto salvation.

The blood of the Lamb is applied by the hyssop of faith to the heart of any person. When that happens, He becomes the saving Lamb.

Not only was Jesus a special Lamb, a slain Lamb, a saving Lamb, but Jesus was also the shared Lamb. You see, the Lamb that saves is the Lamb that strengthens us.

Just as they fed upon Moses's lamb so long ago, we are to feed upon Mary's Lamb. By faith, we are to commune with the Lamb.

Look at **1 Corinthians chapter 10**. Remember that **1 Corinthians chapter 5** told us to keep the feast. Now, you may say "How can I keep the Passover?"

Let me show you how.

📖 **(1 Corinthians 10:16) The cup of blessing which we bless, is it not the communion of the blood of Christ? The bread which we break, is it not the communion of the body of Christ?**

As they fed upon that lamb so long ago, we feed upon the Lamb. The Lord's Supper pictures our feeding upon the Lamb.

📖 **(1 Corinthians 11:23-26) For I have received of the Lord that which also I delivered unto you, That the Lord Jesus the same night in which he was betrayed took bread: 24And when he had given thanks, he brake it, and said, Take, eat: this is my body, which is broken for you: this do in remembrance of me. 25After the same manner also he took the cup, when he had supped, saying, This cup is the new testament in my blood: this do ye, as oft as ye drink it, in remembrance of me. 26For as often as ye eat this bread, and drink this cup, ye do shew the Lord's death till he come."**

Let me tell you something about the Lord's Supper: when you come to the Lord's Supper, you do not have to be mournful and weep. The Lord's Supper is a celebration. We are not mourning a corpse; we are hailing a Conqueror. The Lord's Supper is a meal with a friend, the Lord Jesus. Let me tell you what it celebrates: the Lamb has slain the serpent. The Lamb has slain the snake.

📖 **(Revelation 5:11-14) And I beheld, and I heard the voice of many angels round about the throne and the beasts and the elders: and the number of them was ten thousand times ten thousand, and thousands of thousands; 12Saying with a loud voice, Worthy is the**

Lamb that was slain to receive power, and riches, and wisdom, and strength, and honour, and glory, and blessing. [13]And every creature which is in heaven, and on the earth, and under the earth, and such as are in the sea, and all that are in them, heard I saying, Blessing, and honour, and glory, and power, be unto him that sitteth upon the throne, and unto the Lamb for ever and ever. [14]And the four beasts said, Amen. And the four and twenty elders fell down and worshipped him that liveth for ever and ever."

Glory be to the Lamb of God, that taketh away the sins of the world.

Chapter 20
Herod and the Slaughter of the Innocents

Matthew 2:16-18, Then Herod, when he saw that he was mocked of the wise men, was exceeding wroth, and sent forth, and slew all the children that were in Bethlehem, and in all the coasts thereof, from two years old and under, according to the time which he had diligently enquired of the wise men. 17Then was fulfilled that which was spoken by Jeremy the prophet, saying, 18In Rama was there a voice heard, lamentation, and weeping, and great mourning, Rachel weeping for her children, and would not be comforted, because they are not.

In researching various aspects of this book, several Herod the Great video documentaries were reviewed. These new historians virtually worship the architectural ability and construction capability of Herod the Great. There seems to be an innate quality in the natural man that wants to build and provide a lasting memorial for oneself. So, it was with Herod.

Modern unreliable historians are quick to point out that the slaughter of the innocents by Herod cannot be found in secular history. They, in turn, conclude that a man with the political brilliance and construction acumen of Herod would never be prone to slaughter innocent children. Really?

In response please note, the Bible is the most published and well attested history book in the history of mankind and the biblical account is explicit. In addition, the slaughter of the innocents is in perfect context with the personal demeanor and psychotic acts of behavior which characterized the life of Herod.

The biblical narrative records that the Wise Men come to Jerusalem seeking Jesus. Herod called a meeting of the chief priests and scribes to find where this prophesied king was to be born. Then, Herod met with the Wise Men. All of this occurs at Jerusalem.

When the Wise Men convened with Herod, he was critically ill. The command for the slaughter of innocents would be one of Herod's last acts in Jerusalem. It is speculated that Herod had a combination of kidney disease and gonorrhea. Ancient records detailed Herod's symptoms as painful intestinal problems, convulsions in every limb, intense itching, breathlessness, and gangrene of the genitalia. The illness would cause Herod to "stink to high heaven" and the pain would be excruciating. In a short time after the visit of the Wise Men, Herod would be moved to Jericho and soak in the thermal and mineral springs nearby to try to achieve a cure.

A few years before the visit of the Wise Men, Antipater, son of Herod the Great, conspired against his half-brothers Aristobulus and Alexander to prevent their possible succession to the throne of Judaea. Herod took the bait and believed the plot of Antipater. Herod, in turn, had his two sons executed in 7 or 6 BC. About a year or so thereafter Antipater was rightly accused of conspiring against Herod and Pheroras, Herod's brother. Herod had Antipater tried in a puppet court. Antipater was kept in prison for several months and was executed five days before his father's death at Jericho.

Shortly before Herod died, and aware of his impending death, he correctly reasoned that no one would mourn for him. Rather, Judah would be in a great state of rejoicing and jubilation. Note this excerpt from The Annals of The World by James Ussher:

Herod by an edict, convened to Jericho from every place, the most noble of the Jews and locked them up in a place called the hippodrome. He ordered his sister Salome and her husband Alexas, that as soon as he was dead, they would order the soldiers to kill all those that were confined so that the people should have cause for sorrow otherwise they would rejoice at the death of their king that they hated so much.

Salome and her husband feared political repercussions from the Jews in Rome and let the Jewish nobles go free.

An episode of rebellion occurred shortly after Herod traveled to Jericho in hopes of recovery. This episode was precipitated because the Jews knew Herod was on his deathbed. Again, we quote from The Annals of The World by James Ussher:

Judas, the son of Saripheus and Matthias, the son of Margalothus, were two of the most learned of the Jews and best interpreters of the law. When they knew that the king's sickness was incurable, they persuaded some young men who were their scholars that they should throw down the golden eagle that Herod erected over the large gate of the temple. They went at noon day, they pulled and hewed down with their axes the eagle while a large number in the temple witnessed their actions. As soon as it was told the captain, he came with a strong band of soldiers and laid hold upon some forty of the young men together with their masters and brought them to Herod. These continually defended their

actions and Herod ordered them to be bound and sent to
Jericho. He convened the rulers of the Jews and was brought
into the assembly in a litter because he was so weak. He
complained not so much of the wrong done to himself as to
God, as he said. They denied that it was done according to
their order and Herod dealt more mildly with them. He took
away the high priesthood from Matthias since he knew of this
affair and replaced him with Jazar the brother of his wife,
(Mariamme, the daughter of Simon the high priest.) He
burned alive the other Matthias that was partner of this
sedition along with his companions. That night the moon was
eclipsed {Josephus, Antiq., l. 17. c. 8 <c. 5. 1:461,462>} on
March 13th, three hours after midnight according to the
astronomical tables.

Herod died a short time after this incident. During the last
few days of his life, Herod changed his will and gave the kingdom to
his son Archelaus. You remember that Herod was a client king. The
will of Herod for Archelaus to be the new King was subject to
approval of Augustus Caesar. You remember that Jesus in the parable
of the pounds tells of a certain nobleman who went to a far country
to receive for himself the kingdom, and return. Before Archelaus
could gather his entourage of ambassadors and leave for Rome to get
his Kingship approved, we have the following accounts from
Josephus:

After the funeral ceremony was over, Archelaus came to
Jerusalem, and solemnized the mourning for his father for
seven days according to the traditions of the Jews. At the end
of the mourning, he made a funeral banquet to the people. He
went up into the temple and wherever he went he was
congratulated. He went up to a higher place and sat on a
golden throne. He spoke graciously and honestly to the
people. However, he said that he would not take the name of
king until Caesar had confirmed his father's will. After the
sacrifices were over, he banqueted with his friends.
{Josephus, Antiq. l. 17. c. 10. <c. 8. 1:464>}

The friends of those whom Herod had put to death for
throwing down the golden eagle, made a sedition. They
reproached the dead king and demanded some of his friends
also to be punished. Moreover, they desired that Joazar, the
high priest to be removed from the priesthood. Archelaus
tried to appease them but in vain. It happened that about the

feast of the passover, Archelaus sent the whole army against them and 3000 men were killed by the cavalry around the temple. The rest fled to the adjoining mountains. {Josephus, Antiq. l. 17. c. 11. <c. 9. 1:465,466>}

Archelaus proved himself to be the same type of bloodthirsty tyrant as his father. The Jews, inspired by the death of Herod, were not entirely guiltless and pushed Archelaus to the point that something had to be done to prevent anarchy. Archelaus overreacted and killed three thousand Jews.

Shortly thereafter, Archelaus left for Rome. While Archelaus was gone, various Jews committed all types of treasonous and seditious crimes. The Jewish saboteurs pretended that their efforts were being done for religious and patriotic reasons. These so-called patriots were nothing more than vandals taking advantage of no clear-cut lines of authority. Judea was in such a bad state of affairs that surrounding governors sent armies to Jerusalem to stop the sedition and keep the peace.

Getting back to Herod, his slaughter of the innocents was in perfect context with the rest of his life. Herod was a schizophrenic, power-crazed, evil, and exceedingly cruel tyrant. This poor writer has not the words to paint a picture of just how bad Herod was.

Herod ordered that all Jewish children the age of two years and under to be slain. For some perfectly ignorant reason, a good number of Bible commentators think that the Wise Men came to Jerusalem somewhere around two years after the birth of Christ. We need to make no mistake and completely understand Herod's wicked and evil ways of thinking. If the Wise Men had told Herod that the star had appeared two years prior, Herod would have ordered all the children killed up to four years old. Even though Herod was still at Jerusalem carrying on affairs of government, he was deathly sick. Herod had to know at that time that he only had a short time to live.

The number of children slaughtered by the soldiers of Herod is estimated to be around twenty. It is this writer's understanding that some commentators from yesteryear have estimated ridiculously high numbers. The population of Bethlehem during the time of Christ was estimated to be about 300. This estimation was based upon extensive archaeological research done by the famous archaeologist WF Albright (1891 – 1971). It is believed that Herod's soldiers canvassed a five-mile radius from Bethlehem in search of children two years of age and under.

Chapter 21
The Mystery of the Anticipation of Christmas

(Luke 2:22-35) And when the days of her purification according to the law of Moses were accomplished, they brought him to Jerusalem, to present him to the Lord; 23(As it is written in the law of the Lord, Every male that openeth the womb shall be called holy to the Lord;) 24And to offer a sacrifice according to that which is said in the law of the Lord, A pair of turtledoves, or two young pigeons. 25And, behold, there was a man in Jerusalem, whose name was Simeon; and the same man was just and devout, waiting for the consolation of Israel: and the Holy Ghost was upon him. 26And it was revealed unto him by the Holy Ghost, that he should not see death, before he had seen the Lord's Christ. 27And he came by the Spirit into the temple: and when the parents brought in the child Jesus, to do for him after the custom of the law, 28Then took he him up in his arms, and blessed God, and said, 29Lord, now lettest thou thy servant depart in peace, according to thy word: 30For mine eyes have seen thy salvation, 31Which thou hast prepared before the face of all people; 32A light to lighten the Gentiles, and the glory of thy people Israel. 33And Joseph and his mother marvelled at those things which were spoken of him. 34And Simeon blessed them, and said unto Mary his mother, Behold, this child is set for the fall and rising again of many in Israel; and for a sign which shall be spoken against; 35(Yea, a sword shall pierce through thy own soul also,) that the thoughts of many hearts may be revealed."

Do you remember when you were a child, and it was near Christmas? Perhaps the Christmas tree was in the living room, and it was decorated. Maybe your family hung stockings by the chimney and there were gifts under the tree, and you could hardly wait until Christmas morning.

In this chapter we will look at the story of a man who was anticipating Christmas. He was waiting for Christmas, the very first Christmas, and the very best Christmas ever. His name was Simeon. He was looking. He was waiting. He was longing. He was anticipating the coming of Jesus Christ into this world. How did Simeon know to anticipate this first Christmas? It had been revealed to Simeon by the Spirit of God. This is all a part of the great mysteries of Christmas.

There were many who missed the first coming of Jesus that first Christmas morning because they did not understand, or they did not believe the clear Bible prophecies of His first coming to the world. It was clear. It was plain. It was there in the Word of God; and yet, they missed it, either through ignorance or unbelief.

That same Jesus who came before is coming again! You need to be careful or you will miss the Second Coming of Jesus Christ by ignorance or unbelief, because the same scriptures that clearly prophesied His first coming prophesied His Second Coming. Just as Jesus's first coming was literally fulfilled, His Second Coming will be literally fulfilled. You need to be ready for Christmas by being ready for the Second Coming of our Lord and Saviour Jesus Christ.

So, let us think about how to be ready for Christmas, and how to be ready for the coming of our Lord and Saviour Jesus Christ. There are some things that were true about Simeon that surely ought to be true about everyone reading this book.

First, may I ask you this question: Are you saved? I did not ask if you were Baptist, Methodist, or a nice person. I did not ask: "Do you give to charity, are you generous, kind, and compassionate?" I asked are you saved?

Jesus came to save His people. The Bible says in **Matthew 1:21, "Thou shalt call his name JESUS: for he shall save his people from their sins."**

In **Luke 2:25** the Bible says, **"And, behold, there was a man in Jerusalem, whose name was Simeon; and the same man was just."** Simeon was a just man. That means he was right with God. We are "justified by faith." You say, "now, wait a minute. How could Simeon be saved if Jesus had not yet died on the cross? If Jesus is just a little baby, how could this man be a saved man?" The Old Testament saints were saved by looking forward in faith to the coming of Jesus. The Bible teaches that Abraham was justified by faith. Jesus said, in **John 8:56, "Your father Abraham rejoiced to see my day: and he saw it, and was glad."**

Today we are saved by looking backward to the death of Christ. All saints are looking, whether forward or backward, we are all looking upward in faith to the Lord Jesus Christ. Are you saved? Are you certain beyond the shadow of any doubt that if Jesus Christ, who came the first time, were to come again this time, that you are absolutely certain that you are saved? If you do not receive Christ as your personal Saviour and Lord, you are not ready for Christmas, nor are you ready for the Second Coming of Jesus Christ. So, the first question is, are you saved?

The second question is: Are you surrendered? The same verse that says that this man Simeon was a just man, also says he was a devout man. In **Luke 2:25** the Bible says, **"And, behold, there was a man in Jerusalem, whose name was Simeon; and the same man was just and devout."** The word devout is an adjective that we do not use a lot these days. Are you devout? That means, do you have a deep, burning, passionate love in your heart for the Lord Jesus Christ? Luke goes on to say that Simeon had been **"waiting for the consolation of Israel," (Luke 2:25)** which is why he can be described as being devout. The mark that you are ready for Jesus to come again is that you are devout. The Apostle John said in **1 John 3:3, "And every man that hath this hope in him purifieth himself, even as he is pure."** If you are dabbling in the world, living in sin, carelessly, recklessly, you are not ready for either the first coming or the second coming of Jesus. You are not ready for Christmas. You are not ready for Jesus Christ to come again. Blessed hope leads to blessed holiness. Are you devout? Are you holy? What is the passion of your life? It ought to be the Lord Jesus Christ. Are you saved? Are you surrendered?

Here is the third question: Are you spiritual? In **Luke 2:25** the Bible says, **"And, behold, there was a man in Jerusalem, whose name was Simeon; and the same man was just and devout, waiting for the consolation of Israel:"** (notice the last phrase) **"and the Holy Ghost was upon him."** Is the Holy Ghost upon you? Are you filled with the Spirit of God? If you are saved, you have the Holy Spirit, but does the Holy Spirit have you? Can you say that your body is a surrendered vessel? Does the Spirit have all of you? Simeon was a man who was spiritual. He was filled with the Holy Spirit of God.

Next question: Are you sensitive? So, we have asked: Are you saved? Are you surrendered? Are you spiritual? Are you sensitive? Do you know what the name Simeon means? It means "one who hears." It means "listening one." In Luke 2:26 the Bible says, **"And it was revealed unto him by the Holy Ghost, that he should not see death, before he had seen the Lord's Christ."** Simeon was a man who was in contact with God and sought God to lead him. The Lord spoke to him specifically and told him he was not going to die until he saw Messiah. Simeon was a man who was truly led by the spirit of God. The same Spirit that led Simeon to the temple so long ago to meet the Lord Jesus and hold the baby Jesus in his arms is the same Holy Spirit who wants to guide you. **Romans 8:14** says, **"As**

many as are led by the Spirit of God, they are the sons of God." The same Holy Spirit that revealed to Simeon the first coming of Jesus is the Holy Spirit that wants to reveal to you the Second Coming of the Lord Jesus Christ. Are you sensitive? Can God speak to you?

What about your prayer life? So often in our prayer life we are telling God these things. We think God is some sort of heavenly Santa Claus, and we come to Him with a shopping list of the things we want, and we say, "Now listen, Lord, your servant is speaking," when we ought to say, "Speak, Lord, your servant is listening." We ought to be the listening one.

Simeon was a man who was eagerly awaiting Christmas. He was saved. He was surrendered. He was spiritual. He was sensitive. Lastly, he was a man who was satisfied. In **Luke 2:28** the Bible says that Simeon took **"him up in his arms, and blessed God."** Simeon took the baby Jesus up in his arms when Mary and Joseph came to the temple for certain purification rites. Old Simeon had been waiting for the Messiah. Simeon had been led by the Holy Spirit into the temple. He saw the Lord Jesus Christ. The Holy Spirit of God said to Simeon, "That's the One. That's the Baby." Simeon held this Baby to his chest and praised God. **Luke 2:28-29** says, **"Then took he him up in his arms, and blessed God, and said, ²⁹Lord, now lettest thou thy servant depart in peace, according to thy word..."**

This is a wonderful scene! Here we have the Word of God, and the Spirit of God, and the Son of God coming together. When the Word of God, and the Spirit of God, and the Son of God come together, that brings the peace of God in our heart. Do you have peace? If you do not have peace, you are not ready for Christmas. Are you ready to die? If you are not ready to die, you are not ready for Jesus to come. You are not ready to live until you are ready to die. Simeon said, "Lord, just take me on home. Take me home. I am ready to depart in peace," for "precious in the sight of the LORD is the death of his saints." No man, no woman, boy or girl is ready to live until they are no longer afraid to die. Thank God, one of these days the Lord is going to return and when He returns, He will deliver us from death, but we may die before He comes. You can know that you are ready for Christmas and that you are ready for the Second Coming of Jesus Christ if you meet the qualifications that were in the life of this man Simeon.

The Lord Jesus Christ lived an incomparable life. Simeon said six things about the incomparable life of the Lord Jesus Christ. Simeon was a prophet, a man anointed and filled with the Holy Ghost of God. There are some important things that we can learn from Simeon about our Saviour who stepped out of heaven and came to earth.

Who is this Baby that Simeon held in his arms? First, Jesus is the One who <u>brings deliverance</u>. In **Luke 2:40** Simeon said, "I am ready to go to heaven." **"For mine eyes have seen thy salvation, Which thou hast prepared before the face of all people."** Why did Jesus come? To deliver us. The baby that Mary delivered was the One who would deliver us. He is our Deliverer. This is a hell-bound world. This is a sin-bound world. This is a world that needs a Saviour, and that is the reason that Jesus came to earth. He was born of a virgin that we might be born again. The world does not understand the true reason we celebrate Christmas. The world does not understand that Jesus Christ is come as a Saviour to save them from their sins. They celebrate the Babe in the manger without understanding that that Baby is the Saviour of the world. When Simeon held Him in his arms, he said, "I've seen your salvation." Jesus is the Christ of deliverance.

Jesus is the One who <u>dispels darkness</u>. In **Luke 2:32 and 33**, Simeon said that Jesus is **"A light to lighten the Gentiles, and the glory of thy people Israel. And Joseph and his mother marvelled at those things which were spoken of him."** Jesus is the Light of the World. There is no reason for you to stumble in darkness when you can walk in the light. You will never understand the meaning of life until you know the Light of the world, whose name is the Lord Jesus Christ. There are some people who are afraid of Jesus. We laugh at children being afraid of the dark. More absurd than that is an adult who is afraid of the light. Men hate the light, and they will not come to the light because their deeds are evil. But He is the Light, and He is a delight, and there is no greater joy than knowing the Lord Jesus Christ. He is the only One who dispels darkness. If you are stumbling in darkness and if you want to know the way, He is the way. If you need light, He is the Light. If you are seeking for understanding, He is the Truth.

> *Friends all around me are trying to find*
> *What the world yearns for, by sin undermined;*
> *I have the secret, I know where 'tis found:*
> *Only true pleasures in Jesus abound.*
> *Blindly men strive, for sin darkens the way.*
> *O to draw back the grim curtains of night--*
> *One glimpse of Jesus, and all will be bright.*
> *By Harry Dixon Loes*

Jesus is all this world needs today. He is the One who dispels darkness.

Jesus is the One who <u>determines destiny</u>. **Luke 2:34: "And Simeon blessed them, and said unto Mary his mother, Behold, this child is set for the fall and rising again of many in Israel; and for a sign which shall be spoken against;..."** Jesus is the Christ of destiny. You will rise or fall on Jesus. Jesus will either be a steppingstone or a stumbling block to you, but your destiny is determined by what you will do with the Lord Jesus Christ.

⚲ **1 Peter 2:6-8** says, **Wherefore also it is contained in the scripture, Behold, I lay in Sion a chief corner stone, elect, precious: and he that believeth on him shall not be confounded. 7Unto you therefore which believe he is precious: but unto them which be disobedient, the stone which the builders disallowed, the same is made the head of the corner, 8And a stone of stumbling, and a rock of offence, even to them which stumble at the word, being disobedient: whereunto also they were appointed."**

What does that mean? Christ is the Solid Rock. Christ is the Foundation Stone. Christ is the Cornerstone. He is before you today. You can build on Him or stumble over Him, but you cannot go around the Lord Jesus Christ. Christ is the One who determines destiny. Either Jesus Christ will be your Saviour, or Jesus Christ will be your Judge. He will be a steppingstone or a stumbling block, but you have an appointment with Jesus Christ. He is inescapable. He is inevitable. He is unavoidable. You have a date with Jesus. You are going to meet Him as Saviour or Judge. I am telling you with all the emphasis, and all the emotion of my soul, this baby that Simeon held in his hands is the Christ of your destiny, one way or the other. He is either the door that lets you in or the door that keeps you out, but you have a date with the Lord Jesus Christ. What Jesus Christ will do with you is determined by what you will do with the Lord Jesus Christ. **John 3:36** says: **"He that believeth on the Son hath everlasting life: and he that believeth not the Son shall not see life, but the wrath of God abideth on him."** This Baby is the one who determines destiny.

Next, He is the One who <u>provokes derision</u>. In **Luke 2:34** the scripture says, **"And Simeon blessed them, and said unto Mary his mother, Behold, this child is set for the fall and rising again of many in Israel; and for a sign which shall be spoken against;..."** Notice the phrase: **"for a sign which shall**

be spoken against." Jesus, this Baby, is going to face derision. He is going to face mockery. He is going to face blasphemy.

When the Lord Jesus Christ was here on earth, some said, "You're mad." Others said, "He has a demon." Others said, "He is a winebibber and a glutton." He is a sign that will be spoken against. If He is not spoken against, then the gospel is not being preached. There are many who preach in a way that fill up a church and who do not draw any derision from the worldly crowd.

If a false teacher wants to draw a large crowd, all he must do is preach a Jesus who is not virgin born, who is not sinless, and who is not God. If you want to draw people in, do not preach a gospel that demands a new birth, and do not set a standard of right and wrong. Preach that there is no judgement of God. And especially this, preach that there is more than one way to heaven and that man can choose his own path to God. You could fill up a stadium. Some have. Today we are all politically incorrect if we do not put our arms around everybody else and say, "Your faith is just as good as ours." That is not so. That is a lie out of hell. **"Neither is there salvation in any other...there is no other name under heaven given among men, whereby we must be saved" (Acts 4:12).** That name is the name of Jesus.

You see, if Jesus is not the only way, He cannot be any of the ways. If Jesus is not the only way, He is a liar, for He said, **"I am the way, the truth, and the life: no man cometh unto the Father, but by me."** Either that is true, or it is not true. You cannot just tip your hat to Jesus; you must bow the knee to Jesus. The early Christians could have escaped martyrdom had they just burnt a little incense to Caesar and said, "Caesar is Lord and Christ is Lord." But they said, "No! Jesus is the Lord. He is the only one." You see, this is the Christ of derision. He is the One who is spoken against. The Bible says in **Matthew 9:24, "they laughed him to scorn."** Can you imagine, laughing, pointing to Jesus, and laughing Him to scorn? That is exactly what is happening in the world today. Jesus is the One who is derided. He is the One who is spoken against.

Have you ever thought about how this world hates Jesus Christ? They use His name in vain. Have you ever heard a person curse and say, "Oh Buddha!" or "Oh Confucius!" or "Oh Mohammed!"? No, they say, "Oh Jesus! Oh Christ!" They take the name of our Lord and Saviour and mix it in the muck and in the mire and slime of their profanity and take that holy name upon their lips. There are people who mock Jesus, and they mock Him more and more, for He is a sign that is spoken against.

Dear reader, if you are His disciple, you also will be spoken against. The Bible says in **Luke 6:26, "Woe unto you, when all men shall speak well of you! for so did their fathers to the false prophets."** Jesus said, in **Matthew 5:11-12, "Blessed are ye, when men shall revile you, and persecute you, and shall say all manner of evil against you falsely, for my sake. ¹²Rejoice, and be exceeding glad: for great is your reward in heaven: for so persecuted they the prophets which were before you."** It is time that the preachers in America stopped trying to win popularity contests and preach Jesus Christ, who may be the Christ of derision, but He is the only Saviour of the world.

Jesus is also the One who <u>causes division</u>. In **Luke 2:35** the Bible says, **"(Yea, a sword shall pierce through thy own soul also,) that the thoughts of many hearts may be revealed."** Simeon is speaking to Mary. He is saying, "Mary, a sword is going to pierce through your own soul also, that the thoughts of many hearts may be revealed." Jesus is the most divisive force that has ever come into this world. Jesus divides human hearts. The author of Hebrews said:

📖 **(Hebrews 4:12) For the word of God is quick, and powerful, and sharper than any twoedged sword, piercing even to the dividing asunder of soul and spirit, and of the joints and marrow, and is a discerner of the thoughts and intents of the heart.**

Simeon said, "Mary, this baby is going to be like a sword in your heart. He is going to divide between your natural emotions as a mother and your desire for the will of God, and you're going to find this conflict between natural emotions, and the spiritual life, between your soul and the spirit."

All of us who have received the Lord Jesus Christ as our personal Saviour and Lord feel that sword on the inside, do we not? There is the pull of the old life and the desire of the new life. Do you ever feel that conflict?

You say, "I do not have any conflict. I'm doing just fine." You are not doing as fine as you think you are doing. If you have never met the devil on the road of life, it is because you and the devil have been going in the same direction. If you turn around, and give your heart to Jesus Christ, you become born again, you let the Spirit of God come into you, and you're going to find that there is going to be a division in your life between the old nature and the new nature. The Lord Jesus divides an individual.

Jesus also <u>divides families</u>. You say, "Oh, no, no. Jesus unites families. Well do you know what the Bible says? Jesus said:

📖 **(Matthew 10:34-39) Think not that I am come to send peace on earth: I came not to send peace, but a sword. 35For I am come to set a man at variance against his father, and the daughter against her mother, and the daughter in law against her mother in law. 36And a man's foes shall be they of his own household. 37He that loveth father or mother more than me is not worthy of me: and he that loveth son or daughter more than me is not worthy of me. 38And he that taketh not his cross, and followeth after me, is not worthy of me. 39He that findeth his life shall lose it: and he that loseth his life for my sake shall find it.**

Jesus is the unifier of families that are built on Him. Jesus is the unifier of those who believe in Him. How sweet it is to have this fellowship, because we are one in the bond of love. But **Amos 3:3** asks this question: **"Can two walk together, except they be agreed?"** Now, when Jesus said that if we love father or mother, children, or anyone else more than Him, we are not worthy of Him. That does not mean that we are not to love our families. But Jesus Christ needs to be number one in our lives. Married men ought to love their wives so much that they would lay down their life for them. That is a biblical principle. The Bible says in **Ephesians 5:25, "Husbands, love your wives, even as Christ also loved the church, and gave himself for it..."**

Fathers and mothers ought to love their children so much that they would lay down their lives for them. If Jesus Christ is number one in your life, then you will love your spouse and you will love your children more than you could love them without Jesus. There can be no one other than Jesus Christ who is number one in your life.

Jesus Christ can divide families. There are children in this world today whose parents do not want them to come to Jesus. There are those in this world today who would say to us, "I would have to disavow the tradition of my family, and I would be disowned by my family if I come to Jesus." Our message ought to be "Come to Jesus anyway. Give your heart to Him."

Jesus is the Christ who divides the human spirit. He is Christ who divides families. He is the <u>Christ who may divide a church</u>. When you come to church on Sunday you put on your "Sunday best." You look holy. But not everyone who goes to church is holy. Not everyone who has their name on the church roll is saved. There are husbands and wives who sit together in church on Sunday morning and Sunday night and Wednesday night, but there is a division between them as far as east is from the west, as far as heaven is from hell, because one is saved and the other is lost. And should the Rapture come, or should they die, they would be separated for all eternity. The Lord divides churches. The Lord looks at those who sing in church, and the Lord knows how many of those choir members understand and believe what they are singing and those who do not.

The Lord sees when the offering is taken. The Lord knows who is giving with a cheerful heart and a right attitude.

The Lord knows whether that preacher is preaching the Word of God out of a heart that is pure and clean or whether that man is just mouthing something as a hireling.

The Lord knows when a congregation sings, "Oh, How I Love Jesus" whether they really love Jesus or not. The Lord Jesus Christ is the One who divides the professing church.

He is the Great Divider. Not all that profess faith in Jesus Christ possess faith in Jesus Christ. Jesus said, **"[At the Judgment] many will say to me in that day, Lord, Lord, have we not prophesied in thy name? and in thy name...cast out devils? and in thy name done many wonderful works? And then will I profess unto them... depart from me, ye that work iniquity. I never knew you."**

What a sad division there will be when Jesus comes again. Jesus is dividing, and He will divide for all eternity. At the Judgment, Jesus will divide between the sheep and the goats, the saved and the lost. When He stands in judgement, His decision is not going to be based upon the bankbook of finance or the bluebook of society, but on the Lamb's Book of Life. We divide people by status. We say, "upper class," "middle class," and "lower class." But God divides right and left, saved or lost. He is the Christ with the sword in His hand. He is the One who divides.

The final thing we need to see is that Jesus is the One who reveals decisions. In **Luke 2:35** Simeon says, **"(yea, a sword shall pierce through thy own soul also,)"** and notice this, **"that the thoughts of many hearts may be revealed."**

Do you know what the preaching of the Word does? It reveals your thoughts. It exposes you to yourself and to God. God is the One who is revealing decisions. You see, the gospel is a sword of life unto life or death unto death. When a pastor is preaching you may say, "I don't agree with that. I will not accept that. I refuse that. I will not yield to that." God is revealing your heart. There are others who say, "That is true. What he says is true. I need a Saviour. I need to be saved." Once you are saved, your response will be, "I need to love Him more, I need to know Him better, I need to walk closer to him." God's Word is revealing your heart.

What makes the difference in individuals? It is not education. It is not social status. It is not environment. Children can be raised in the same family, and one child will love God and the other child will not love God. Cain and Abel were brought up in the same environment. Two thieves were crucified with Jesus. One was crucified on Jesus's right hand and one on the left. One of those thieves cursed and blasphemed and spit blasphemies in the face of Jesus. The other one of those dying thieves said, **"Lord, remember me when thou comest into thy kingdom."** The Lord revealed what was in the heart of those individuals. **(Luke 2:35)** says, **"(yea, a sword shall pierce through thy own soul also,) that the thoughts of many hearts may be revealed."** What you do with Jesus is going to determine what Jesus does with you.

Simeon took this baby, held him in his arms, brought him to his chest, and said, "Lord God, I'm ready to go. Let me depart in peace. I have seen your salvation."

Today, if you are saved, you accepted Christ's first coming, and you see him not just as a baby in a manger but your salvation. Just as surely as He came the first time, Jesus is coming again! Are you looking for His return? Are you waiting expectantly on the Lord? Simeon lived his entire life looking for the Saviour. I think he got up every morning and said, "Lord is this the day that I will see your salvation?" How many of us get up every morning and say Lord is this the day that You are going to return? How many of us live every day of our lives like this could be our last day on earth? It could be! We could go up through the Rapture or out through the grave. This could be our last day. How many of us are witnessing and working like the Lord could return at any time?

Can I tell you something? I do not think Simeon kept his message to himself. I believe he told anyone who would listen that he was looking for the coming of the Lord. Is your heart pierced because your family is divided? Do you have lost loved ones who would be left behind if Jesus were to return today? We ought to pray every day and witness every day and work every day like today could be the day that the Lord returns. We ought to wake up every morning as Simeon did looking for the coming of the Lord. But in many cases, we are not living like the Lord could return. In many cases we are living like the world and the world sees no difference between us and them.

Do you know what the problem with the modern-day church today is? The church looks so much like the world that the world looks at the church and the church is so worldly that they say, "If those people are going to heaven then so am I." It is time to get serious. This author believes that we are getting close to the return of the Lord. Simeon was looking for the Lord to come. Are you? If we are truly looking for the Lord to come, it will change our way of living. I want to challenge you, dear reader, to be like Simeon and live each day looking for Jesus to come. Witness and pray and study God's word and believe God like He could come any day.

Chapter 22
The Story of Christmas Grace

(Luke 2:36-38) "And there was one Anna, a prophetess, the daughter of Phanuel, of the tribe of Aser: she was of great age, and had lived with an husband seven years from her virginity; 36And she was a widow of about fourscore and four years, which departed not from the temple, but served God with fastings and prayers night and day. 37And she coming in that instant gave thanks likewise unto the Lord, and spake to all them that looked for redemption in Jerusalem.

The Baby Jesus, when He was forty days old, traveled with His parents from Bethlehem to the temple of Jerusalem. Jewish law required that certain ceremonial rites, as an act of worship, be carried out there. After Simeon encountered the Baby Jesus and spoke his prophetic words, Anna, a lady of great age, entered.

Anna was a prophetess, and from the context we know that the subject of her prophecies was the coming of the Christ, the Redeemer of all mankind. We can also conclude from the previous verses that she fully expected to see the Lord's Christ before her death, just as Simeon did.

Anna means "grace." It is only by the grace of God that we "see" Christ for who He really is. **Ephesians 2:8** says, **"by grace are ye saved through faith..."** Someone has said that grace is "God's Riches At Christ's Expense." You see, the problems of this world are not social or economic, but stem from the very nature of man. Man is a fallen creature and has a sin problem, a wicked heart, and only through God's grace can we even see that we have this problem.

Anna was the daughter of Phanuel, and "Phanuel" means "the face of God." When Anna looked in the arms of Mary, she saw "the face of God." Jesus was the Son of God and God the Son. He was fully God and fully man. The angel of the Lord appeared to Joseph in a dream **(Matthew 1:20-25) and said, "His name shall be called Emanuel, which being interpreted is, God with us."** What a blessed thought to have God come to this sin cursed world to be with us. In **Hebrews 13:5,** the Lord gave this quite simple promise to the Christian, **"I will never leave thee, nor forsake thee."**

Do you know that the Lord, the Christ of Christmas is with

you today?

Anna was of the tribe of Aser, and "Aser" means "blessed." The apostle Paul quotes David in **Romans 4:7-8, "Blessed are they whose iniquities are forgiven and whose sins are covered. Blessed is the man to whom the Lord will not impute sin."**

The message of Anna was the message of redemption. Look at it in the last line of the passage above. Redemption means "to deliver by paying a price." The picture portrayed here is of the Lord walking through a slave market and buying us out of the slave market. Paul says we were all **"sold under sin." 1 Peter 1:18-19** says, **"Ye are not redeemed with corruptible things, but with the precious blood of Christ."** Christ came to die for our sin and to be our sin sacrifice on the brutal cross of Calvary. He was buried and after the third day arose proving that God the Father accepted His sacrifice. Trust His goodness and grace for your redemption and have a Merry Christmas!

Chapter 23
The Gifts of the Wise Men

(Matthew 2:1-11) Now when Jesus was born in Bethlehem of Judaea in the days of Herod the king, behold, there came wise men from the east to Jerusalem, ²Saying, Where is he that is born King of the Jews? for we have seen his star in the east, and are come to worship him. ³When Herod the king had heard *these things,* he was troubled, and all Jerusalem with him. ⁴And when he had gathered all the chief priests and scribes of the people together, he demanded of them where Christ should be born. ⁵And they said unto him, In Bethlehem of Judaea: for thus it is written by the prophet. ⁶And thou Bethlehem, *in* the land of Juda, art not the least among the princes of Juda: for out of thee shall come a Governor, that shall rule my people Israel. ⁷Then Herod, when he had privily called the wise men, enquired of them diligently what time the star appeared. ⁸And he sent them to Bethlehem, and said, Go and search diligently for the young child; and when ye have found *him,* bring me word again, that I may come and worship him also. ⁹When they had heard the king, they departed; and, lo, the star, which they saw in the east, went before them, till it came and stood over where the young child was. ¹⁰When they saw the star, they rejoiced with exceeding great joy. ¹¹And when they were come into the house, they saw the young child with Mary his mother, and fell down, and worshipped him: and when they had opened their treasures, they presented unto him gifts; gold, and frankincense, and myrrh.

The story of the Wise Men is one of mystery, majesty, and high adventure. In Matthew chapter two we have the account of the visit of the Wise Men and the gifts they brought to Jesus. We all know the story of the Wise Men. However, there is much about these Wise Men that we do not know. For example, as stated in a previous chapter, we are not certain that there were three Wise Men. There may have been three. There may have been more. We sing the song, "We Three Kings of Orient Are," but there may have been more. Dr. J. Vernon McGee says that he doubts whether three Wise Men would have disturbed Herod or have excited Jerusalem. He said that he does believe that three hundred men would have done so. Dr. McGee told on his radio program that he received a Christmas card from a member of his congregation with three Wise Men on it. The member wrote on the inside of the card, "The other two hundred and ninety-seven are on their way." The point is we are not sure how many there were.

We know that there were three categories of gifts that are listed; there may have been more gifts. We do not know for certain what country these Wise Men came from. They came from the east. The author believes like most scholars that they came from Babylon.

The Bible says in **Galatians 4:4, "But when the fullness of the time was come, God sent forth his Son, made of a woman, made under the law."** God in "the fullness of time" prepared the world to receive His Son. The children of Israel were "chosen" to bring the Christ Child into the world. This chosen people had rebelled against God, and God used Nebuchadnezzar to invade Israel and deport them to Babylon in 586 BC. From Babylon, Israel was scattered throughout the rest of the world. Throughout the world, there were little colonies of Jews and the synagogues where they worshipped. Each synagogue possessed a copy of the Holy Scriptures, our Old Testament. The scriptures told of a coming Saviour. God had planned for this very period in history in which He would send His Son to be born, to walk among sinful men, to live a sinless life, to go to an old rugged cross, to die for you and me, to raise from the dead and then to depart back into heaven.

The world at that time had one world government and one common language, Greek. Greek was the language of choice among the learned and businesspeople of that day. God would use this language to write the New Testament and to spread the good news of Jesus to Jews and Gentiles alike.

God required that His Son be born in Israel and specifically in Bethlehem. God had gathered a remnant of His chosen people back to Israel and had reestablished them as a nation. God in His providence set in motion the world events to suit Himself, and to make a way for His Son.

God also prepared the hearts of many to look for His Son. The children of Israel had not heard from God in over 400 years, but some knew the promises of God and looked for the long-awaited and faithfully promised Saviour.

The prophets of old foretold of Him countless times. Daniel, as a small Israelite boy, was carried away as a captive slave to

Babylon. There Daniel rose to a mighty position of power reporting directly to the kings during three dynasties. Daniel even became "chief of the governors over all the wise men of Babylon." I believe the Wise Men heard about the prophecies of Christ from Daniel in Babylon.

The Wise Men believed in the ancient scriptures about the Lord Jesus. These fearless Wise Men, bearing precious gifts overcame great difficulties to worship Christ. They had a lot of barriers to overcome. For example, there was the barrier of distance. In **Matthew 1:1** the scriptures say, **"Behold, there came wise men from the east to Jerusalem."** If the Wise Men did come from Babylon, which is modern day Iraq, to Jerusalem, that would be a great distance to travel even by today's standards. These men likely traveled 700 to 800 miles just to worship the King of Kings, the Lord Jesus Christ.

There was the barrier of difficulty. In that day there were no planes, no trains, no automobiles. There were no hotels, there no restaurants, there were no superhighways. Over rough terrain they came.

There was literal danger. When the Wise Men arrived, they faced the wicked King Herod. Herod was a murderous old man with no conscience and took no thought of killing people. He was the one who killed all the little babies under two years of age. But before he killed those little babies, he had already murdered his wife. He had already murdered his mother. He had already murdered his sons. As a matter of fact, when Herod died, he knew he was going to die, and just before he died, he said, "Get some of the best known citizens of our land, and when I die, put them to death because," he said, "if they don't shed any tears for me, maybe they'll shed some tears for them. I want there to be some tears when I die." So, he had people killed just because he himself had to die. He was a hateful, hellish, murderous old man. These Wise Men were in danger from Herod himself.

It is with great difficulty and peril that the Wise Men came to worship the Christ child. These Wise Men sought the Lord Jesus Christ. Despite distance and danger and difficulty, they came to worship Him. When the Wise Men worshiped the Lord Jesus, they brought Him three kinds of gifts.

Matthew 2:11 says, **"And when they were come into the house, they saw the young child with Mary his mother, and fell down, and worshipped him: and when they had opened their treasures, they presented unto him gifts; gold,**

and frankincense, and myrrh." These most precious gifts were chosen with care and forethought. They will stand forever as indisputable evidence that these Wise Men already knew this Holy Child. You see, these gifts are symbolic in nature and each gift will tell us something incredibly significant and special about this Divine Babe. In this chapter we will see what these gifts are, what they represent, and what they speak of.

The first gift was gold. So why gold? Why was this gift given first? The gold shows us that Christ is a King. Gold is a gift that would be presented to a king. Gold was the most precious metal of that day. In Bible times, and even today, gold is symbolic of royalty. When the Wise Men came to the Lord Jesus Christ and presented gold to Him, they were saying that Christ was born a king. They learned it from the prophet Daniel.

📖 **Daniel 9:25: "Know therefore and understand, that from the going forth of the commandment to restore and to build Jerusalem unto the Messiah the Prince shall be seven weeks, and threescore and two weeks: the street shall be built again, and the wall, even in troublous times."**

Daniel had called the baby that would be born, "Messiah, the Prince." The word prince means king, ruler, or sovereign. Technically, a prince is a son waiting to take his father's throne. When the Wise Men brought gold to Christ, they demonstrated that they recognized His sovereign dominion. Have you recognized Christ as king? The prophet Isaiah said:

📖 **(Isaiah 9:7) Of the increase of *his* government and peace *there shall be* no end, upon the throne of David, and upon his kingdom, to order it, and to establish it with judgment and with justice from henceforth even for ever. The zeal of the LORD of hosts will perform this."**

This Baby that we are speaking of is the King of Kings and Lord of Lords. This Christmas will you bow your knee to the Lord Jesus Christ to acknowledge Him as your King? Romans 14:11 says, **"For it is written, *As* I live, saith the Lord, every knee shall bow to me, and every tongue shall confess to God."** When these kings came to the baby Jesus, they did not cuddle Him. They did not play games with Him. These powerful kings from the East bowed the knee in reverence to Him, and they recognized that He is a King. In **Matthew 2:2,** they said, **"Where is he that is born King of the Jews."** Jesus Christ is King of Kings and Lord of Lords. One day the great leaders of this world will bow their knees to him. One day every human being who has ever lived on this earth will bow their knee to Jesus Christ.

He is King. When the Wise Men came, they said in **Matthew 2:2**: **"Where is he that is born King of the Jews? for we have seen his star in the east and are come to worship him."** A great gift you can give the Lord today is to recognize Him as King of Kings and Lord of Lords.

The second gift was frankincense. Frankincense reveals that the Baby Jesus was God! If gold was a gift fit for a king, frankincense was used to worship Almighty God. You see in Biblical times a special holy mixture of frankincense was prepared and used exclusively for worship. Note the scripture in **Exodus 30:34-38.**

📖 **(Exodus 30:34-38) And the LORD said unto Moses, Take unto thee sweet spices, stacte, and onycha, and galbanum;** *these* **sweet spices with pure frankincense: of each shall there be a like** *weight:* **35And thou shalt make it a perfume, a confection after the art of the apothecary, tempered together, pure** *and* **holy: 36And thou shalt beat** *some* **of it very small, and put of it before the testimony in the tabernacle of the congregation, where I will meet with thee: it shall be unto you most holy. 37And** *as for* **the perfume which thou shalt make, ye shall not make to yourselves according to the composition thereof: it shall be unto thee holy for the LORD. 38Whosoever shall make like unto that, to smell thereto, shall even be cut off from his people.**

The frankincense was the base of this holy incense used in worship. It was to be given to God. In the Old Testament they would burn incense in the tabernacle and in the temple. The Bible teaches that a sweet savor would rise out of the tabernacle and the temple. That sweet savor speaks of the prayers and the worship of the saints that go to Almighty God. No one, no not one, deserves worship except God.

The Wise Men brought frankincense because they recognized the sinless deity of Jesus Christ. Jesus Christ is God. He is the Son of God and God the Son. His name is Immanuel which means "God with us." He is the Mighty God, and the Everlasting Father. When the Wise Men came, they came worshipping the Lord Jesus. Again, the Bible says in **Matthew 2:11, "And when they were come into the house, they saw the young child with Mary his mother,**

and fell down, and worshipped him:" They worshiped Him. Well, you may wonder what is so important about that? **Matthew 4:10** says, **"Thou shalt worship the Lord thy God, and him only shalt thou serve."** If Jesus is not the Lord God, this is the ultimate blasphemy. Nobody should worship anything or anybody except God Himself. They worshiped Him. Why? Because this Baby was God.

I love the song <u>Mary Did You Know?</u> One line of it says, "Mary, did you know that your baby boy has walked where angels trod? And when you kiss your little baby, you have kissed the face of God?"

Isaiah 9:6 says, **"For unto us a child is born, unto us a son is given: and the government shall be upon his shoulder:..."** (that is the gold which speaks of Christ the King) and His name shall be called Wonderful, Counsellor, the Mighty God, the Everlasting Father, the Prince of Peace. That is the frankincense. You see Christ was not only born a King. He was God. He was God in human flesh. Because of His sinless deity, Jesus is the only one who deserves our worship and praise.

The Wise Men brought Christ a third gift. Myrrh points to Jesus as the suffering, bleeding, and dying Saviour. Myrrh was an expensive, bitter herb used as a burial ointment to embalm the dead. Why would the Wise Men bring a baby an ointment that was used to embalm the dead? You see the Wise Men recognized that Jesus was born to die. In **Mark 15:22-23** the Bible says, **"And they bring him unto the place Golgotha, which is, being interpreted, The place of a skull. 23And they gave him to drink wine mingled with myrrh: but he received *it* not."** Myrrh was also used as a narcotic to dull pain. But Jesus came and tasted death for every man. He refused the taste of the myrrh there upon the cross.

In **John** we see the preparation of Jesus' body for burial.

📖 **(John 19:38-40) And after this Joseph of Arimathaea, being a disciple of Jesus, but secretly for fear of the Jews, besought Pilate that he might take away the body of Jesus: and Pilate gave *him* leave. He came therefore, and took the body of Jesus. 39And there came also Nicodemus, which at the first came to Jesus by night, and brought a mixture of myrrh and aloes, about an hundred pound *weight*. 40Then took they the body of Jesus, and wound it in linen clothes with the spices, as the manner of the Jews is to bury.**

This was the manner of the Jews to bury someone. What did they use to bury someone? It was their custom to bring myrrh. Did you know that the Bible never records the early church celebrating the birth of Jesus? I do not think it is wrong to celebrate the birth of Jesus. The Holy Spirit of God recorded it in the Bible. We have all of this scripture, and the birth of Jesus is very important. It gives us an opportunity to preach and to teach and to worship and yes to witness to a lost and dying world. But we do not have any record that the early church was told to remember His birth. We are told to remember what? His death. The real Christmas tree is this: that Jesus in His own body bore our sins on a tree.

These Wise Men, at the birth of Jesus, were there remembering that one day, Jesus would die upon the tree. No wonder heaven's choir came down to sing, they proclaimed heaven's King came down to bring salvation to the world. He was born, but His destiny was to die as a sin sacrifice for your sins and my sins and the sin of the whole world.

Christ did not come to be a teacher, philosopher, or good example. Christ came to die and pay the sin debt for all who would receive and believe in Him. He suffered our hell and our torment on Calvary's cross. His death was no accident. Wise men see this. Eternal life through Jesus Christ is the true Christmas Gift. **Romans 6:23** says, **"For the wages of sin *is* death; but the gift of God *is* eternal life through Jesus Christ our Lord."**

This chapter is meant to be a special blessing to those who have received the Christ of Christmas and to give the world's most glorious invitation to those who have not received Christ. The invitation is to receive Christ this Christmas. There can be no Christmas without Christ. The Wise Men **"opened their treasures."**

The Wise Men gave Him gold because He is the King of Kings. Is Jesus the Lord of your life today? Do you know Him? Do you know you are saved? Have you given Him your will?

The Wise Men gave frankincense. Have you given him your worship and praise?

The last gift given by the Wise Men was myrrh. Because of the sacrificial death of Christ, He deserves our witness for him. Will you witness for Him? It should be your desire to tell the world that He died for you. Our wealth, our worship, and our witness belong to Christ this Christmas season.

The greatest gift you could give Christ is to open your heart by repenting of sin and allowing Christ to come in. Your heart is a treasure to Christ. Yes, God and you can exchange Christmas gifts. Christ has already been given for you, and you can give your life to Him.

Chapter 24
The Chronology of the Wise Men and
The Flight to Egypt by the Christmas Family

The episode of the Wise Men in their venture to see Jesus has everything necessary for a great story. We will see intrigue, mystery, and high adventure. We find the complete story in **Matthew chapter 2.**

We wish to discuss the chronology and order of events surrounding the visit of the Wise Men. Of course, the visit of the Wise Men is significantly tied to Joseph, Mary, and the Christ child and their flight to Egypt. There are many misconceptions and false assumptions about the visit of the Wise Men.

The author can remember reading a worldwide Sunday school quarterly which stated that the estimated time of the visit of the Wise Men to Bethlehem was about two years after the birth of Christ. The reason postulated for the two-year interval was caused by travel time from the presumed Babylon and the fact that Jesus was called a "young child" instead of a "babe."

The prevailing view is that the Wise Men came from Babylon. Remember, the children of Judah were deported to Babylon in about 581/582 BC. The tenure of the children of Israel in Babylon was seventy years, and after that a remnant returned. Certainly, copies of the Scripture were retained in Babylon. The Wise Men were familiar with the scriptures and the star drew them to Jesus.

Traveling through the normal routes and roads of Christ day, the distance would be about 700 to 800 miles. Roman roads and highways would have permitted much faster travel than six or seven centuries prior when the remnant of Jews returned to Judah from Babylon.

The returning remnant was a large contingent of Jews traveling to repopulate Judea. This relocation would have required loads of cumbersome baggage. They had to transport clothing, furniture, tools, dishes, and everything else you would need to start a new life. According to the book of **Ezra 7:7-8**, it took Ezra and his group exactly four months to make the trip.

A camel carrying a man or luggage up to around 300 pounds can travel eighty miles a day. However, eighty miles a day would not be sustainable. In any case, it is realistic that the Wise Men could have arrived in Jerusalem within a thirty-day timeframe traveling using horses, camels, or donkeys. There could be no doubt that the Wise Men had the assets to fund their travel.

Note that the Bible says Jesus was a young child and some think no longer an infant. **Matthew 2:11, "And when they were come into the house, they saw the young child with Mary his mother, and fell down, and worshipped him: and when they had opened their treasures, they presented unto him gifts; gold, and frankincense, and myrrh."** Biblical commentators note that Jesus is not in a stable but in a house. The taxing at Bethlehem would have been completed quickly, and Joseph and Mary would have moved Jesus in one or two days after His birth.

Much is made of the fact that Jesus is called a "young child" in this text. The Greek word (G3816) for "child" is "paidion" pronounced "pahee-dee'-on" is a "childling (of either sex)" and can mean "a half-grown boy or girl." Now you see that Jesus is a half-grown boy by the time the Wise Men get there. Really?

Look at these two verses that speak of the shepherd's visit to the manger. **Luke 2:16-17, "And they came with haste, and found Mary, and Joseph, and the babe lying in a manger. 17And when they had seen it, they made known abroad the saying which was told them concerning this child."** The word "child" is the same Greek word used in **Matthew 2:11**. There are three Greek words for child, but in these two passages the same Greek word is used.

Notice that in the above passage of Luke, "babe" is equal to "child." There are some lessons about Bible interpretation here:
1. Biblical context determines the final and the exact meaning of a word.
2. The Greek definition can easily be altered to prove a point.
3. The King James Bible is always right.

If a Greek definition is used to reword or redefine your KJV, that Greek meaning is bogus. The problem is the interpretation of the Greek word. The fifty-five King James translators were the most linguistically qualified group of English translators ever assembled.

The Greek word (G3816) for "paidion" translated child in the above has a primary meaning of "infant." You were set up by this writer. We will soon find out; Jesus was an infant when the Wise Men made their visit to Him. The reader needs to be cautioned about the use of Bible commentaries. A Bible commentator can be completely truthful in the provision of definitions and extra biblical information and yet, at the same time be deceiving or misleading by not providing all the information.

The idea of a two year later visit of the Wise Men appears to have been postulated in the last century. It is interesting that a few commentators who believe the Wise Men's visit was at about two years even speculate that the Wise Men visited the Christ child at Nazareth. This clearly violates the biblical narrative. Bethlehem is clearly in view in the text, and there can be no doubt that the Wise Men traveled to Bethlehem.

The question is: when did the Wise Men arrive to see Jesus?

Remember the holiday Christmas song, "The Twelve Days of Christmas?" The number of gifts correspond to the number of the day. New gifts are offered each day. The first day's gift is "a partridge in a pear tree." Traditionally, the 12 days start on Christmas day. Some Catholic churches celebrate The "Feast of Epiphany" or "The Three Kings Day." This feast day is meant to commemorate the day in which the Wise Men arrived to see the Baby Jesus. This is strictly tradition with no biblical or historical confirmation.

The chronology of events surrounding the birth of Jesus, the visit of the Wise Men, and the flight to Jerusalem is difficult to discern. However, we can be assured that the narratives of Matthew and Luke are entirely correct. In addition, the Bible does not give us enough information to be dogmatic about the chronology of the nativity of our Lord and subsequent events. The following list comes from trusted sources who record their opinion of the approximate time that the Wise Men visited Jesus.

- Dr. Floyd Nolan Jones in his unexcelled work entitled The Chronology of the Old Testament presents an excellent case for the Wise Men's visit to Jesus when He was one or two days old.
- Archbishop James Ussher wrote about 1650 AD. His chronological history entitled The Annals of the World places the Wise Men's visit between the circumcision of Jesus (8th day) and the temple visit (40th day).
- Alfred Edersheim, D. D., Ph. D. was a Jewish convert to Christianity and published over a dozen major works. Edersheim is best known for his Christian classic entitled The Life and Times of Jesus the Messiah. Here is a direct quote from that book. "Shortly after the Presentation of the Infant Saviour in the Temple, certain Magi from the East arrived in Jerusalem with strange tidings."
- The New Testament of our Lord and Saviour Jesus Christ: In the original Greek with introduction and notes by Christopher Wordsworth, Volume 4 (January 1, 1862) provide an

introductory chronological listing at the beginning of their book and locate the Wise Men's visit to the holy family after the Temple visit to Jerusalem.

☉ The Encyclopedia Americana: A Library of Universal Knowledge, Volume 18 (1918 ed?) pinpoints the visit of the Wise Men after the forty-day Temple visit.

☉ Philip Schaff (1819-1893), the German Bible scholar and commentator wrote an extensive meticulous History of the Christian Church. Schaff does not give a direct statement concerning the timing of the Wise Men's visit. However, the excellent chronological information provided by Schaff makes it evident that the Wise Men's visit was shortly after the temple visit.

We will sketch two chronological timelines of the visit of the Wise Men to bring their gifts to Jesus and then the subsequent flight of the holy family to Egypt. The first is by Dr. Floyd Nolan Jones as presented in his excellent history, The Chronology of the Old Testament. Dr. Jones' chronology is exhaustive and complete. In addition, this writer agrees with Dr. Jones on the fundamentals of the faith, his confidence in the word of God as preserved in the KJV, and his view of prophecy and end time events.

In brief, Dr. Jones believes that the Wise Men arrived at Jerusalem almost immediately after the birth of Jesus and before the news of Jesus' birth could get back to Herod. The Lord Jesus was moved out of His birthplace into a house the next day. The Wise Men came to see Jesus one or two days after his birth. Mary and Joseph then took the Baby Jesus and fled to Egypt. Herod died within forty days. The holy family returned to Jerusalem and immediately to the temple for the presentation of Jesus and the purification rites of Mary. They found out that Archelaus had taken the throne and go back to Nazareth. This chronology of the Wise Men's visit as presented by Dr. Jones is certainly viable.

However, we like this second timeline better, and it is the preferred scenario used by the commentators of yesteryear. In this timeframe, the Wise Men visited shortly after the temple visit. We will track the biblical narrative as to what we believe to be the chronological order of the Christmas events. The format will be verse by verse using the verses and passages which have chronological textual value. Comments will be made as appropriate. These comments will mainly relate to the chronological scenario we are presenting.

📖 (Luke 2:1-2) And it came to pass in those days, that

there went out a decree from Caesar Augustus, that all the world should be taxed. ²(And this taxing was first made when Cyrenius was governor of Syria.)

The biblical critics and naysayers of yesteryear could not fit this taxing into their historical chronological scheme and were sure that the Bible was in error. New historical information has been uncovered and, as usual, the inspired word of the living God was correct and perfectly preserved for us.

📖 **(Luke 2:3-5) And all went to be taxed, every one into his own city. ⁴And Joseph also went up from Galilee, out of the city of Nazareth, into Judaea, unto the city of David, which is called Bethlehem; (because he was of the house and lineage of David:) ⁵To be taxed with Mary his espoused wife, being great with child.**

Many have questioned why Mary made this trip. Various foolish and bogus answers have been offered, and we have previously commented on these. Mary made the trip because she was doing the Lord's bidding. Joseph and Mary certainly planned to keep the law; thus, it appears their plan was to stay forty days and return. There were certainly kinfolks in the area to provide cheap lodging. Mary could recuperate and visit. The economy was booming, and Joseph would have found day work readily. The religious rituals would be observed, and they would return.

📖 **(Luke 2:6-17) And so it was, that, while they were there, the days were accomplished that she should be delivered. ⁷And she brought forth her firstborn son, and wrapped him in swaddling clothes, and laid him in a manger; because there was no room for them in the inn. ⁸And there were in the same country shepherds abiding in the field, keeping watch over their flock by night. ⁹And, lo, the angel of the Lord came upon them, and the glory of the Lord shone round about them: and they were sore afraid. ¹⁰And the angel said unto them, Fear not: for, behold, I bring you good tidings of great joy, which shall be to all people. ¹¹For unto you is born this day in the city of David a Saviour, which is Christ the Lord. ¹²And this shall be a sign unto you; Ye shall find the babe wrapped in swaddling clothes, lying in a manger. ¹³And suddenly there was with the angel a multitude of the heavenly host praising God, and saying, ¹⁴Glory to God in the highest, and on earth peace, good will** toward men. ¹⁵And it came to pass, as the angels were gone away from them into heaven, the shepherds said one to another, Let us now go even unto Bethlehem, and see this thing which is come to pass, which the Lord hath made known unto us. ¹⁶And they came with haste, and found Mary, and Joseph, and the babe lying in a manger. ¹⁷And when they had seen it, they made known abroad the saying which was told them concerning this child.

We make the point again to the mule-faced and somber professed Christians who say that nowhere in the Bible are we told to celebrate Christmas. It certainly appears to me that God is putting on a show. God lit up the sky and paraded out a glorious angel. The multitude of the heavenly host displayed a praise and worship service. These angels called Christ "a Saviour" and "Christ the Lord."

The shepherds went forth and published the angel's message abroad. There can be no doubt that some versions of the shepherds account reached back to Herod's palace. However, Herod was amid prosecuting his own son, Antipater, for sedition. Antipater was sent to Rome and Caesar for education and political reasons. While in Rome, Antipater plotted to have his father poisoned. Letters were intercepted and Herod sent for Antipater.

When Antipater returned, Herod promptly charged him with sedition. Varus, the president of Syria, just happened to be visiting with Herod. Herod enlisted Varus to be the judge. The palace was in an uproar and the shepherds account would not have been a priority. Also, when information is passed on through verbal accounts, the message often becomes corrupted and distorted.

📖 (Luke 2:18-21) And all they that heard it wondered at those things which were told them by the shepherds. ¹⁹But Mary kept all these things, and pondered them in her heart. ²⁰And the shepherds returned, glorifying and praising God for all the things that they had heard and seen, as it was told unto them. ²¹And when eight days were accomplished for the circumcising of the child, his name was called JESUS, which was so named of the angel before he was conceived in the womb.

Joseph, Mary, and the Christ Child apparently are still in Bethlehem. The taxation and registration would be completed in a couple of days. Joseph probably moved Mary and the Baby Jesus into a house the next day. Joseph is a man on the move and would secure work quickly. Mary now has time to recuperate from the labor process.

For Joseph and Mary to go back to Nazareth and then to return for the purification process would have taken 8 to 10 days both ways. Joseph would have come out ahead by staying and working in Bethlehem.

📖 **(Luke 2:22-39) And when the days of her purification according to the law of Moses were accomplished, they brought him to Jerusalem, to present him to the Lord; 23(As it is written in the law of the Lord, Every male that openeth the womb shall be called holy to the Lord;) 24And to offer a sacrifice according to that which is said in the law of the Lord, A pair of turtledoves, or two young pigeons. 25And, behold, there was a man in Jerusalem, whose name was Simeon; and the same man was just and devout, waiting for the consolation of Israel: and the Holy Ghost was upon him. 26And it was revealed unto him by the Holy Ghost, that he should not see death, before he had seen the Lord's Christ. 27And he came by the Spirit into the temple: and when the parents brought in the child Jesus, to do for him after the custom of the law, 28Then took he him up in his arms, and blessed God, and said, 29Lord, now lettest thou thy servant depart in peace, according to thy word: 30For mine eyes have seen thy salvation, 31Which thou hast prepared before the face of all people; 32A light to lighten the Gentiles, and the glory of thy people Israel. 33And Joseph and his mother marvelled at those things which were spoken of him. 34And Simeon blessed them, and said unto Mary his mother, Behold, this child is set for the fall and rising again of many in Israel; and for a sign which shall be spoken against; 35(Yea, a sword shall pierce through thy own soul also,) that the thoughts of many hearts may be revealed. 36And there was one Anna, a prophetess, the daughter of Phanuel, of the tribe of Aser: she was of a great age, and had lived with an husband seven years from her virginity; 37And she was a widow of about fourscore and four years, which departed not from the temple, but served God with fastings and prayers night and day. 38And she** coming in that instant gave thanks likewise unto the Lord, and spake of him to all them that looked for redemption in Jerusalem. 39And when they had performed all things according to the law of the Lord,

The holy family returned to Bethlehem after the temple visit. Joseph probably went back to work the next day as Mary packed for the return to Nazareth.

📖 **(Matthew 2:1-3) Now when Jesus was born in Bethlehem of Judaea in the days of Herod the king, behold, there came wise men from the east to Jerusalem, 2Saying, Where is he that is born King of the Jews? for we have seen his star in the east, and are come to worship him. 3When Herod the king had heard these things, he was troubled, and all Jerusalem with him.**

Many writers of yesteryear calculate the Wise Men's visit to Herod at Jerusalem within two or three days of the presentation of Christ and purification of Mary on the fortieth day at the temple.

Herod had heard the rumors of the Christ child. The angels presented Jesus as "Christ" and a "Saviour," but the biblical narrative in Luke does not use the title "King." Now the Wise Men arrive and call this Child "King of the Jews." "King of the Jews" is Herod's cherished and relished title, so the situation is now personal with Herod. Traveling from a far country, the Wise Men evidently had no inkling of the reputation of the psychotic and cruel nature of King Herod.

📖 **(Matthew 2:4-5) And when he had gathered all the chief priests and scribes of the people together, he demanded of them where Christ should be born. 5And they said unto him, In Bethlehem of Judaea: for thus it is written by the prophet,**

It is worthy of note that the Wise Men are not at this meeting. The chief priests and the scribes are kept separate from the Wise Men. Read on and note below:

📖 **(Matthew 2:6-8) And thou Bethlehem, in the land of Juda, art not the least among the princes of Juda: for out of thee shall come a Governor, that shall rule my people Israel. 7Then Herod, when he had privily called the wise men, enquired of them diligently what time the star appeared. 8And he sent them to Bethlehem, and said, Go and search diligently for the** young child; and when ye have found him, bring me word again, that I may come and worship him also.

Some documentaries show Herod assigning a soldier to travel with the Wise Men. There is no evidence that this happened. Herod, in a sense, had good administrative and political skills. Had Herod sent a soldier with the entourage of the Wise Men, Herod would have raised their suspicions.

Herod's affection for deception was instinctively part of his nature. When Antipater tried to poison his father, he was just being the chip off the proverbial block. In this case, Herod is just being Herod.

📖 **(Matthew 2:9) When they had heard the king, they departed; and, lo, the star, which they saw in the east, went before them, till it came and stood over where the young child was.**

From the narrative, it appears that the Wise Men got their answer on the day they visited Herod and headed toward Bethlehem. The star likely appeared at twilight. The Wise Men followed the Star to find Mary and the Baby Jesus. Joseph is not there and is probably working.

📖 **(Matthew 2:10-11) When they saw the star, they rejoiced with exceeding great joy. ¹¹And when they were come into the house, they saw the young child with Mary his mother, and fell down, and worshipped him: and when they had opened their treasures, they presented unto him gifts; gold, and frankincense, and myrrh.**

The arrival of the Wise Men was without fanfare. Of course, the gifts were actual gifts and yet symbolic in nature. The symbolism of the gifts demonstrates to us that the Wise Men knew who they were seeking. Upon leaving the house, the Wise Men either found lodging close by, or made camp.

📖 **(Matthew 2:12) And being warned of God in a dream that they should not return to Herod, they departed into their own country another way.**

These Wise Men knew the Lord God and the Lord God knew them. The next morning, the Wise Men departed with haste through an unknown route. Judea was not that big of a place. By the time Herod the deceiver would have discerned about his own deception, the Wise Men would have been out of Herod's jurisdiction. Certainly, Herod was a powerful man as the client King of Judea. However, where the border of Judea ended, Herod's power ended. Herod would never have dared to send his soldiers outside the borders of Judea.

📖 **(Matthew 2:13)And when they were departed, behold, the angel of the Lord appeareth to Joseph in a dream, saying, Arise, and take the young child and his mother, and flee into Egypt, and be thou there until I bring thee word: for Herod will seek the young child to destroy him.**

It is my opinion that Joseph came home from work late the same night that the Wise Men visited.

📖 **Matthew 2:14, When he arose, he took the young child and his mother by night, and departed into Egypt:**

No sooner than Joseph went to sleep, the Lord appeared to him in a dream. Joseph and Mary gathered their belongings and the Baby Jesus then left almost immediately.

Egypt's border was not located where it is now. One biblical researcher and commentator says that Egypt's border was forty miles away. According to my research, the border of Egypt appeared to be about seventy miles from Bethlehem. Mary had recuperated from childbirth and would be in excellent condition to travel. The holy family communicated with no one before leaving for Egypt.

Herod waited two or three days before ordering the slaughter of the innocents, and the Lord's family would have been safely across the border of Egypt. Again, Herod's authority does not extend outside of Judea. History records that Herod's search for the Christ child extended no further than a five-mile radius around Bethlehem.

Here we depart for a note of interest. The following is from: (http://egypt.travel/en/stories/the-journey-of-the-holy-family-to-egypt) an Egyptian touring and travel website. Their account of Jesus in Egypt makes great fiction. Incidentally, this great fiction is also Catholic tradition and considered truth in some Catholic circles.

The arrival of Jesus Christ and the Holy Family is an important event that took place in Egypt. The story starts with a group of Wise Men declaring Jesus as the next king of the Jews. That's why King Herod (Ruler of Judea at the time) felt threatened and decided to kill him.

The Holy Family left from Bethlehem to Egypt after an angel warned Joseph to leave with Jesus and Virgin Mary. They started their journey through northern Sinai until reaching Farama. The places they stayed in have now been transformed to churches and monasteries.

The next destination from their journey was Tel Basta where Jesus performed a miracle. He blessed the place by causing a water spring to well up from the ground.

The Family then reached Mostorod, also known as el Mahamaah, meaning the bathing place. A name that was given to the town Virgin Mary bathed in child Jesus and washed his clothes.

After that, the Holy Family made their way to Belbeis where they sat under the shades of a sycamore tree, later known as the "Virgin Mary's Tree." When they crossed the Nile to the city of Samanoud, Jesus hollowed another water well. While in Sakha, it is believed Jesus touched a stone and pure water thrust from it.

The Holy Family then traveled westward to the Valley of Natroun. The Valley was the monasticism's first home in the world to practice chastity and meditating God.

The Family eventually headed to Cairo's districts of Matariyah and Ain Shams where Jesus created a water well and blessed it. Then Virgin Mary washed Jesus's cloth pouring the water onto the ground which blossomed the Balsam tree. Balsam essence is used for the preparation of the Holy Myron.

The Holy Family moved on to Old Cairo where they took refuge in a cave. At this site the Church of Abi Serja, within the walls of the Fortress of Babylon, was built years later. The whole area has become a place of pilgrimage for Egyptians and Christians from around the globe.

They then set out to Al-Maadi, where the Virgin Mary Church was built by the Nile. From where the Family embarked a sailing boat heading southwards. The Family then headed to Minya from which they crossed to the east bank of the Nile. There stands the Monastery of the Virgin on top of the Gabal Al-Kaf (Mountain of the Palm). It is believed that Jesus left an imprint of his palm on a stone in the mountain.

From that spot, the Family crossed the Nile back west, to Qussqam in Assiut. They stayed for more than six months, longer than any other place in Egypt. In that area, the Monastery of Al-Moharraq was built. Later, in the same spot, an angel appeared in Joseph's dream telling him to return to Palestine as Herod was dead.

The Holy Family took almost the same route on their

journey back to Palestine, after spending over three years in Egypt. (end of travel tour information)

Chronological calculations and efforts to mesh legitimate history with the biblical narrative yield a short visit in Egypt for the holy family. If Jesus were born in 4 BC, the maximum time of the holy family's tenure in Jerusalem would be about six weeks. Joseph did not have to go far into Egypt to hide. Herod's command of the slaughter of the innocents would be one of the last things that Herod did while he was still in Jerusalem. Shortly thereafter, Herod was transported to Jericho hoping to recover from his putrefying sicknesses. Herod died a month before Passover in early April.

Remember, the Jews started an insurrection almost immediately after the death of Herod. The Passover was at hand, and the Jews were incited because they hated the defilement of the Eagle insignia placed by Herod on the side of the Temple. Archelaus commanded the Jews to be dispersed and slew 3000 Jews of the Passover. This was before the official appointment of Archelaus as king by Caesar.

📖 **(Matthew 2:15-20) And was there until the death of Herod: that it might be fulfilled which was spoken of the Lord by the prophet, saying, Out of Egypt have I called my son. ¹⁶Then Herod, when he saw that he was mocked of the wise men, was exceeding wroth, and sent forth, and slew all the children that were in Bethlehem, and in all the coasts thereof, from two years old and under, according to the time which he had diligently enquired of the wise men. ¹⁷Then was fulfilled that which was spoken by Jeremy the prophet, saying, ¹⁸In Rama was there a voice heard, lamentation, and weeping, and great mourning, Rachel weeping for her children, and would not be comforted, because they are not. ¹⁹But when Herod was dead, behold, an angel of the Lord appeareth in a dream to Joseph in Egypt, ²⁰Saying, Arise, and take the young child and his mother, and go into the land of Israel: for they are dead which sought the young child's life.**

The Lord was providing step-by-step instructions to Joseph.

📖 **Matthew 2:21, "And he arose, and took the young child and his mother, and came into the land of Israel.**

And as usual, Joseph without delay moved his family to Israel.

The journey back probably took three or four days at most.

📖 **Matthew 2:22, But when he heard that Archelaus did reign in Judaea in the room of his father Herod, he was afraid to go thither: notwithstanding, being warned of God in a dream, he turned aside into the parts of Galilee:**

Herod had commanded the gathering of the Jewish nobles with the intent for them to be killed upon his death. However, when Herod died, Salome, the sister of Herod, and her husband were afraid to follow through with Herod's command. The Jewish nobles were set free without their knowledge of Herod's death. Subsequently, the palace officials notified the soldiers of Herod's intent to appoint Archelaus as the new king. Immediately, plans were made for the burial of Herod. Due to palace secrecy, the news of Herod's death could have taken two or three days to reach Jerusalem. Joseph returned to Israel with his family and heard the news of the reign of Archelaus and perhaps the slaughter of the 3000 Jews at the Passover.

In any case, the news of the Archelaus' reign caused Joseph to fear. That night the Lord instructed Joseph to head toward home and probably by a different route. Apparently, Joseph had planned to go through Bethlehem and to Jerusalem and then home. Joseph turned "aside" to the left and went up the coast to Nazareth.

📖 **Matthew 2:23 And he came and dwelt in a city called Nazareth: that it might be fulfilled which was spoken by the prophets, He shall be called a Nazarene.**

Joseph, Mary, and the baby Jesus are finally home. The entire journey from the time Joseph and Mary left Nazareth until their return to Nazareth would have taken four to seven months.

📖 **Luke 2:39 And when they had performed all things according to the law of the Lord, they returned into Galilee, to their own city Nazareth.**

Joseph and Mary return home with the Christ child. We have no news or account of the childhood of Jesus except the Temple episode when Jesus was twelve years old. **Luke 2:52** states that Jesus grew "in wisdom, in stature, and in favor with God and man." In other words, the Bible infers that Jesus would lead a somewhat ordinary childhood: working, playing, going to school and the synagogue, participating in normal day to day family and social activities. Note: "in favor with God and man." Jesus was well respected and highly esteemed in his hometown and surrounding area.

Chapter 25
The Mystery of Immanuel - God With Us

Through the ages, mankind has wondered about the mystery of God. The Old Testament prophet Isaiah, over 700 years before the birth of Christ, foretold of a day that would come when God would become man. **Isaiah 7:14** says, **"Therefore the Lord himself shall give you a sign; Behold a virgin shall conceive, and bear a son, and shall call his name Immanuel."**

In Matthew, we have had an opportunity to listen in as the angel of the Lord told Joseph that the time had come for God to become man; and at last, God would be with man.

Yes, the little baby Jesus was none other than the Son of God and God the Son. He was God incarnate. He was divine deity. Many infidels and heathen have hated and denied the very plain biblical truth that Jesus was Immanuel and thus "God With Us." The Bible even gives us some insight on how God became man.

The "virgin birth" and the "deity of Christ" are wrapped up in one another and are inseparable. These two great truths form the wrappings of God's true Christmas Gift to you.

The miracle event and supernatural story of the virgin birth is told in **Matthew:**

📖 **(Matthew 1:18-25) Now the birth of Jesus Christ was on this wise: When as his mother Mary was espoused to Joseph, before they came together, she was found with child of the Holy Ghost. 19Then Joseph her husband, being a just man, and not willing to make her a publick example, was minded to put her away privily. 20But while he thought on these things, behold, the angel of the Lord appeared unto him in a dream, saying, Joseph, thou son of David, fear not to take unto thee Mary thy wife: for that which is conceived in her is of the Holy Ghost. 21And she shall bring forth a son, and thou shalt call his name JESUS: for he shall save his people from their sins. 22Now all this was done, that it might be fulfilled which was spoken of the Lord by the prophet, saying, 23Behold, a virgin shall be with child, and shall bring forth a son, and they shall call his name Emmanuel, which being interpreted is, God with us. 24Then Joseph being raised from sleep did as the angel** of the Lord had bidden him, and took unto him his wife: **25And knew her not till she had brought forth her firstborn son: and he called his name JESUS.**

Also, Luke plainly declares the virgin birth in the same manner as Matthew in the parallel account of the Christmas Story in **Luke 1:26-35.**

Yes, many evil and wicked minds have imagined that the virgin birth was a man-made doctrine and has rejected Christ, Christmas, and Christianity. But only God can foretell an event and bring it to pass.

Jesus was not only the Son of God, but also God the Son. It is amazing that many will acknowledge Jesus as the Son of God but not God the Son. The Bible certainly declares that He absolutely must be both. John begins his gospel, **"In the beginning was the Word, and the Word was with God, and the Word was God. The same was in the beginning with God. All things were made by him; and without him was not anything made that was made." (John 1:1-3).**

John 1:14 says, **"And the Word was made flesh, and dwelt among us, (and we beheld his gory, the glory as of the only begotten of the Father,) full of grace and truth."**

You see, Jesus was there in the beginning with the Father and was the Creator of the heaven and the earth. You are a product of His creation. Jesus has always been God's **Word** to us. Jesus the Christ is God's revelation to man of what God is like. Yes, Jesus is God's Word. The Bible vividly announces, **"the Word was God"** and **"the Word was made flesh."**

The fact that Jesus is the eternal, pre-existent Son of God and God the Son should not be new to anyone who has a remedial knowledge about the Bible. **Colossians 1:16** says, **"For by him (referring to Christ) were all things created, that are in heaven, and that are in earth."** In **Hebrews 1:1-2**, Jesus is seen as the Creator again, and we quote, **"God...hath in these last days spoken unto us by his Son...by whom also He made the worlds."** In **Isaiah 9:6,** Jesus is called **"the Mighty God"** and **"The Everlasting Father."**

Man sinned and fell breaking his relationship with God. The Bible says, "all have sinned." Mankind is tainted by the tendency to sin. Adam's sin syndrome has been passed on from generation to generation **(Romans 5:12)** and thus death has been passed on from generation to generation. Man, and his wicked sin, has separated himself from a good, righteous, and holy God and thus could not know God. So, Jesus laid aside His garments of deity and came in the likeness of sinful flesh to reveal God to man.

Jesus reveals three things about God. First, God is holy and hates sin. Jesus came in the **"likeness of sinful flesh."** Yet, the Bible says that Jesus **"Knew no sin" (II Corinthians 5:21).** Jesus was God and therefore could not sin.

Second, God will judge sin. When God talks of death in the Garden of Eden, He was referring to physical and spiritual death. This spiritual death is called the **"second death"** in **Revelation 21:8** which says, **"But the fearful, and unbelieving, and the abominable, and murderers, and whoremongers, and sorcerers, and idolaters, and all liars, shall have their part in the lake which burneth with fire and brimstone: which is the second death."** Jesus, who was God, declared and confirmed God's judgment of sin.

Third, God loved sinful, fallen mankind, and came to pay the sin debt for everyone who would receive and believe in Him. The love of God is openly displayed as we pull back the curtain of Calvary. Look there at the suffering, bleeding, and dying Saviour. In **Romans 6:23** the Bible declares, **"For the wages of sin is death; but the gift of God is eternal life through Jesus Christ our Lord."** The true Christmas Gift is eternal life.

Jesus loved you and me enough to die for us and to pay our sin debt. There is more! On the third day after the death of our Saviour, the Son of God proved Himself to be so by the bodily resurrection of the dead. The angel of the Lord, while sitting upon the stone he had rolled away from the tomb, said calmly, **" I know that ye seek Jesus, who was crucified, He is not here; for He is risen."** The bodily resurrection from the dead gives our Saviour the credibility to offer salvation to "whosoever" that will come to Him.

This should be a special blessing to those who have received the Christ of Christmas and give the world's most glorious invitation to those who have not received Christ. The invitation is to have Christmas this Christmas. There can be no Christmas without Christ, without Immanuel, without having God with you. You can have the greatest gift and have God with you by repenting of sin and allowing Christ to come in and forgive you of that sin.

There is only one way to receive Christ and only one way to give your heart to Him, and that is by faith, belief, or trust (they are the same). **John 3:16** says, **"Whosoever believeth in Him should not perish but have everlasting life."** Yes, you can have

God with you, and He will abide with you forever. Listen to the great invitation of Christ and accept it today. **Revelation 3:20** says, **"Behold, I stand at the door and knock: if any man hear my voice, and open the door, I will come in to him and will sup with him and he with Me."**

Chapter 26
The Reason for the Season

John 1:1-3 "In the beginning was the Word, and the Word was with God, and the Word was God. ²The same was in the beginning with God. ³All things were made by him; and without him was not any thing made that was made.

      The Apostle John, who wrote these words, was not a wordy writer. Yet, he was a weighty writer. He has packed as much theology in three verses as could possibly be packed into three verses.

      There are a lot of things that the other gospel writers write about that John does not write about. The genealogy of Jesus is not given in the Gospel of John. You do not find anything about the manger or the birth experience of the Lord Jesus in the gospel of John. You find no reference to the boyhood of Jesus in the Gospel of John. In the Gospel of John, you do not find the story of the temptation of the Lord Jesus. When this writer traveled to Israel, we visited the ruins of the Old City of Jericho. Jericho is the oldest city in the world. We had lunch there, and I will never forget the name of the restaurant where we ate. It is probably the best named restaurant I have ever been to. It was named the Temptation Restaurant. It was so named because it is located in the valley below the mountain of temptation where Jesus went to be tempted by the devil. This is a well-known instance in the life of Christ, yet John does not speak of it. In the Gospel of John, you do not find any of the parables of Jesus.

      John has a purpose in writing his gospel, and John tells us what his purpose is at the end of the book. He says in **John 20:31: "But these are written, that ye might believe that Jesus is the Christ, the Son of God; and that believing ye might have life through his name."** John's purpose in writing the gospel of John is to bring you to a saving knowledge of Jesus Christ. In these verses that you have just read, there are three great truths that John teaches.

      The very first thing is "the sovereign majesty of Jesus." John opens his gospel with a theological mountain peak. He speaks to us directly without stutter, stammer, or apology. He tells us as clearly and as plainly as human language can tell us that Jesus Christ is God and that He is unquestionably God, and that He is eternally God. When John wrote this, he wrote this as an old man. This is not the opinion of a moment. He has had fifty or sixty years to think about it. This is his mature, unshakeable conviction: that Jesus Christ is God.

Not only is Jesus Christ God, He is eternally God. John says in **John 1:1: "In the beginning was the Word."** When John says, **"In the beginning,"** he is not talking about a start, he is talking about a state. Jesus Christ is eternally God. He has always been God. **"In the beginning was the Word."** That noun, **"Word,"** speaks of Jesus Christ. One of the names of Jesus is "the Word." Why would you call Jesus "the Word?" Notice that the **Word** is written with a capital letter. **"In the beginning was the Word."** Jesus' name is **"the Word."** So why does God describe His Son by calling Him **"the Word?"** Well, a word is an expression of an invisible thought. A person has thoughts in their head, but you cannot see those thoughts. However, you can hear that person's words, and you know what they are thinking by their words. So, a word is an expression of an invisible thought. Jesus Christ is the expression, the visible expression, of the invisible God. Jesus Christ expresses the Father. **John 1:1** says, **"In the beginning was the Word"** and notice what it says, **"and the Word was with God, and the Word was God."** The verb "was" in this verse is in the imperfect tense. What does that mean? It means that it does not speak of something that just simply took place in the past and now it is completed. It speaks of something that goes on, and on, and on. What John is saying is, in the beginning, before there was any earth, sun, moon, and stars and before there was any creation, and any cosmos, Jesus was there. He was dwelling in the dimension where time does not exist.

Dear reader, you need to understand, that when you think of Jesus, you do not begin with the manger. You do not begin with Mary. Jesus never, ever had a beginning. Dr. B. R. Lakin used to say, "He is the beginning of beginnings." He always was. **"In the beginning was the Word" (John 1:1).** Jesus is eternally God.

Jesus is equally God. Notice again that John states: **"In the beginning was the Word, and the Word was with God and the Word was God" (John 1:1).** In the Godhead, there is more than one person. We worship one God, but He has revealed Himself to us in three persons: the Father, the Son, and the Holy Spirit. The Bible teaches this from the very beginning. In **Genesis 1:26** it says, **"God said, "Let us make man in our image."** The word God in **Genesis 1:26** is the Hebrew word Elohim, and that is a plural noun.

We do not worship three Gods. That would be idolatry. That would be blasphemy. But we worship one God who has revealed Himself eternally in three persons. There are those who go from door to door and house to house in almost every major American city, and they tell us that the doctrine of the Trinity is a pagan invention. There was an individual in Greene County, Tennessee, who claimed to be a Christian missionary and street preacher, who literally went around to churches with a bullhorn, and he would stand on the curb outside of churches in Greeneville and Greene County. He would yell at the congregants entering or leaving their churches and say there is no such thing as a Trinity. He called it a "luciferian doctrine." There are groups in our world today that ridicule the doctrine of the Trinity. They say, "You worship three Gods: you have God the Father, God the Son, and God the Holy Spirit, and one plus one, plus one, equals three." But one times one, times one, equals one! We worship one God who has revealed Himself to us eternally in three persons. Jesus is eternally God and Jesus is equally God. He is as much God as God the Father is God. He is as much God as God the Holy Spirit is God.

So, Jesus Christ is God, He is equally God, He is eternally God and Jesus Christ is essentially God. Everything that God does, Jesus does. Everything that God thinks, Jesus thinks. Everything that God has, Jesus has. **John 1:3** says, **"All things were made by him; and without him,"** (that is, **"the Word,"** Jesus) **"was not anything made that was made."** Everything that God is, does, or has—Jesus is, Jesus does, and Jesus has.

It was Jesus that spoke this universe into existence. Have you ever thought about the enormity of the universe? This author did some research on the size of the universe. In the Milky Way galaxy, it is estimated that there are one hundred billion stars. If you were to turn a telescope to the outer reaches of space, you would find that space goes on and on. NASA estimates, based on pictures taken by the Hubble space telescope, that there are 100 billion galaxies in the universe. They say that the number of galaxies that are discovered could increase as telescope technology improves. We know that light travels through space at one hundred and eighty-six thousand miles per second. That means that light travels six trillion miles a year. If you could travel through space, you would see stars everywhere strewn like grains of sand through the blackness of space. Behind all this, the Creator of all this, was Jesus. **"Without him was not anything made that was made."**

Then you could put down your telescope and pick up your microscope to study the minutia of creation. Study the atomic building blocks of our cells, the atoms. An atom is one hundred and fifty millionth of an inch in diameter. Yet, each of those atoms, which is completely invisible to the naked eye, is a whirling powerhouse of sheer energy. One atom is a miniature solar system with a central nucleus with electrons in orbit around it.

I read something interesting: if you were to take a drop of water and take the molecules in one drop of water and translate or transform those molecules in one drop of water into grains of sand, you would have enough sand to build a concrete highway one and a half miles wide and one foot thick from New York to San Francisco. That is how many molecules that are in one drop of water.

Think about the complexity of the smallest parts of creation. Think of the vastness of creation. Jesus Christ made it all. **"Without him was not anything made that was made."** Jesus is God. We are talking about the sovereign majesty of Jesus. **Hebrews 1:8** says, **"unto the Son he saith, Thy throne, O God, is for ever and ever."** God the Father calls His Son "God." **Titus 2:13** tells us that we are to be **"looking for that blessed hope, and the glorious appearing of the great God and our Saviour Jesus Christ."** Our Saviour Jesus Christ is the great God. The apostle Thomas, "doubting Thomas," when he was finally convinced that Jesus had been raised from the dead, fell before Him and said in **John 20:28: "My LORD and my God."**

The first thing that John teaches about Jesus is His sovereign majesty. Jesus is eternally God. Jesus is equally God. Jesus is essentially God. Jesus is God. If you take that doctrine out of Christianity, you do not have Christianity anymore. What you have is a cult. I would not invite an individual into my home who comes to my door holding in their doctrine a belief that Jesus Christ is not God. Do you realize there are groups of people who claim to believe the Bible who say that Jesus Christ is the Son of God, but He is not God? I would not invite them into my home. I would not bid them good day. You say, "that is mean." That is scriptural. **2 John 1:10, "If there come any unto you, and bring not this doctrine, receive him not into your house, neither bid him God speed:"**

So first, John teaches us of the sovereign majesty of Jesus. He is the supreme creator and ruler of this universe. The next thing we need to see is Jesus' simple humanity. In **John 1:14** John says, **"And the Word was made flesh, and dwelt among us, (and we beheld his glory, the glory as of the only begotten of the Father,) full of grace and truth."** This scripture that you have just read had to be translated from the Greek into a word that we could understand. God translated Jesus into a language that we could understand, and the language that we could understand is human flesh. **"The Word was made flesh, and dwelt among us."** Jesus manifested the Father. In **John 1:18** the Bible says, **"No man hath seen God at any time; the only begotten Son, which is in the bosom of the Father, he hath declared him."** The word "declared" here means that Jesus Christ reveals God to us. God is invisible. Man can see God revealed in nature and in His mighty works in history, but he cannot see God Himself.

Jesus Christ reveals God to us, for He is **"the image of the invisible God" (Colossians 1:15)** and **"the express image of His person" (Hebrews 1:3).** The word translated "declared" gives us our English word "exegesis," which means "to explain, to unfold, to lead the way." Jesus Christ explains God to us and interprets Him for us. We simply cannot understand God apart from knowing His Son, Jesus Christ. The Bible says in **John 1:18**, that the Lord Jesus Christ has declared the Father, He has manifested the Father. The Word is translated into flesh.

The mystery of the manger is this: that God would be able to translate deity into humanity without discarding His deity or distorting His humanity. Jesus did not discard His deity, nor did He distort His humanity. This *is* the great mystery of the manger. Jesus Christ is the God-Man. He was not all God and no man. He was not all man and no God. He was not half-man and half-God. Jesus was all God and all man at the same time.

Jesus is the God-Man. There has never been another like Him. The Word was translated into flesh without discarding His deity and without distorting His humanity. He was as much man as any man who has ever lived and yet He was still God.

What a mystery this is! That little baby wrapped in swaddling clothes and lying in a manger that we celebrate and sing about was the eternal, uncreated, self-existing Word made flesh. The Baby in swaddling clothes of **Luke 2** is the mighty God of **Genesis 1.** This is Bible truth, and it is so fundamental to being a Bible Christian.

That little two-year-old toddler that held Mary's hand as she went about her tasks around the house was the mighty God who swung the planets into space. That busy little boy playing in Joseph's carpenter shop is God manifested in the flesh. That man who hung upon a cross and cried, "I thirst," was the mighty God who made all of the oceans, and all of the rivers, and all of the springs, and every drop of rain. He was God.

Notice what the Bible says here in **John 1:14, "the Word was made flesh, and dwelt** (or tabernacled) **among us."** That word dwelt is an interesting word; it literally means "He pitched His tent among us," or "He tabernacled with us." The word translated dwelt here is the word for a tabernacle. Back in the Old Testament, God gave the people a tabernacle.

Do you know what the tabernacle was? It was a tent of worship. If you had seen the tabernacle in the wilderness, you would not have thought that it was beautiful. On the outside of the tabernacle it was covered with badger skins. They were just rough, drab blue gray leather. It was unlovely, there was nothing beautiful to look at.

There were no windows in the tabernacle. The only light that the tabernacle had was from a golden lampstand, a seven-pronged menorah. We visited the Temple Institute in Israel. The Jews are preparing now for the building of the third temple in Israel. All the furniture and the altars are prepared for the day the temple will be rebuilt. This author believes we are drawing close to the return of the Lord. In the Temple Institute they had a replica of the solid gold menorah that will go in the third temple. It stood taller than my head.

On the inside of that tabernacle in the wilderness it was completely, indescribably beautiful. There was fine twined linen. There was scarlet, and purple, and blue, and white, and shimmering gold there. It was exquisite. Millions of dollars would have been spent to decorate the inside of that tent. Solid gold was everywhere. It was all glowing by the lamp of the seven-pronged candlestick that was there.

From the outside you would never have known the beauty that was on the inside, but once you went in and saw that candlestick, that lamp-stand fed by oil, which is a symbol of the Holy Spirit of God, it's beauty would take your breath away.

This is a picture or a type of the Lord Jesus Christ. **"The Word was made flesh, and dwelt among us."** If you looked at the Lord Jesus Christ, outwardly, you would not have been impressed. I am not being disrespectful. I am just telling you what the Bible teaches. In **Isaiah 53:2** the prophet Isaiah tells us: **"He hath no form nor comeliness; and when we shall see him, there is no beauty that we should desire him."** Jesus did not stand out before men. His appearance was average. He was a nondescript man. But, for those of us who have come to Christ and for those of us who are illuminated by the Holy Spirit of God, we see the indescribable, exquisite beauty of the Son of God.

John said, **"The Word was made flesh, and dwelt among us, and we beheld his glory..."** John the apostle had a glimpse of that hidden glory. He said, **"We beheld his glory."** John saw God in the flesh living and breathing, laughing, and crying, eating, and drinking. He saw Him in public. He saw Him in private. He saw Him as He was hailed as a Messiah and nailed as a malefactor. He saw Him when He was consulted, and when He was contradicted. He saw Him when He was cheered, and w hen He was crucified. He saw Him when He was buried and saw Him when He was resurrected. He saw the Word, the eternal God made flesh.

No wonder the Apostle Paul said in **1 Timothy 3:16, "great is the mystery of godliness: God was manifest in the flesh."** We must thank God for His sovereign majesty. He was the Word. But oh, thank God for His simple humanity, because had Jesus not become a man, you and I could not have been saved.

Jesus suffered as a man. It was necessary that He die as a man. You see, our standing before God was lost by a man. **"In Adam all die."** When Adam sinned our relationship to God and our dominion over the earth was legally lost. Adam forfeited it. **"In Adam [we] die."** Adam sold out to the devil. The devil became the prince of this world, and men became slaves of Satan and slaves of sin. The son of a slave could not redeem a slave because all sons of slaves are slaves themselves.

So, God had to do a new thing. No son of Adam could redeem us. God had to send His Son, made in the likeness of sinful flesh and yet without sin. **He... "who knew no sin," became sin for us (1 Corinthians 5:21).** Jesus paid the price. He ransomed us. He suffered, bled, and died as a man. Had Jesus not become a man, you and I could never have been saved. That is the reason for the virgin birth. Jesus Christ is the virgin born son of God. If He were not the son of God and God the son who came to earth as a man, He would not be able to die for the sins of mankind.

Jesus suffered as a man, and not only did He suffer as a man. He subdued as a man. Remember, when Adam sinned in the Garden of Eden, he lost it all. When Jesus Christ came against Satan and was tempted there in the wilderness on the mount of temptation, Jesus, the second Adam, gained back all that Adam lost. There in the wilderness, Jesus met the devil head on, and Jesus overcame the devil.

When Jesus overcame the devil, He did not overcome the devil as God would overcome the devil. He overcame the devil as Man filled with God would overcome the devil. When Jesus came to earth, He emptied himself. He laid aside his deity and He took upon Himself human flesh and the limitations of that human flesh. Then, Jesus Christ, filled with the power of the Spirit, went against the devil, and

He overcame the devil. You say, "Well, what's the point? What difference does it make how He overcame the devil?" Dear reader, if He overcame the devil as God, that is no encouragement to me. Of course, God can overcome the devil. But, when He overcame the devil as a man, then He is my example.

Jesus Christ did not use any power to overcome the devil that is not available to John David Shanks or to you today. Jesus suffered as a man.

Jesus went to a garden on His way to Calvary, the Garden of Gethsemane. Gethsemane means olive press. Here in the Garden, Jesus was surrendered to death. Jesus is the Son of God and He knew full well that He would be raised from the dead, yet His soul experienced agony as He anticipated what lay before Him.

We visited an olive press in Nazareth. They would gather olives place them on a circular stone basin in which a millstone sat. They had a little donkey pulling that stone around, grinding those olives and crushing them. Once the olives have been crushed, a paste forms which is collected in baskets and stacked several layers high over stone pits. A stone weight was placed on top of the baskets, and a heavy wooden beam, and one end of that beam would be placed in a hole in the wall nearby. That beam was then placed across the pile of baskets. Stone weights were hung from the beam, applying enormous pressure to the olives squeezing the oil from the pulp.

As Jesus was in the Garden of Gethsemane and as He reflected on the work He was about to do, He, too, was pressed. The weight of your sin and my sin pressed on Jesus. The weight of all that you have done, and the weight of all that I have done, all the guilt and all the shame pressed upon Him but Jesus told God the Father to "put that weight of sin on me, put it on my back." I will take John David's judgment. I will take John David's sin. I will even leave here, and I will give my life and I will take John David's hell. I will take the anger and the judgment of a Holy God. Because John David can never ever be righteous; he can never be good. God's only Son provided that salvation.

Jesus knew in the hours ahead, He would be humiliated and abused, and suffer shame and pain on the cross. But even more than that, He would be made sin for us and be separated from His Father.

A comparison of the Gospel accounts reveals that Jesus was pressed three times. Three times He prayed, **"Father, if it be possible, let this cup pass from me."** Jesus agonized for you and for me in Gethsemane. **Luke 22:44** says, **"And being in an** agony he prayed more earnestly: and his sweat was as it were great drops of blood falling to the ground."

There is a rare physical phenomenon known as hemosiderosis, in which, under great emotional stress, the tiny blood vessels rupture in the sweat glands and produce a mixture of blood and sweat. My friend, do you understand the agony that Jesus was in as He was pressed in Gethsemane?

He faced the cross and He said, "O Father, please, if there be some other way..." And the silence from heaven said there was no other way. Jesus drank that bitter cup. He suffered as a man, and He subdued as a man. He overcame Satan as a man, and He is our example.

Jesus suffered as a man, and Jesus sympathizes as a man. **Hebrews 4:15** says: **"For we have not an high priest which cannot be touched with the feeling of our infirmities; but was in all points tempted like as we are, yet without sin."** When you hurt, He hurts. He knows how you feel. Thank God!

Jesus did not have to become a man to know how you feel, because He knows all things. But dear reader, Jesus became a man that we might know that He knows. Do you understand what I am saying? Jesus was here, that we might know that He knows, because He suffered, He walked, He felt, He hurt, He lived, He breathed, He wept, He hungered, just like we do. Thank God for His sovereign majesty, but oh, thank God for His simple humanity!

There is one last thing that John tells us about, and this is the reason for the season. This is the reason Jesus came into this world.

Jesus's sovereign majesty and simple humanity leads to His saving ministry. **John 1:11-13** says, **"He came unto his own, and his own received him not. ¹²But as many as received him, to them gave he power to become the sons of God, even to them that believe on his name: ¹³Which were born, not of blood, nor of the will of the flesh, nor of the will of man, but of God.**

In this passage we see three great things. We see the greatest tragedy: **"He came unto his own, and his own received him not."** We see the greatest transaction: **"But as many as received him..."** We see the greatest transformation: **"became the sons of God" (John 1:12).** What a miracle!

Jesus came to earth, that we could go to heaven. He was born of a virgin that we might be born again. He became the Son of man that we might become sons of God. He died that we might live. He came unto His own in order that He might save us.

How are we saved? **John 1:13** says, **"Which were born, not of blood, nor of the will of the flesh, nor of the will of man, but of God."** Now, let us break this verse down. Notice the phrase: **"which were born not of blood."** What does that mean? That means we cannot inherit our salvation. Just because your parents were saved does not make you a Christian. You cannot inherit it. We are born not of blood. It is not handed down through the bloodline. We are not saved by natural generation.

Notice the second phrase: **"Nor of the will of the flesh."** What does this mean? This means salvation is not the works of men's hands. You cannot work your way into heaven. We are not saved by natural determination. We are not born again by the will of the flesh. We are not born again by good deeds. We are not born again by living a good life. We are not born again by natural generation or by natural determination. We are born again by supernatural regeneration; we are **"born, not of blood, nor of the will of the flesh, nor of the will of man, but of God."** That means that God, the God-man who died for us, now provides for us a new birth. This is the reason for the season.

What is this new birth? It means that we are born again because we have received the nature of God. Do you know what it means to be regenerated? It means to be "regened." Do you know that you have in you the genes and chromosomes of your parents? David and Pam Shanks are my parents, and if you know my father you know that we look and act a lot alike.

But when you are regenerated in Christ, you receive the genes of God spiritually. You have a new nature, and you begin to look and act like the Heavenly Father. This is the miracle of the Christmas season. The new birth is not a luxury; it is a necessity. George Whitfield, one of the great preachers of the past, went all over America preaching, "Ye must be born again!" Somebody stopped him and said, "Mr. Whitfield, may I ask you a question?" He said, "Yes." They said, "Why do you always preach, 'You must be born again'?" He said, "that is simple: 'it's because you must be born again."

John has told us about the sovereign majesty of Jesus. He told us about the simple humanity of Jesus. He told us about the saving ministry of Jesus. That is the reason for the season.

If you have read this and you are saved, you ought to love Jesus so much for saving you that you will follow Him wherever He leads you and obey him whenever He speaks. You should never allow yourself to be ashamed of Him.

Chapter 27
Great Expectations

But when the fulness of the time was come, God sent forth his Son, made of a woman, made under the law... (Galatians 4:4)

God in **"the fullness of time"** prepared the world to receive His Son. The children of Israel were "chosen" to bring the Christ Child into the world. This chosen people rebelled against God and God had Nebuchadnezzar invade Israel and deport them to Babylon. From Babylon, Israel was scattered throughout the rest of the world.

Throughout the world, there were little colonies of Jews and their synagogues. Each synagogue possessed a copy of the Holy Scriptures (our Old Testament). The scriptures foretold of the great expectation of a coming Saviour. God had planned for this very period in history in which He would send His Son to be born, to walk among sinful men, to live a sinless life, to go to an old rugged cross, to die for you and me, to raise from the dead, and then to depart back into heaven.

The world of Jesus' day had one world government and one common language (Greek). Greek was the language of choice among the learned people of that day. God would use this language to write the New Testament and to spread His good news of the coming of His Son. God required that his Son be born in Israel and specifically in Bethlehem. God had gathered a remnant of His chosen people back in Israel and had reestablished them as a nation. God in His providence set in motion the world events to suit Himself, and to make a way for His Son.

God also prepared the hearts of many to look for His Son. God gave these people a heart of great expectation. The children of Israel had not heard from God in over 400 years, but some knew the promises of God and looked with great expectation for the long awaited and faithfully promised Saviour.

The story of the Wise Men is a story of great expectation. It is also one of mystery, majesty, and high adventure. These rulers and priests journeyed four months from the Kingdom of Babylon to Jerusalem and asked, "Where is He that is born King of the Jews?" These Magi knew exactly who they were looking for. But how?

The prophets of old foretold of Him countless times. Daniel, as a small Israelite boy, was carried away as a captive slave to Babylon. There Daniel rose to a mighty position of power reporting directly to the king during three dynasties. Daniel even became "chief of the governors over all the wise men of Babylon." Daniel, no doubt, had copies of the Holy Writ available at that time. Prophets Moses, Isaiah, David, and others provided ample proof of the coming King. David investigated the future and says, **"Thou art my Son; this day have I begotten thee" (Psalm 2:7).** Isaiah spoke of the birth of Christ and said, **"Therefore, the Lord himself shall give you a sign; Behold, a virgin shall conceive, and bear a son, and shall call his name Immanuel."** The story of the Samaritan woman at Jacob's well in **John chapter 4** is one of great expectation. The Samaritans were a mixed race of Jew and Gentile blood and were hated by the Jews in that day. This woman had a "reputation" and was an outcast. She was an outcast in a nation of outcasts. Still, she had a great expectation. **John 4:25** says, **"The woman saith unto him, I know that Messias cometh, which is called Christ: when he is come, he will tell us all things."** Yes, this woman of ill repute looked with great expectation for Christ and found him and a whole multitude of these outcasts did as well. **"For unto us a child is born, unto us a son is given: and the government shall be upon his shoulder: and his name shall be called Wonderful, Counselor, the Mighty God, the Everlasting Father, the Prince of Peace. Of the increase of his government and peace there shall be no end, upon the throne of David, and upon his kingdom, to order it, and to establish it with judgment and with justice from henceforth even forever. The zeal of the Lord of hosts will perform this" (Isaiah 9:6-7).**

Moses even records the old hireling prophet Balaam from the East (Babylon) as even he correctly connected the appearing of a star with the appearing of the Saviour-King. **"I shall see him, but not now: I shall behold him, but not nigh: there shall come a star our of Jacob, and a Sceptre shall rise out of Israel..." (Numbers 24:17).**

Remember, Daniel was God's prophet and was carried away

to Babylon. Daniel spent his career as one of the Magi. His prophetic book would be recorded in Babylon. Those Magi believed the ancient Scriptures about this Saviour-King.

These fearless Wise Men, bearing precious gifts, bravely appeared before King Herod. Herod's reputation as one of the most wicked, brutal, vile, and godless kings ever to rule in mankind's history had no doubt been heard of even in the far east province of Babylon. The Wise Men plainly stated they had come to worship the newborn King and boldly asked, **"Where is He that is born King of the Jews?"** Herod called the scribes and they used **Micah 5:2** to point the Wise Men to Bethlehem. As a matter of record, Micah's prophecy about Bethlehem was given many years after the time of Daniel, and thus the Wise Men had no access to this Scripture.

The star that had appeared to the Wise Men reappeared and guided the Magi to the Baby King in Bethlehem. There these Wise Men opened their precious gifts and treasures and presented them to the Christ child. These most precious gifts were chosen with care and forethought and will stand forever as indisputable evidence that these Wise Men already knew this Holy Child. You see these gifts are symbolic in nature. Each gift will tell us something significant and special about this Divine Babe.

Gold shows us that Christ is a King and this is in keeping with earlier Scriptures. **Psalms 2:3** reads, **"Thou settest a crown of pure gold on his head."** Today, we know every country's financial status is controlled by the "gold" standard. Gold is a gift fit for a king.

Christ has never assumed His rightful position as King of the earth. When He came the first time, evil, wicked men crowned Him with thorns, nailed Him to a tree, and slew Him. He was buried. Yet, on the third day His body came out of the tomb perfectly alive and well. He has promised that He will return one day. Glory, majesty, and honor will belong to Christ and at that time the government will be placed upon His shoulders. **Revelation 19 and 20** vividly and literally paint an awesome picture of His return as **"King of Kings and Lord of Lords."** He could return today!

Frankincense reveals that this Baby Jesus was God! In Biblical times a special holy mixture of frankincense was prepared and was used exclusively for worship **(Exodus 30:34-38)**. Worship belongs to God. Worship never belongs to man. Jesus was God incarnate. Yes, He was the Son of God and God the Son. His name is Immanuel which means, **"God with us" (Matthew 1:23).** He is **"The Mighty God,"** and **"the Everlasting Father" (Isaiah 9:6).**

In the New Testament John introduces Jesus as the **"word of God"** **(John 1:1, 14)** and John goes on to say, **"And the Word was God."**

Myrrh points to Jesus as the suffering, bleeding, and dying Saviour. Myrrh was an expensive, yet bitter herb used as a burial ointment. Nicodemus brought myrrh for the burial of Christ **(John 19:39-40)**. Christ was born to die. He did not come to be a teacher, philosopher, or good example. Christ came to die and pay the sin debt for all who would receive and believe in Him. He suffered our hell and our torment on Calvary's Cross. His death was no accident. Wise men see this. Eternal life through Jesus Christ is the true Christmas Gift **(Romans 6:23)**.

The story of Anna, found in **Luke 2:36-38,** gives us an example of the great expectation. **"And there was one Anna, a prophetess, the daughter of Phanuel, of the tribe of Aser:... a widow of about fourscore and four years, which departed not from the temple, but served God with fastings and prayers night and day. And she coming in that instant gave thanks likewise unto the Lord, and spake to all them that looked for redemption in Jerusalem."**

The Baby Jesus, when He was forty days old, traveled with His parents from Bethlehem to the temple of Jerusalem. Jewish law required that certain ceremonial rites, as an act of worship, be carried out there. Upon arrival at the temple, Simeon, a prophet recognized (by revelation from God) the Baby Jesus as the Lord's Christ. Simeon spoke a short prophecy and adoration of the Christ Child and Anna, a lady of great age, entered.

Anna was a prophetess and from the context we know that the subject of her prophetic speaking was the coming of the Christ, the Redeemer of all mankind. We can also conclude from the previous verses that she fully expected to see the Lord's Christ before her death, just as Simeon did. Anna means "Grace." It is only by the grace of God that we "see" Christ for who He really is. The Bible says, "by grace are ye saved through faith." You see, the problems of this world are not social or economic, but stem from the very nature of man. Man is a fallen creature and has a sin problem—a wicked heart—and only through God's Grace can we even see that we have this problem.

Anna was the daughter of Phanuel and "Phanuel" means "the face of God." When Anna looked in the arms of Mary, she saw "the face of God." Jesus was the Son of God and God the Son. He was fully God and fully man. The angel of the Lord appeared to Joseph in a dream **(Matthew 1:20-25)** and said, **"His name shall be called Emanuel, which being interpreted is, God with us."** What a blessed thought to have God come to this sin cursed world to be with us. In **Hebrews 13:5** the Lord gave this amazingly simple promise to the Christian, **"I will never leave thee, nor forsake thee."**

Anna was of the tribe of Aser and "Aser" means "blessed." David said in **Romans 4:7-8, "Blessed are they whose iniquities are forgiven and whose sins are covered. Blessed is the man to whom the Lord will not impute sin."**

The message of Anna was the message of redemption. Look at it in the last line of the passage above. Redemption means "to deliver by paying a price." The picture is of the Lord walking through a slave market and buying us out of the slave market. Paul says we were all "sold under sin." **1 Peter 1:18-19** says, **"Ye are not redeemed with corruptible things but with the precious blood of Christ."** Christ came to die for our sin and to be our sin sacrifice on the brutal cross of Calvary. He was buried and after the third day arose—proving that God the Father accepted His sacrifice. Trust His goodness and Grace for your redemption, and you will have the great expectation of heaven today.

Today, we have the great expectation and hope of the return of the Lord. The Lord Himself promised to return in **John 14:3** where He said, **"And if I go and prepare a place for you, I will come again, and receive you unto myself; that where I am, there ye may be also."** The angels gave us the same promise in **Acts 1:10-11**. Paul tells us of this great expectation and our hope of the resurrection in **1 Thessalonians 4:13-18.** Permit me here to inject a personal note. My prayer is that the Lord would return soon, and I could say to Him, "I was just expecting you."